Jim Henson's
Beneath the
Dark Crystal

ADAM
SMITH

ALEXANDRIA
HUNTINGTON

VOLUME TWO

Published by
ARCHAIA

Jim Henson's
BENEATH THE
DARK CRYSTAL

Written by **Adam Smith**
Illustrated by **Alexandria Huntington**
With Colors by **Laura Langston** (Chapters 6-8)
Lettered by **Jim Campbell**

Cover and Chapter Break Art by **Benjamin Dewey**

Series Designer **Marie Krupina**
Collection Designer **Jillian Crab**
Assistant Editor **Gavin Gronenthal**
Editor **Matthew Levine**

Special Thanks to **Brian Henson, Lisa Henson, Jim Formanek, Nicole Goldman, Carla DellaVedova, Karen Falk, Blanca Lista, Jessica Mansour, the entire Jim Henson Company team, Wendy Froud, Brian Froud, Francesco Segala, Cameron Chittock, and Sierra Hahn.**

ARCHAIA™

Jim Henson
THE JIM HENSON COMPANY™

JIM HENSON'S BENEATH THE DARK CRYSTAL Volume Two, August 2019. Published by Archaia, a division of Boom Entertainment, Inc.

BOOM! Studios, 5670 Wilshire Boulevard, Suite 400, Los Angeles, CA 90036-5679.

Printed in China. First Printing.

ISBN: 978-1-68415-396-1
eISBN: 978-1-64144-379-1

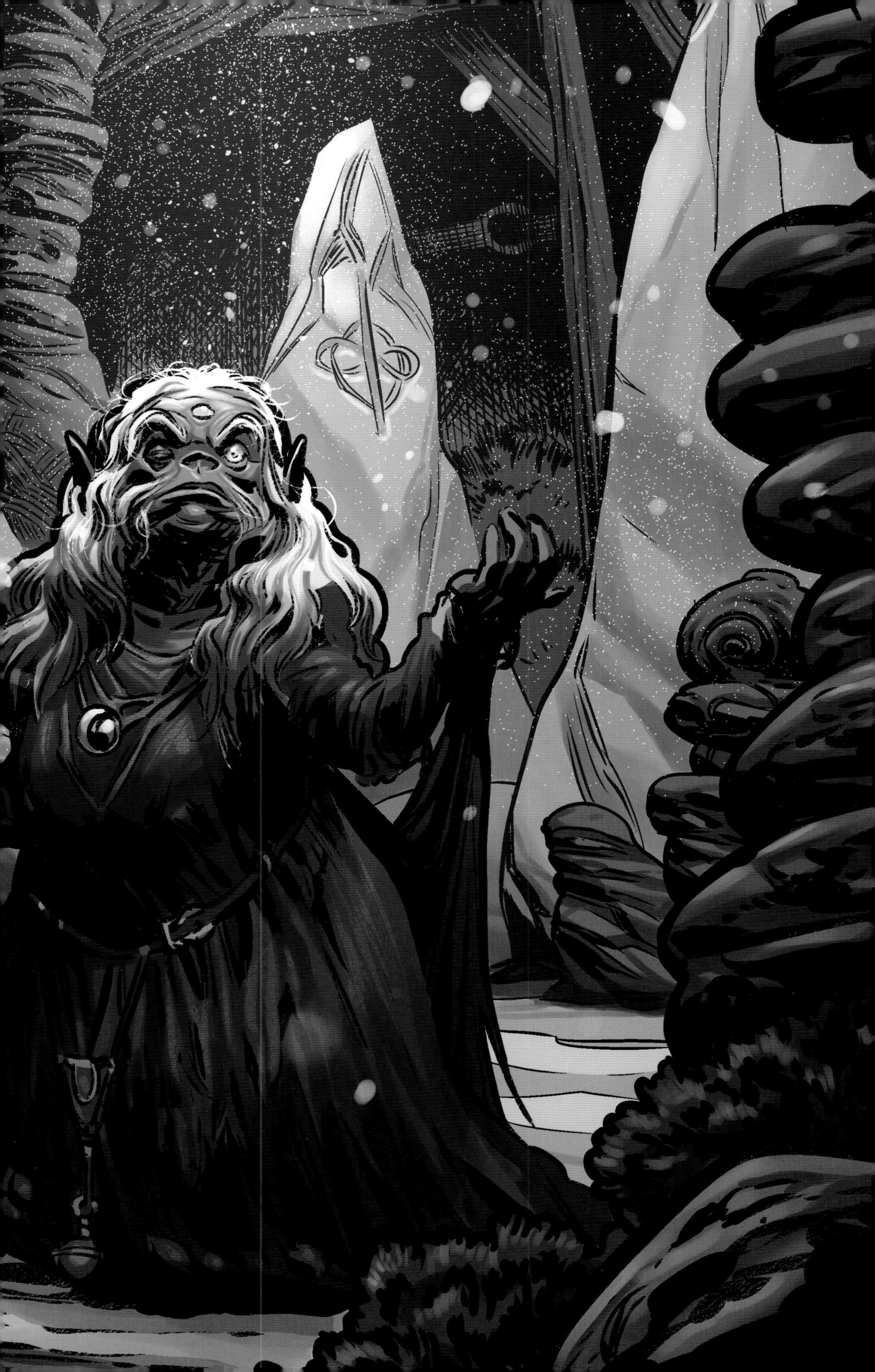

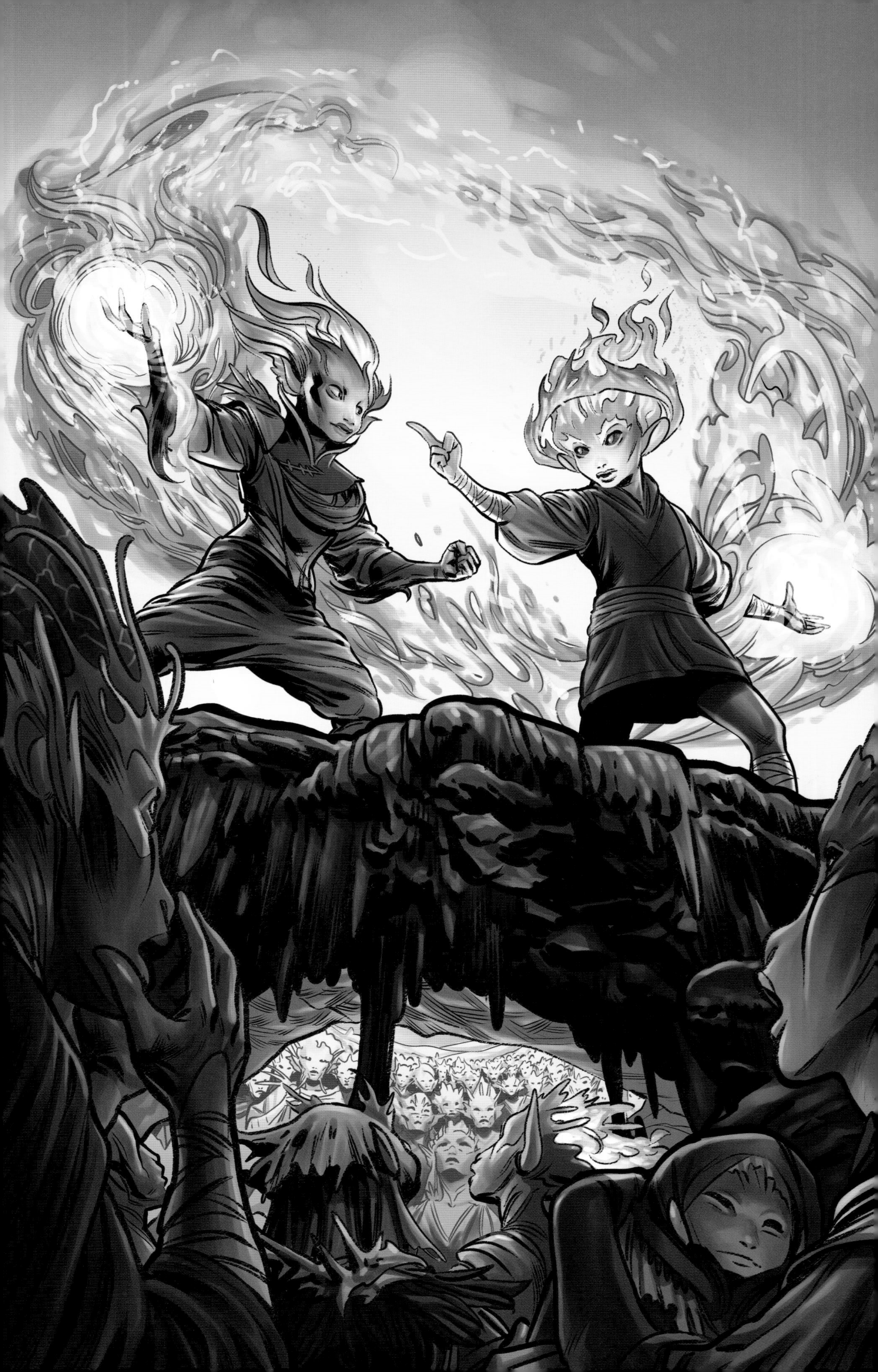

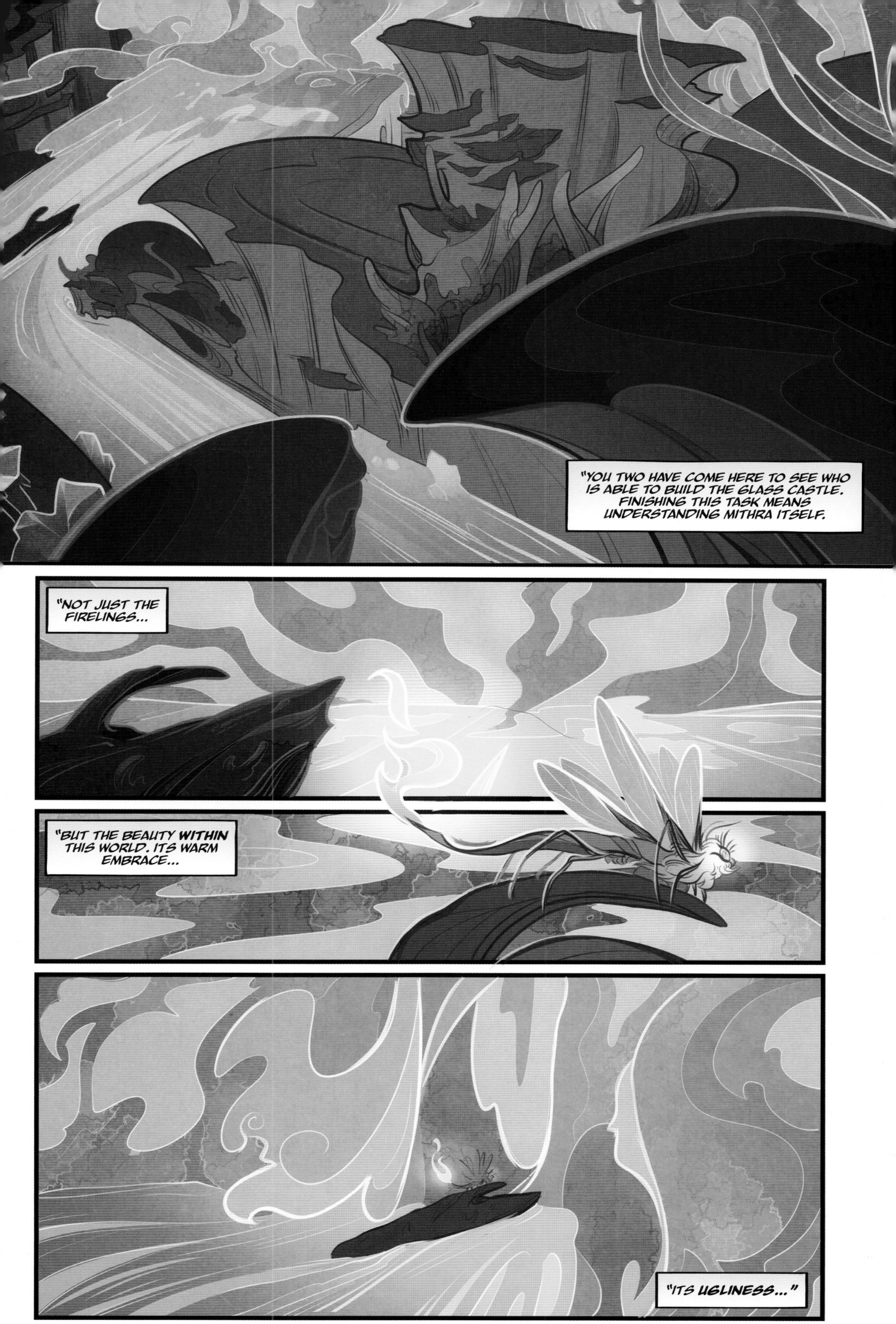
"YOU TWO HAVE COME HERE TO SEE WHO IS ABLE TO BUILD THE GLASS CASTLE. FINISHING THIS TASK MEANS UNDERSTANDING MITHRA ITSELF.
"NOT JUST THE FIRELINGS...
"BUT THE BEAUTY WITHIN THIS WORLD. ITS WARM EMBRACE...
"ITS UGLINESS..."

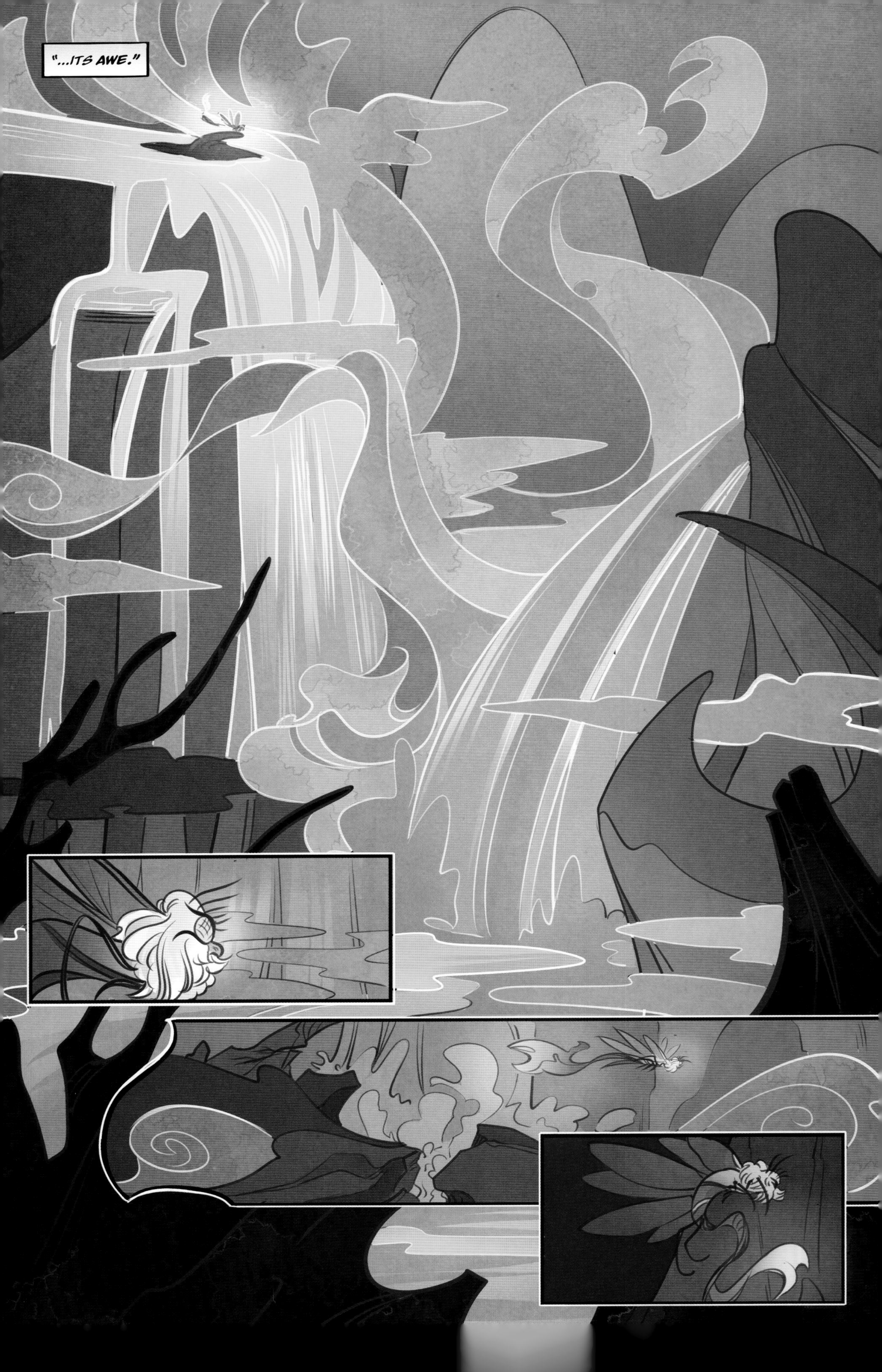
"...ITS AWE."

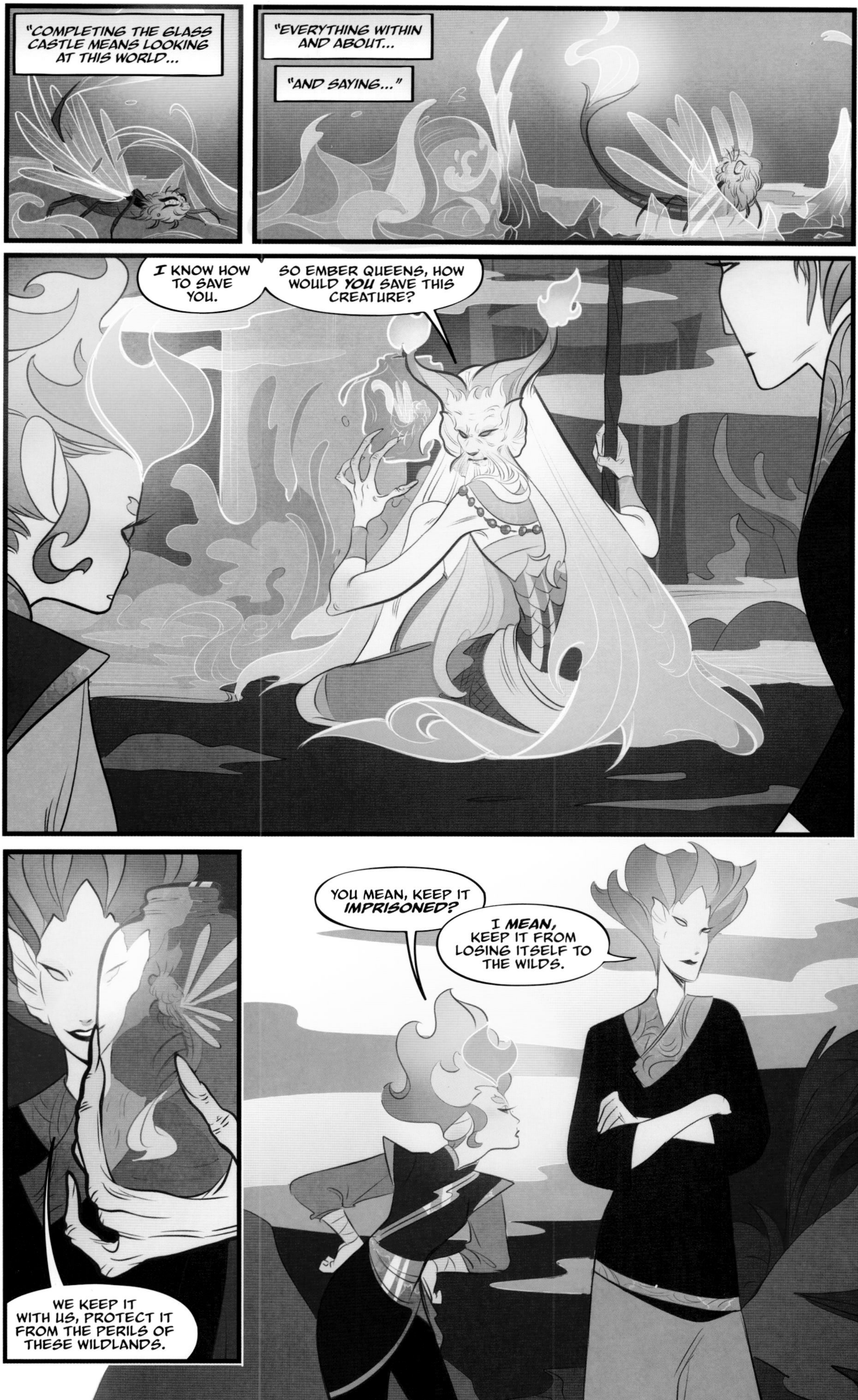
"COMPLETING THE GLASS CASTLE MEANS LOOKING AT THIS WORLD...
"EVERYTHING WITHIN AND ABOUT...
"AND SAYING..."
I KNOW HOW TO SAVE YOU.
SO EMBER QUEENS, HOW WOULD YOU SAVE THIS CREATURE?
WE KEEP IT WITH US, PROTECT IT FROM THE PERILS OF THESE WILDLANDS.
YOU MEAN, KEEP IT IMPRISONED?
I MEAN, KEEP IT FROM LOSING ITSELF TO THE WILDS.

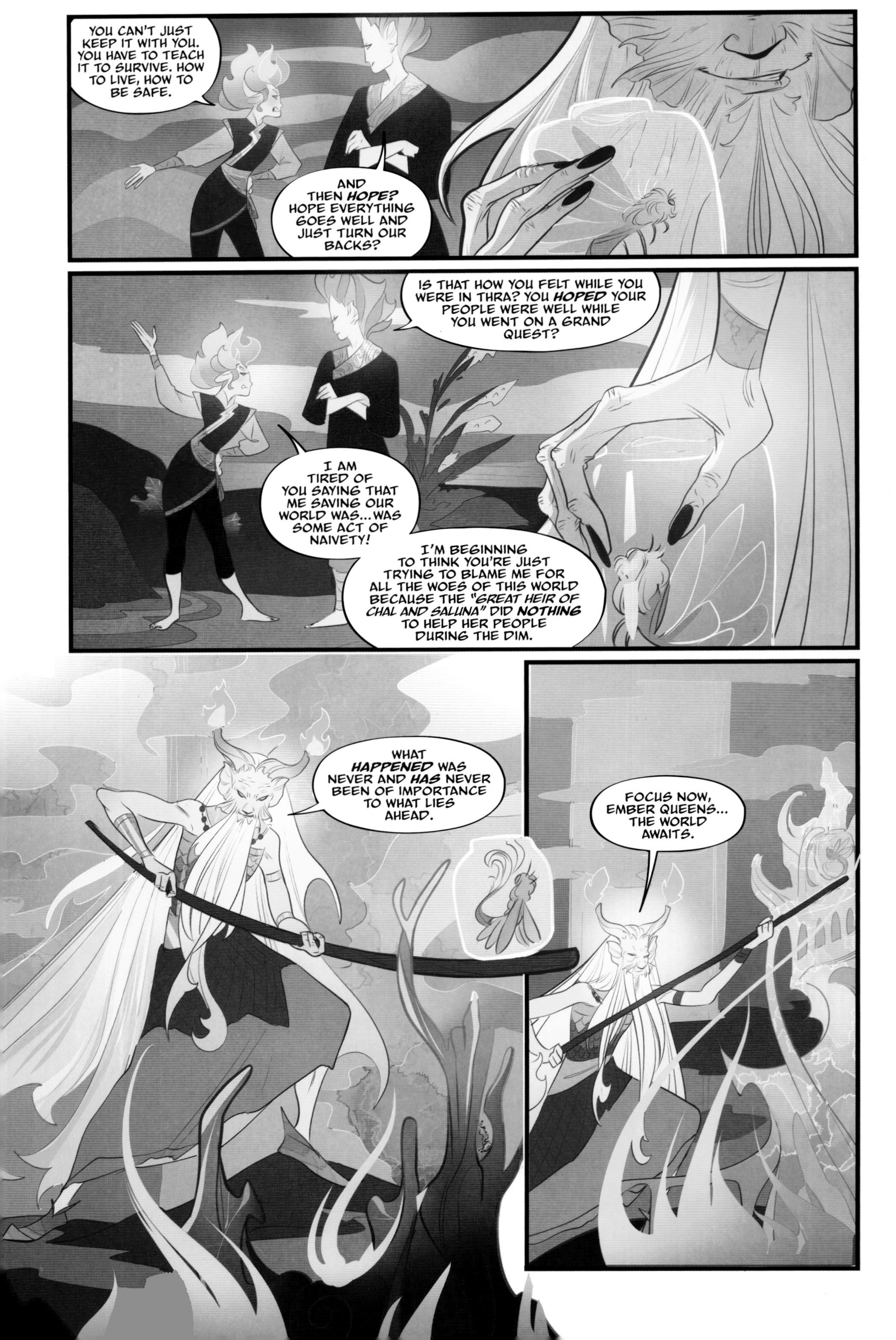
YOU CAN'T JUST KEEP IT WITH YOU. YOU HAVE TO TEACH IT TO SURVIVE. HOW TO LIVE, HOW TO BE SAFE.
AND THEN *HOPE?* HOPE EVERYTHING GOES WELL AND JUST TURN OUR BACKS?
IS THAT HOW YOU FELT WHILE YOU WERE IN THRA? YOU *HOPED* YOUR PEOPLE WERE WELL WHILE YOU WENT ON A GRAND QUEST?
I AM TIRED OF YOU SAYING THAT ME SAVING OUR WORLD WAS...WAS SOME ACT OF NAIVETY!
I'M BEGINNING TO THINK YOU'RE JUST TRYING TO BLAME ME FOR ALL THE WOES OF THIS WORLD BECAUSE THE *"GREAT HEIR OF CHAL AND SALUNA"* DID *NOTHING* TO HELP HER PEOPLE DURING THE DIM.
WHAT *HAPPENED* WAS NEVER AND *HAS* NEVER BEEN OF IMPORTANCE TO WHAT LIES AHEAD.
FOCUS NOW, EMBER QUEENS... THE WORLD AWAITS.

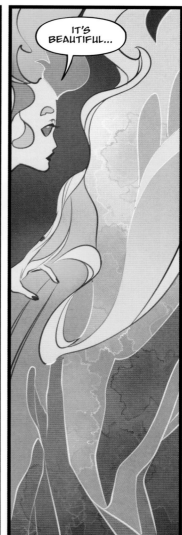

IT'S BEAUTIFUL...

THIS IS NOT BEAUTY, NOT YET. ONE OF YOU WILL LEARN THOUGH...

YOU MUST LEARN TO BUILD YOUR OWN. ONE LARGE ENOUGH TO SAVE OUR PEOPLE.

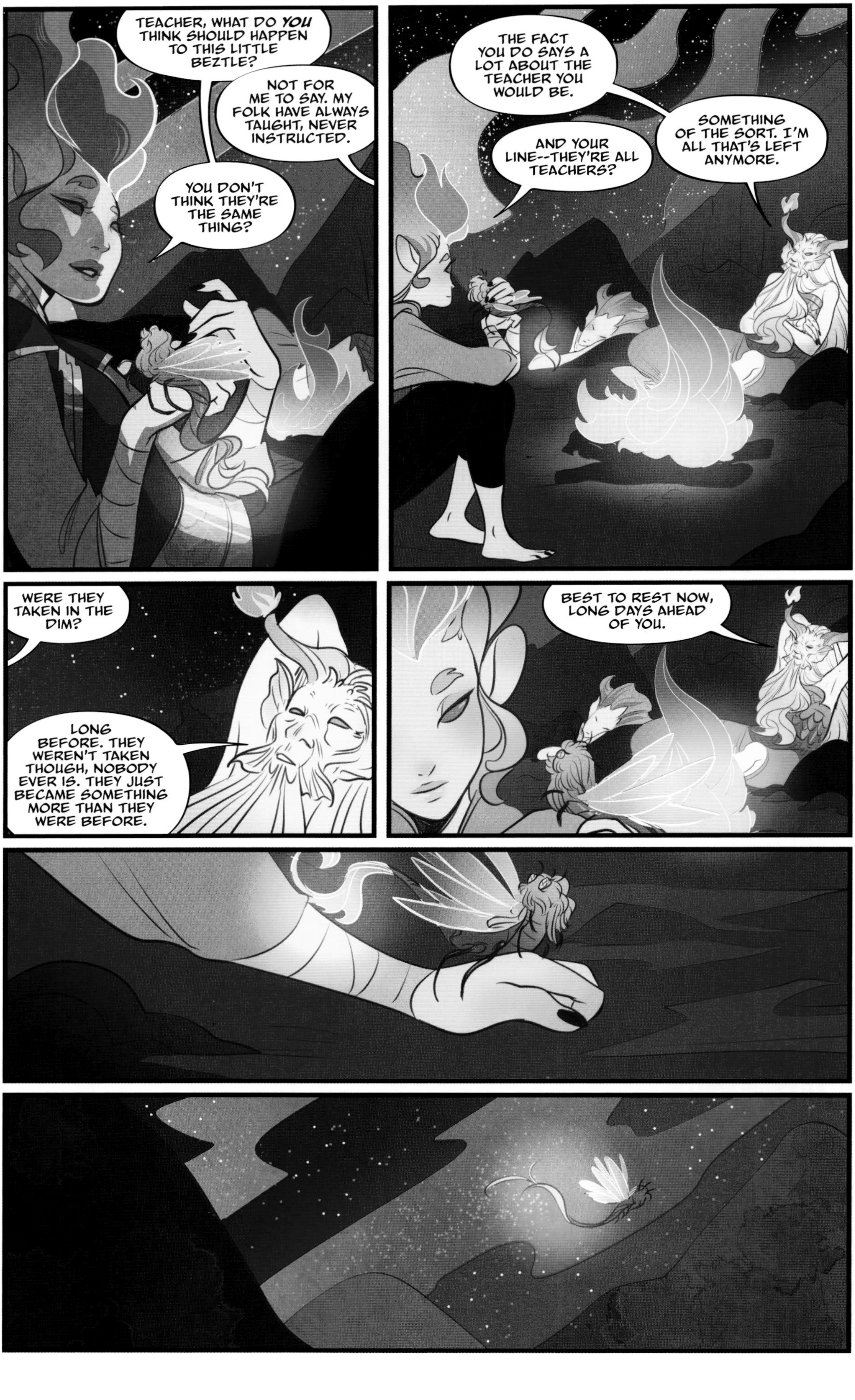
TEACHER, WHAT DO *YOU* THINK SHOULD HAPPEN TO THIS LITTLE BEZTLE?
NOT FOR ME TO SAY. MY FOLK HAVE ALWAYS TAUGHT, NEVER INSTRUCTED.
YOU DON'T THINK THEY'RE THE SAME THING?
THE FACT YOU DO SAYS A LOT ABOUT THE TEACHER YOU WOULD BE.
AND YOUR LINE--THEY'RE ALL TEACHERS?
SOMETHING OF THE SORT. I'M ALL THAT'S LEFT ANYMORE.
WERE THEY TAKEN IN THE DIM?
LONG BEFORE. THEY WEREN'T TAKEN THOUGH, NOBODY EVER IS. THEY JUST BECAME SOMETHING MORE THAN THEY WERE BEFORE.
BEST TO REST NOW, LONG DAYS AHEAD OF YOU.

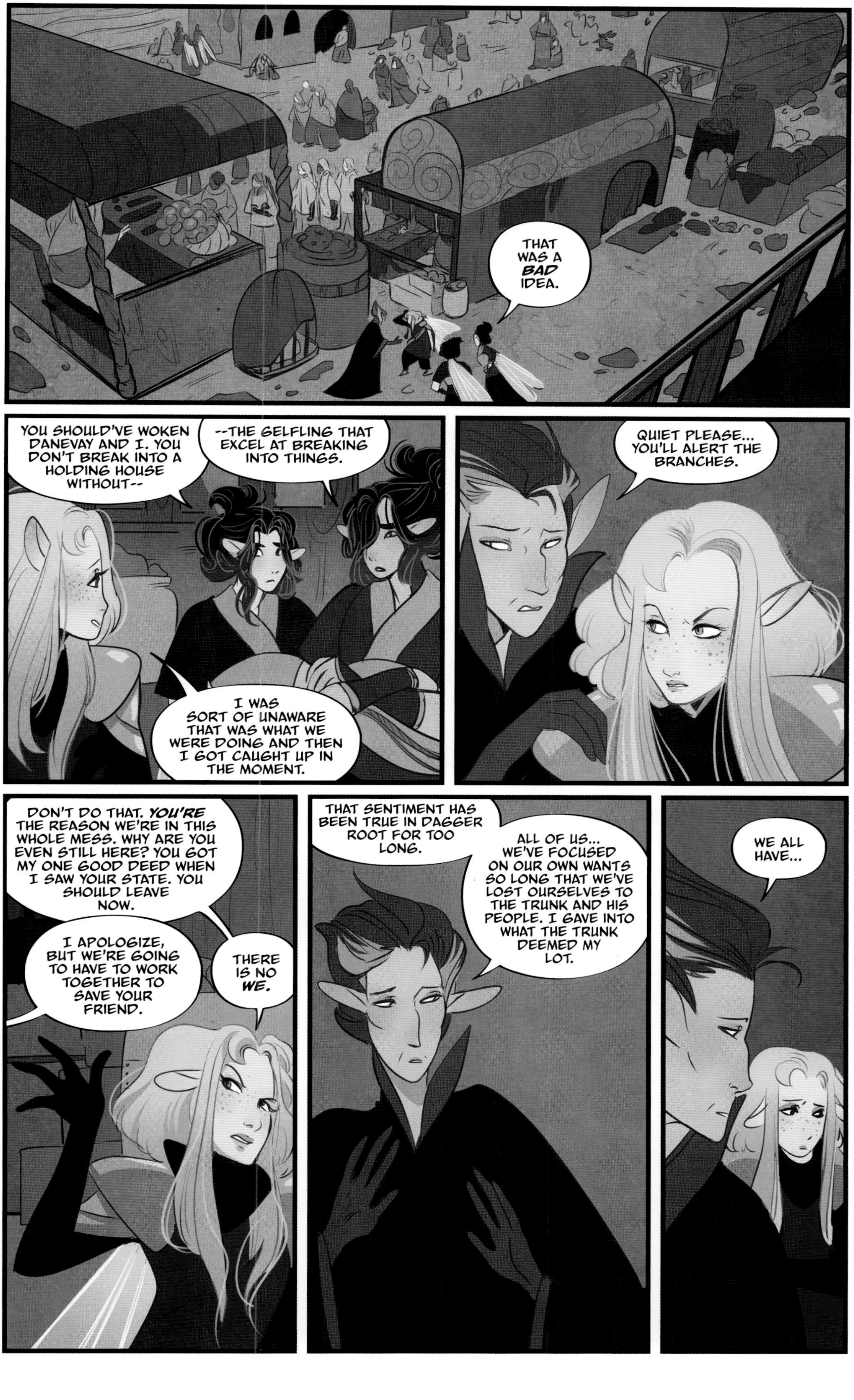
THAT WAS A *BAD* IDEA.
YOU SHOULD'VE WOKEN DANEVAY AND I. YOU DON'T BREAK INTO A HOLDING HOUSE WITHOUT--
--THE GELFLING THAT EXCEL AT BREAKING INTO THINGS.
I WAS SORT OF UNAWARE THAT WAS WHAT WE WERE DOING AND THEN I GOT CAUGHT UP IN THE MOMENT.
QUIET PLEASE... YOU'LL ALERT THE BRANCHES.
DON'T DO THAT. *YOU'RE* THE REASON WE'RE IN THIS WHOLE MESS. WHY ARE YOU EVEN STILL HERE? YOU GOT MY ONE GOOD DEED WHEN I SAW YOUR STATE. YOU SHOULD LEAVE NOW.
I APOLOGIZE, BUT WE'RE GOING TO HAVE TO WORK TOGETHER TO SAVE YOUR FRIEND.
THERE IS NO *WE.*
THAT SENTIMENT HAS BEEN TRUE IN DAGGER ROOT FOR TOO LONG.
ALL OF US... WE'VE FOCUSED ON OUR OWN WANTS SO LONG THAT WE'VE LOST OURSELVES TO THE TRUNK AND HIS PEOPLE. I GAVE INTO WHAT THE TRUNK DEEMED MY LOT.
WE ALL HAVE...

"...AND THE TRUNK IS NEVER KIND TO THOSE WHO REBUKE THEIR LOT.

"HIS REIGN IS BASED ON FEAR...

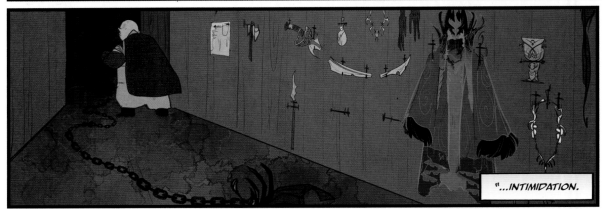

"...INTIMIDATION.

"HORROR. THAT'S WHAT AWAITS YOUR FRIEND..."

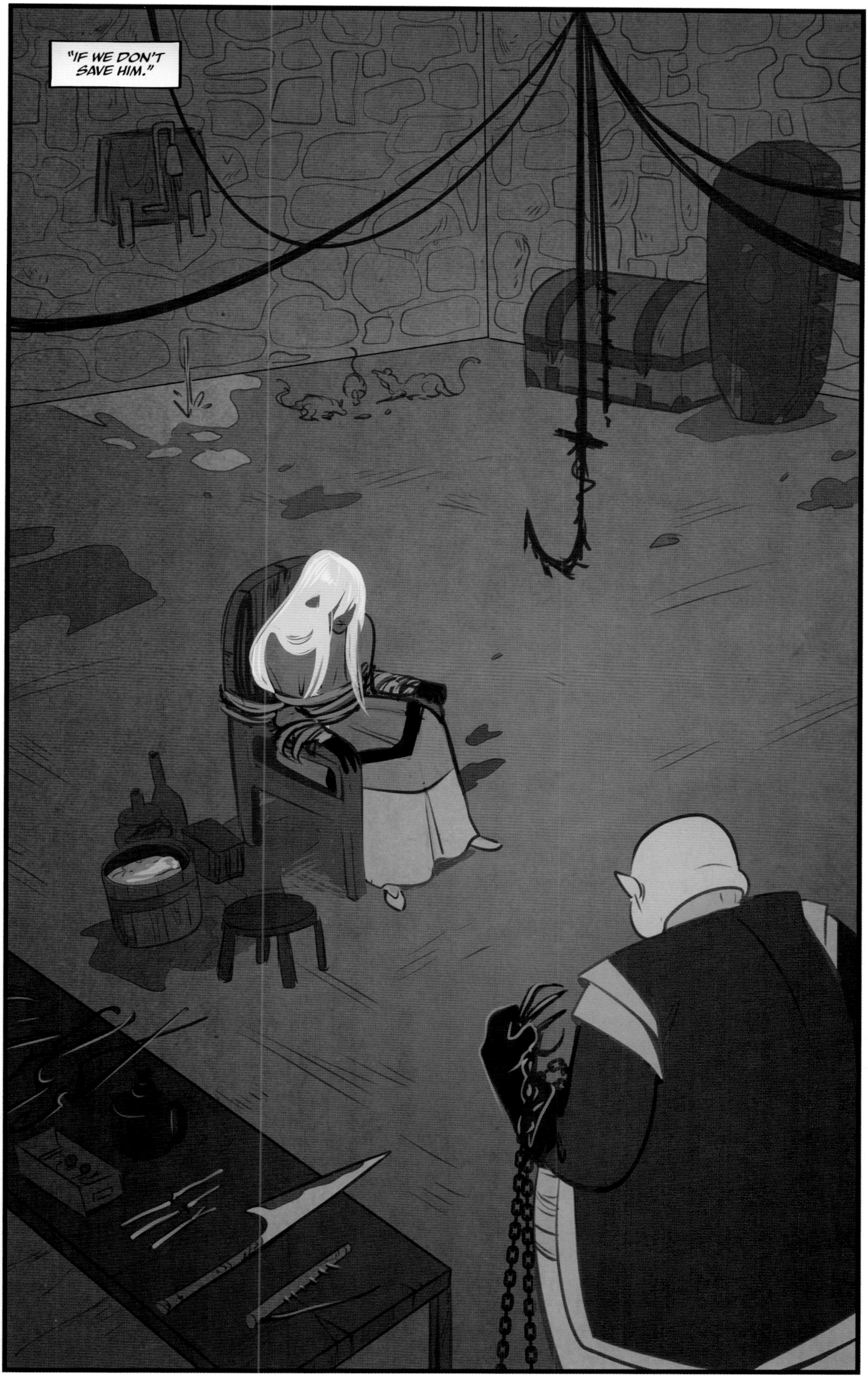
"IF WE DON'T SAVE HIM."

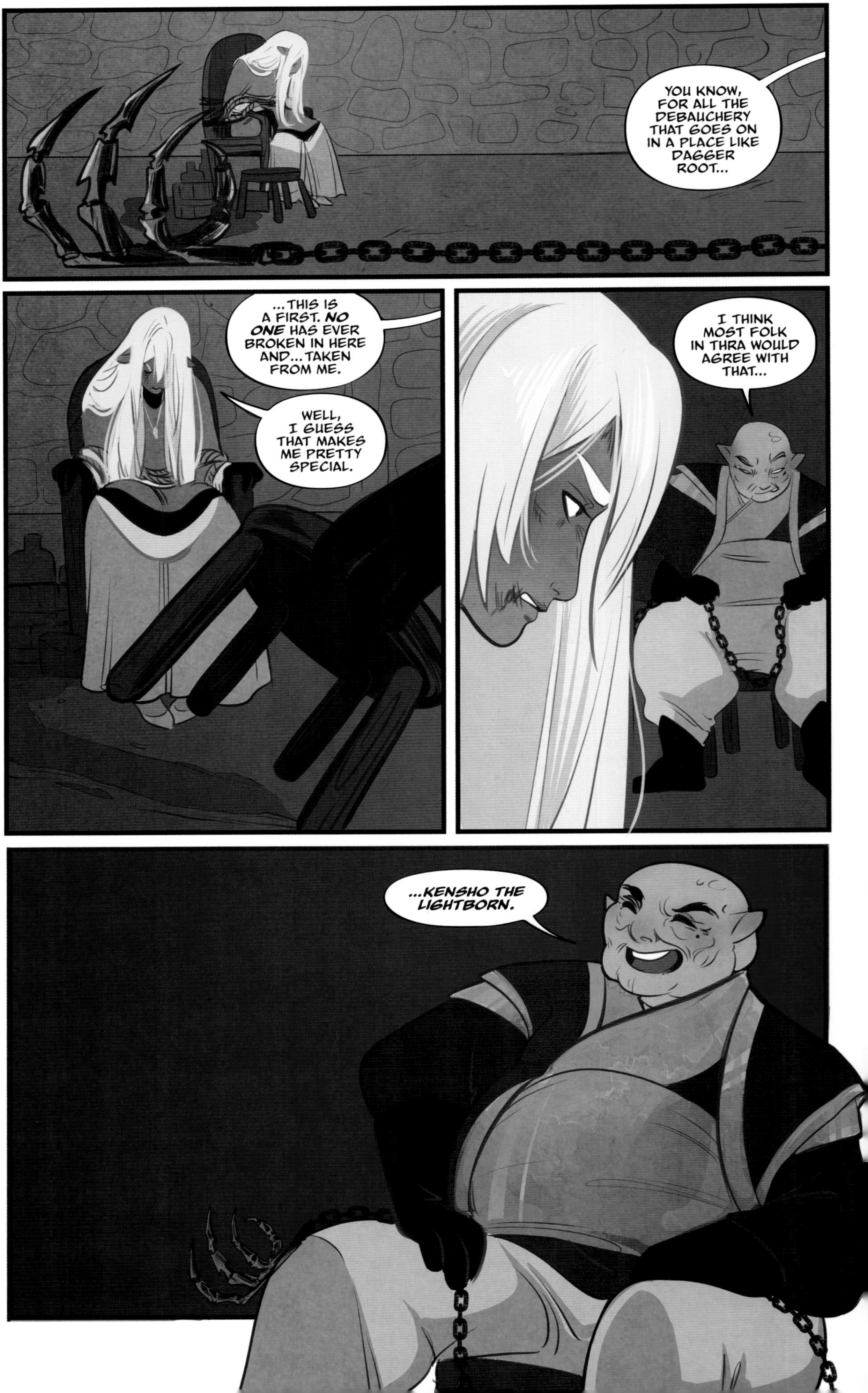
YOU KNOW, FOR ALL THE DEBAUCHERY THAT GOES ON IN A PLACE LIKE DAGGER ROOT...
...THIS IS A FIRST. NO ONE HAS EVER BROKEN IN HERE AND...TAKEN FROM ME.
WELL, I GUESS THAT MAKES ME PRETTY SPECIAL.
I THINK MOST FOLK IN THRA WOULD AGREE WITH THAT...
...KENSHO THE LIGHTBORN.

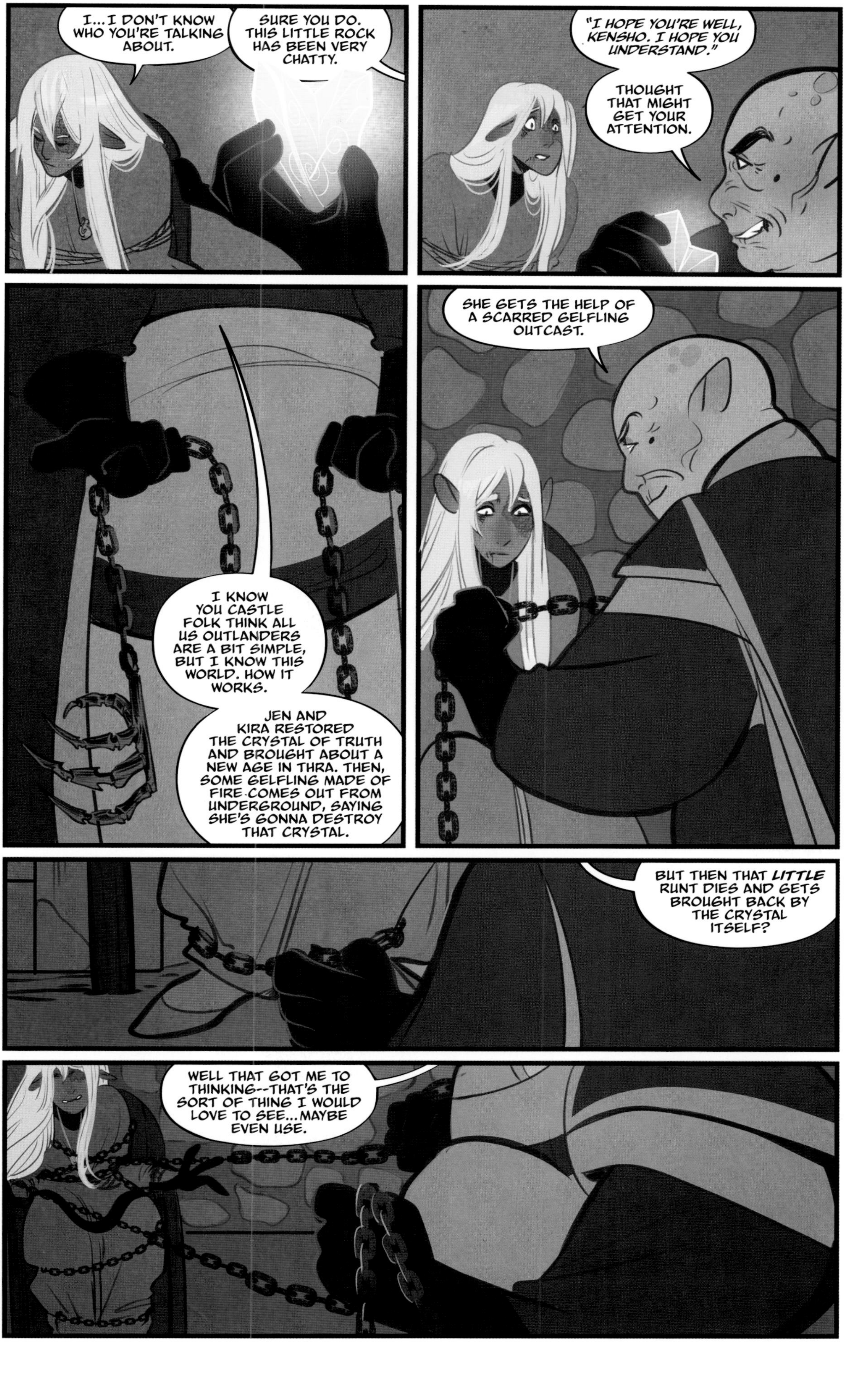
I...I DON'T KNOW WHO YOU'RE TALKING ABOUT.
SURE YOU DO. THIS LITTLE ROCK HAS BEEN VERY CHATTY.
"I HOPE YOU'RE WELL, KENSHO. I HOPE YOU UNDERSTAND."
THOUGHT THAT MIGHT GET YOUR ATTENTION.
I KNOW YOU CASTLE FOLK THINK ALL US OUTLANDERS ARE A BIT SIMPLE, BUT I KNOW THIS WORLD. HOW IT WORKS.
JEN AND KIRA RESTORED THE CRYSTAL OF TRUTH AND BROUGHT ABOUT A NEW AGE IN THRA. THEN, SOME GELFLING MADE OF FIRE COMES OUT FROM UNDERGROUND, SAYING SHE'S GONNA DESTROY THAT CRYSTAL.
SHE GETS THE HELP OF A SCARRED GELFLING OUTCAST.
BUT THEN THAT *LITTLE* RUNT DIES AND GETS BROUGHT BACK BY THE CRYSTAL ITSELF?
WELL THAT GOT ME TO THINKING--THAT'S THE SORT OF THING I WOULD LOVE TO SEE...MAYBE EVEN USE.

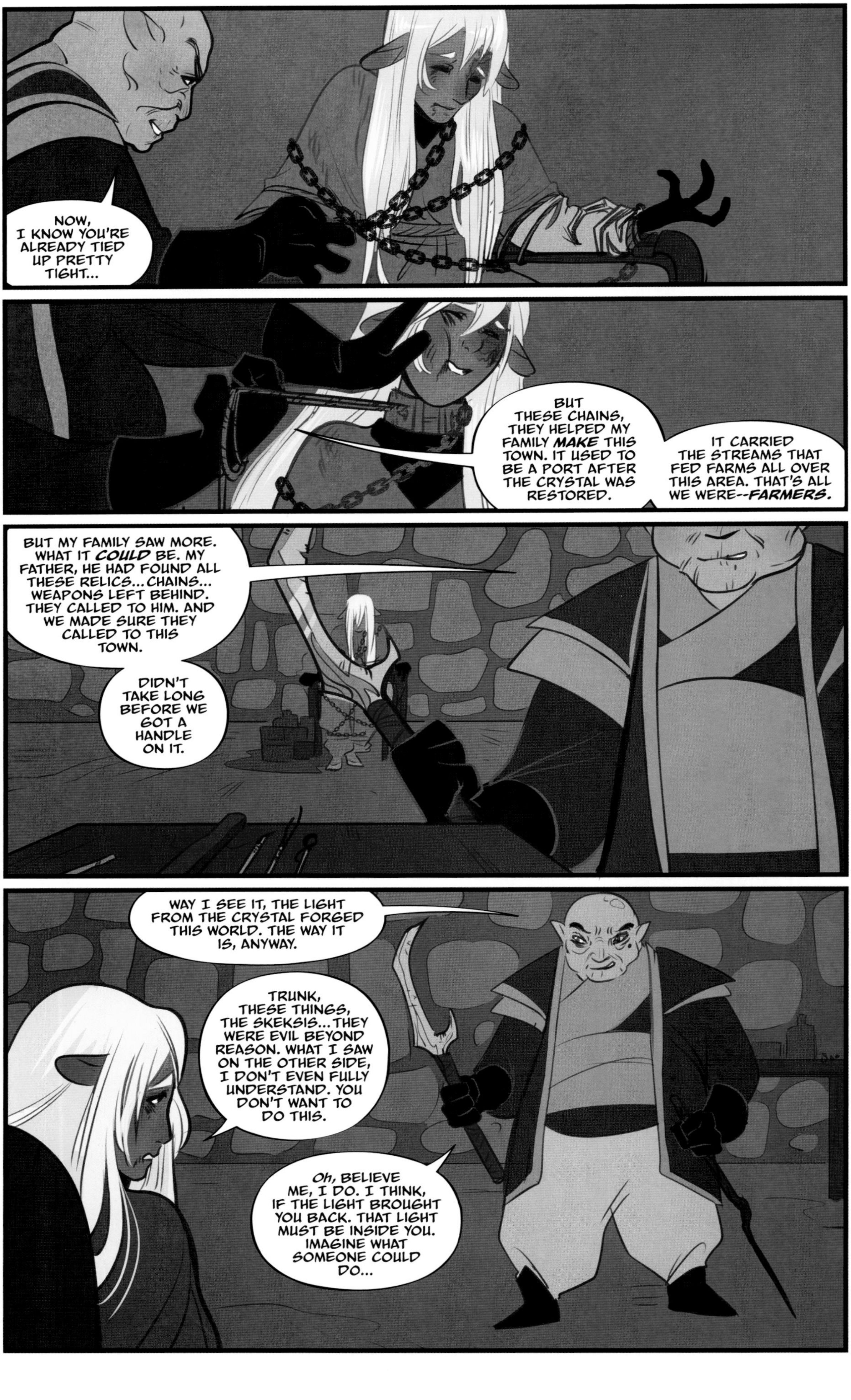
NOW, I KNOW YOU'RE ALREADY TIED UP PRETTY TIGHT...
BUT THESE CHAINS, THEY HELPED MY FAMILY MAKE THIS TOWN. IT USED TO BE A PORT AFTER THE CRYSTAL WAS RESTORED.
IT CARRIED THE STREAMS THAT FED FARMS ALL OVER THIS AREA. THAT'S ALL WE WERE--FARMERS.
BUT MY FAMILY SAW MORE. WHAT IT COULD BE. MY FATHER, HE HAD FOUND ALL THESE RELICS...CHAINS... WEAPONS LEFT BEHIND. THEY CALLED TO HIM. AND WE MADE SURE THEY CALLED TO THIS TOWN.
DIDN'T TAKE LONG BEFORE WE GOT A HANDLE ON IT.
WAY I SEE IT, THE LIGHT FROM THE CRYSTAL FORGED THIS WORLD. THE WAY IT IS, ANYWAY.
TRUNK, THESE THINGS, THE SKEKSIS...THEY WERE EVIL BEYOND REASON. WHAT I SAW ON THE OTHER SIDE, I DON'T EVEN FULLY UNDERSTAND. YOU DON'T WANT TO DO THIS.
Oh, BELIEVE ME, I DO. I THINK, IF THE LIGHT BROUGHT YOU BACK. THAT LIGHT MUST BE INSIDE YOU. IMAGINE WHAT SOMEONE COULD DO...

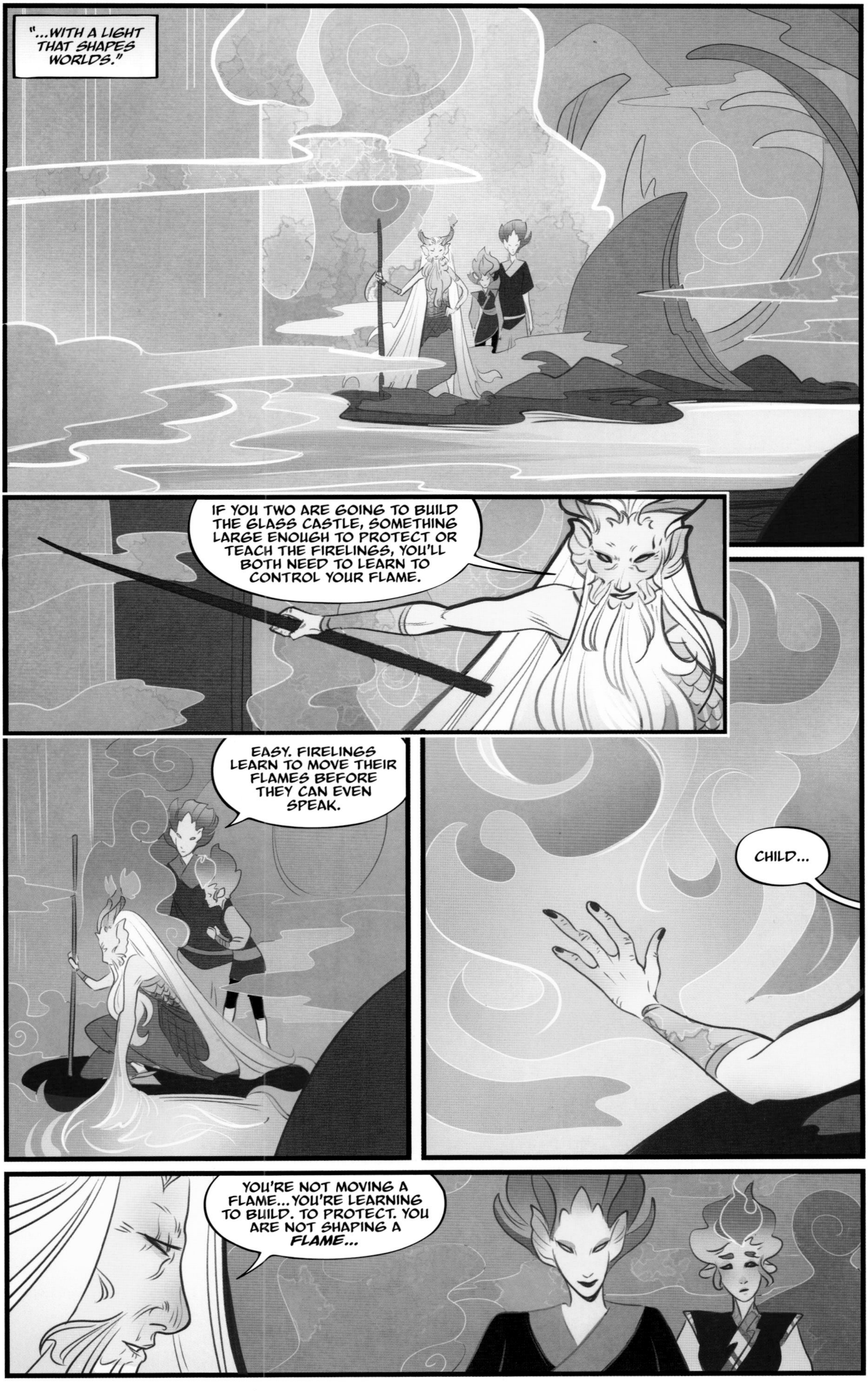
"...WITH A LIGHT THAT SHAPES WORLDS."
IF YOU TWO ARE GOING TO BUILD THE GLASS CASTLE, SOMETHING LARGE ENOUGH TO PROTECT OR TEACH THE FIRELINGS, YOU'LL BOTH NEED TO LEARN TO CONTROL YOUR FLAME.
EASY. FIRELINGS LEARN TO MOVE THEIR FLAMES BEFORE THEY CAN EVEN SPEAK.
CHILD...
YOU'RE NOT MOVING A FLAME...YOU'RE LEARNING TO BUILD. TO PROTECT. YOU ARE NOT SHAPING A *FLAME*...

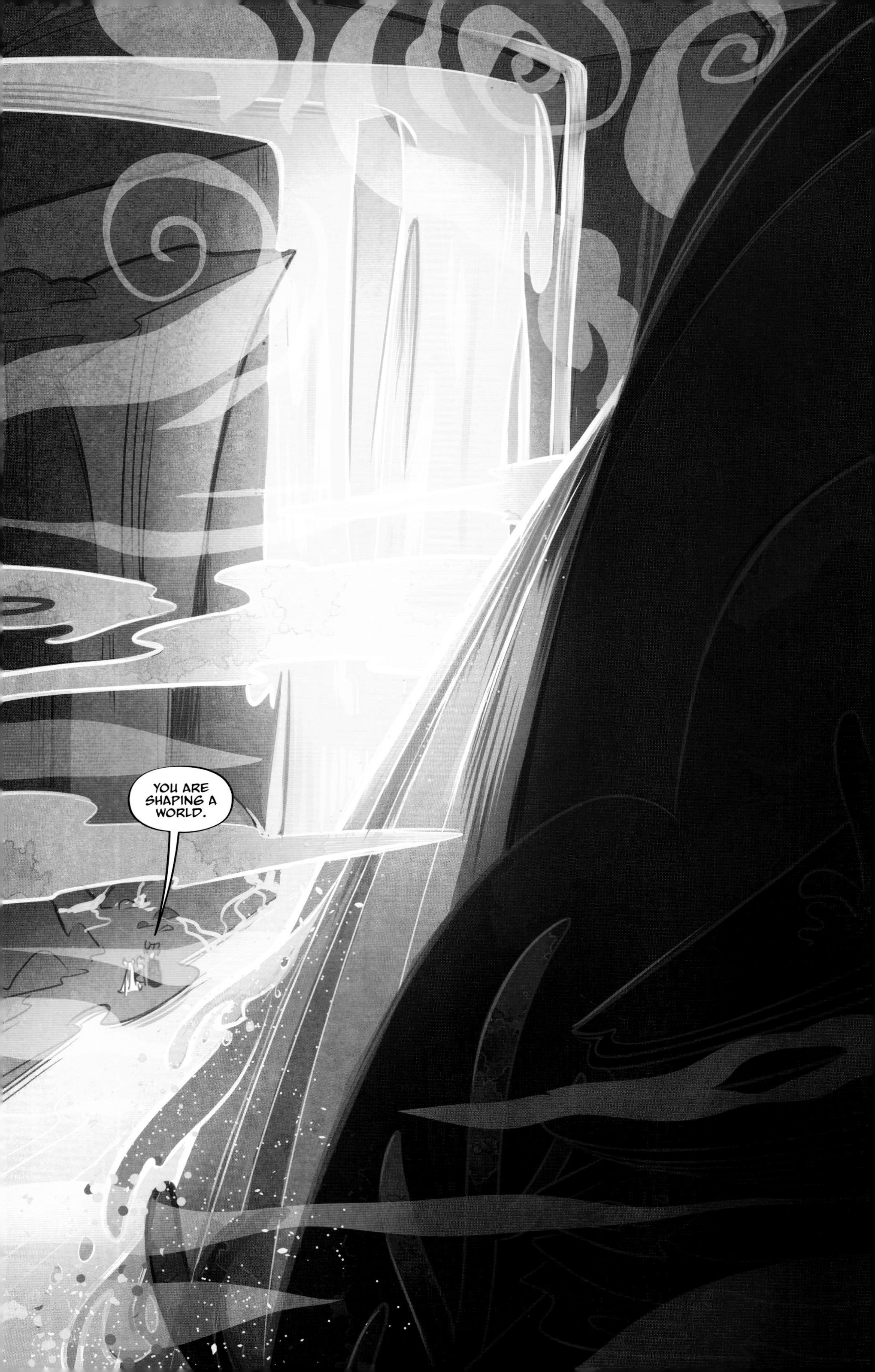
YOU ARE SHAPING A WORLD.

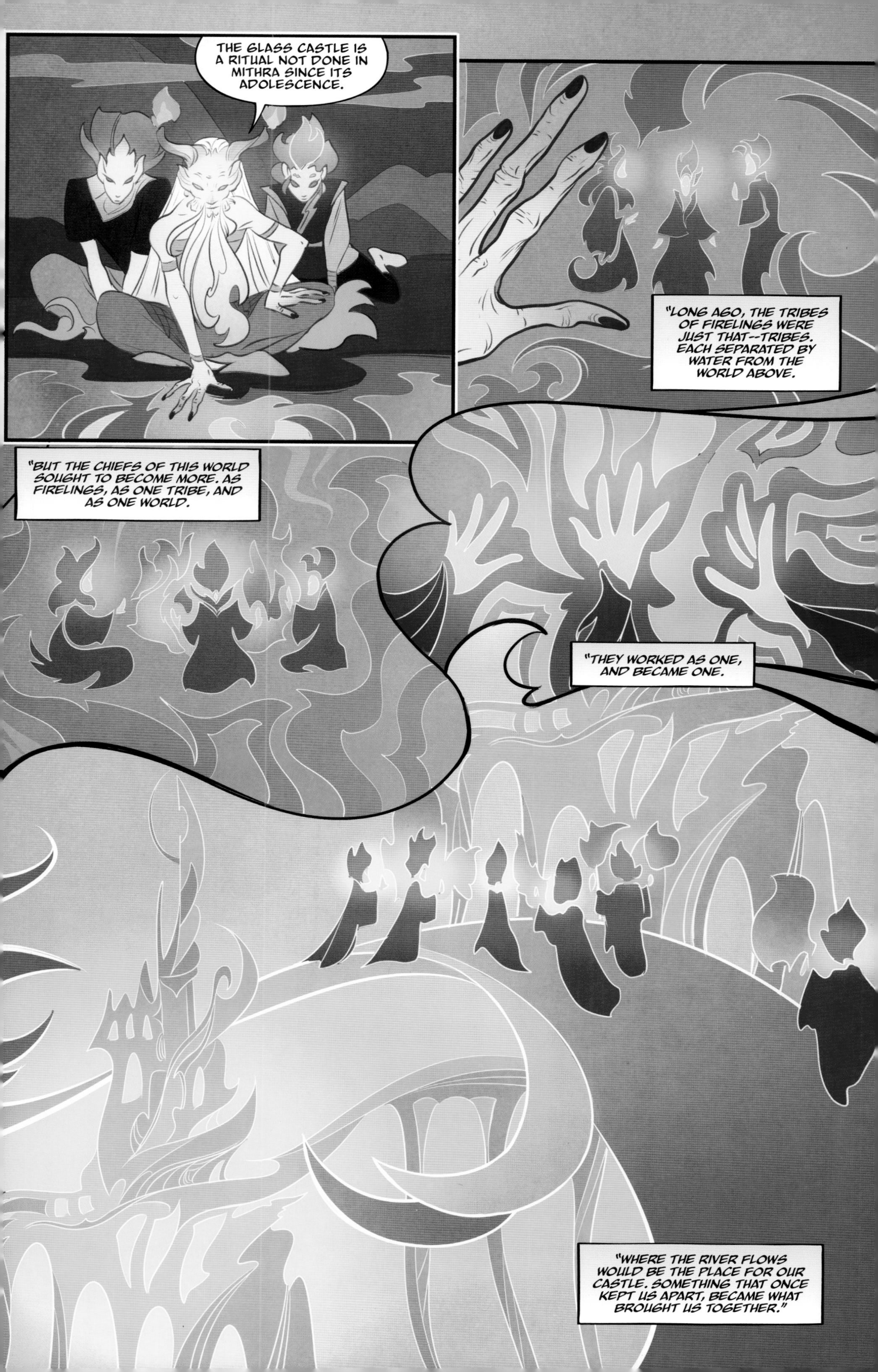
THE GLASS CASTLE IS A RITUAL NOT DONE IN MITHRA SINCE ITS ADOLESCENCE.
"LONG AGO, THE TRIBES OF FIRELINGS WERE JUST THAT--TRIBES. EACH SEPARATED BY WATER FROM THE WORLD ABOVE.
"BUT THE CHIEFS OF THIS WORLD SOUGHT TO BECOME MORE. AS FIRELINGS, AS ONE TRIBE, AND AS ONE WORLD.
"THEY WORKED AS ONE, AND BECAME ONE.
"WHERE THE RIVER FLOWS WOULD BE THE PLACE FOR OUR CASTLE. SOMETHING THAT ONCE KEPT US APART, BECAME WHAT BROUGHT US TOGETHER."

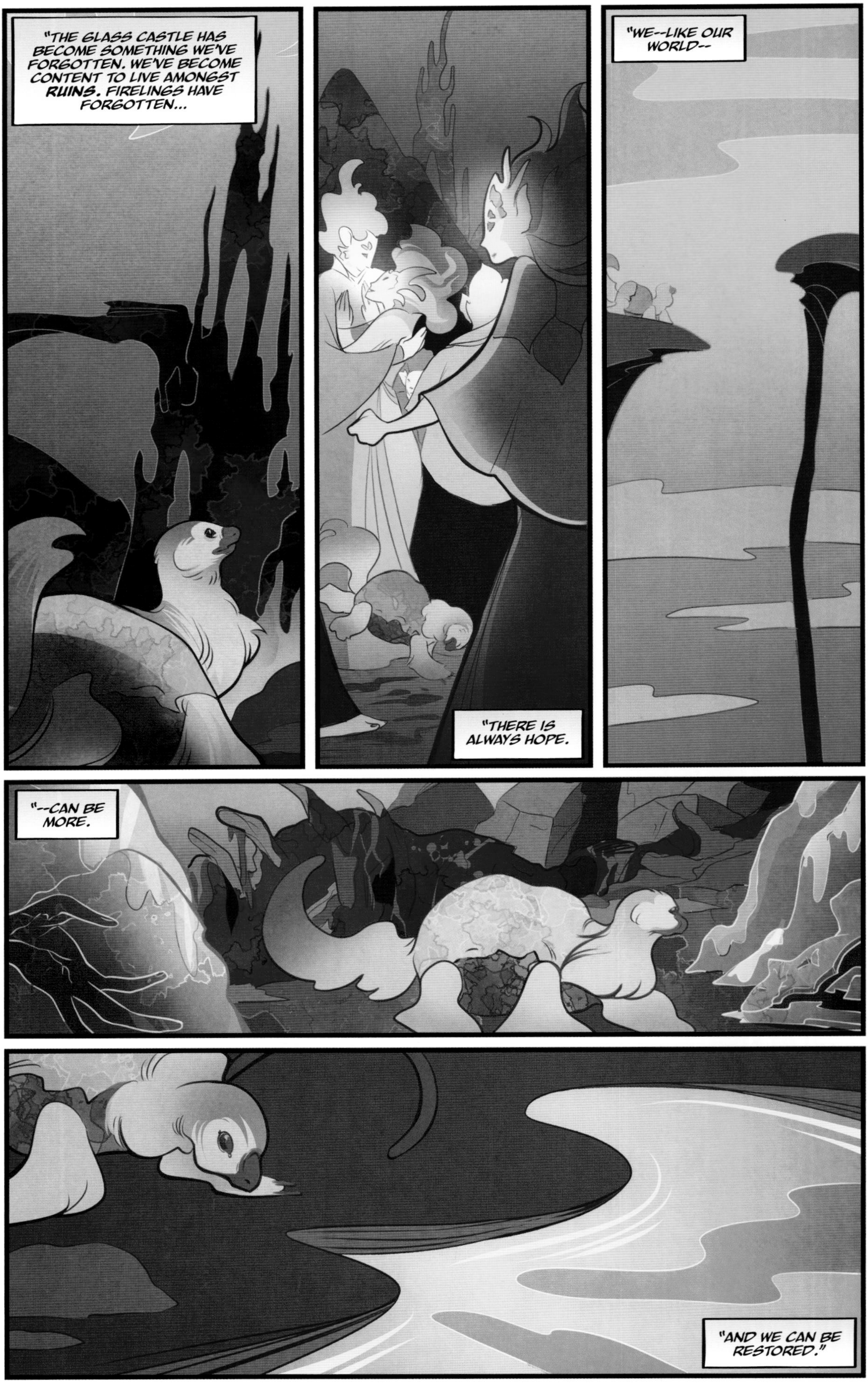
"THE GLASS CASTLE HAS BECOME SOMETHING WE'VE FORGOTTEN. WE'VE BECOME CONTENT TO LIVE AMONGST **RUINS**. FIRELINGS HAVE FORGOTTEN...
"THERE IS ALWAYS HOPE.
"WE--LIKE OUR WORLD--
"--CAN BE MORE.
"AND WE CAN BE RESTORED."

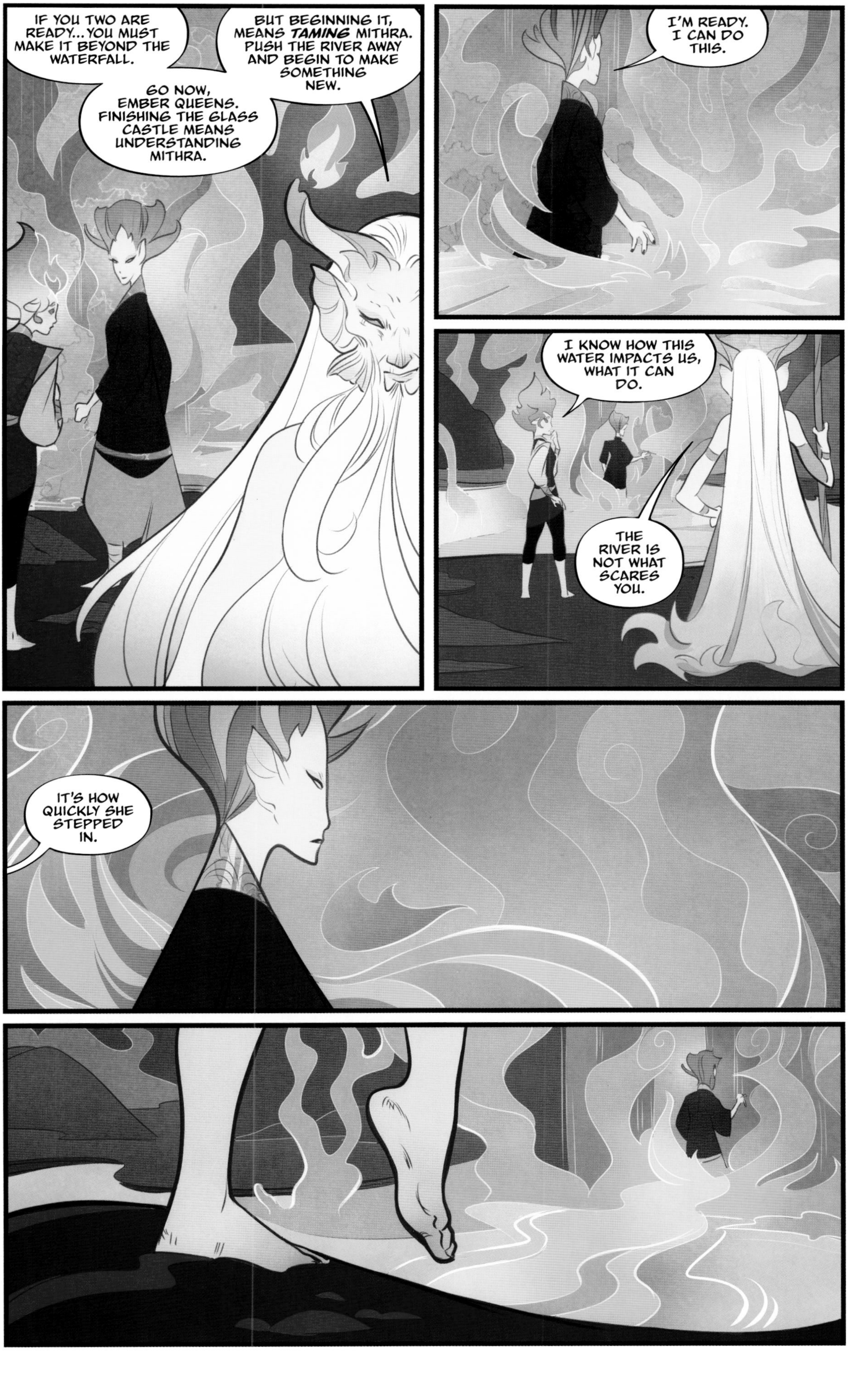
IF YOU TWO ARE READY...YOU MUST MAKE IT BEYOND THE WATERFALL.
BUT BEGINNING IT, MEANS *TAMING* MITHRA. PUSH THE RIVER AWAY AND BEGIN TO MAKE SOMETHING NEW.
GO NOW, EMBER QUEENS. FINISHING THE GLASS CASTLE MEANS UNDERSTANDING MITHRA.
I'M READY. I CAN DO THIS.
I KNOW HOW THIS WATER IMPACTS US, WHAT IT CAN DO.
THE RIVER IS NOT WHAT SCARES YOU.
IT'S HOW QUICKLY SHE STEPPED IN.

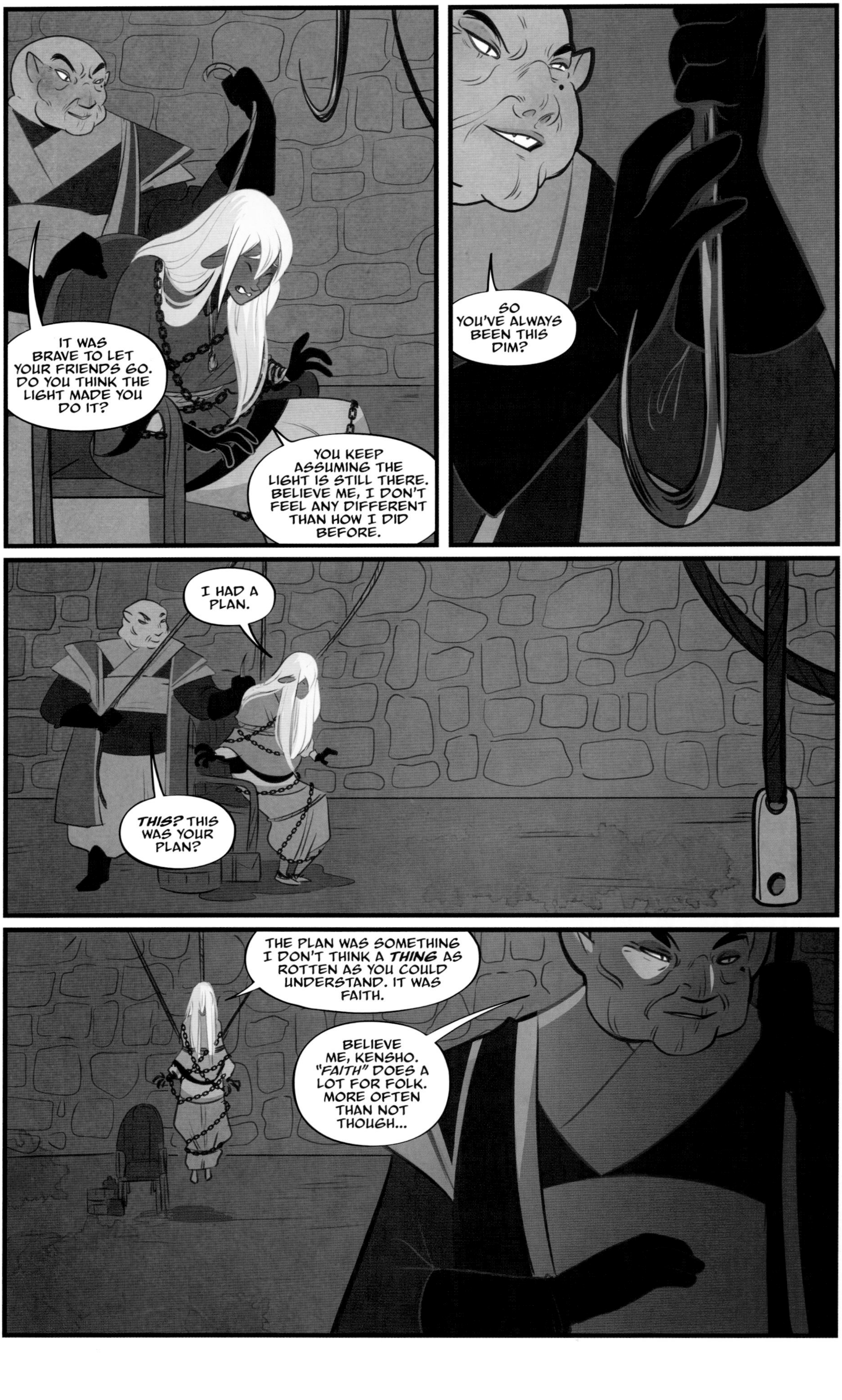
IT WAS BRAVE TO LET YOUR FRIENDS GO. DO YOU THINK THE LIGHT MADE YOU DO IT?
YOU KEEP ASSUMING THE LIGHT IS STILL THERE. BELIEVE ME, I DON'T FEEL ANY DIFFERENT THAN HOW I DID BEFORE.
SO YOU'VE ALWAYS BEEN THIS DIM?
I HAD A PLAN.
THIS? THIS WAS YOUR PLAN?
THE PLAN WAS SOMETHING I DON'T THINK A *THING* AS ROTTEN AS YOU COULD UNDERSTAND. IT WAS FAITH.
BELIEVE ME, KENSHO. "*FAITH*" DOES A LOT FOR FOLK. MORE OFTEN THAN NOT THOUGH...

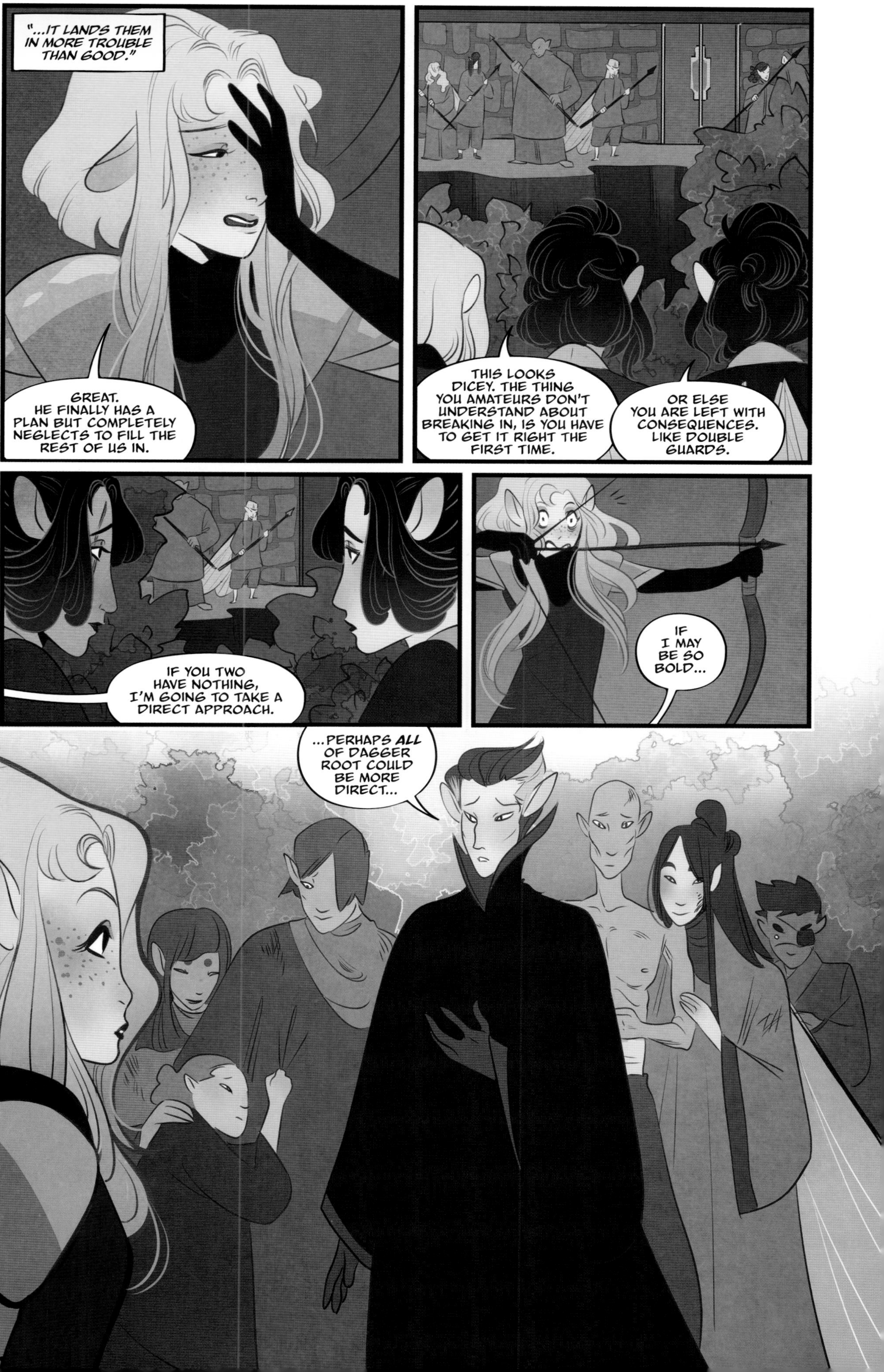
"...IT LANDS THEM IN MORE TROUBLE THAN GOOD."
GREAT. HE FINALLY HAS A PLAN BUT COMPLETELY NEGLECTS TO FILL THE REST OF US IN.
THIS LOOKS DICEY. THE THING YOU AMATEURS DON'T UNDERSTAND ABOUT BREAKING IN, IS YOU HAVE TO GET IT RIGHT THE FIRST TIME.
OR ELSE YOU ARE LEFT WITH CONSEQUENCES. LIKE DOUBLE GUARDS.
IF YOU TWO HAVE NOTHING, I'M GOING TO TAKE A DIRECT APPROACH.
IF I MAY BE SO BOLD...
...PERHAPS ALL OF DAGGER ROOT COULD BE MORE DIRECT...

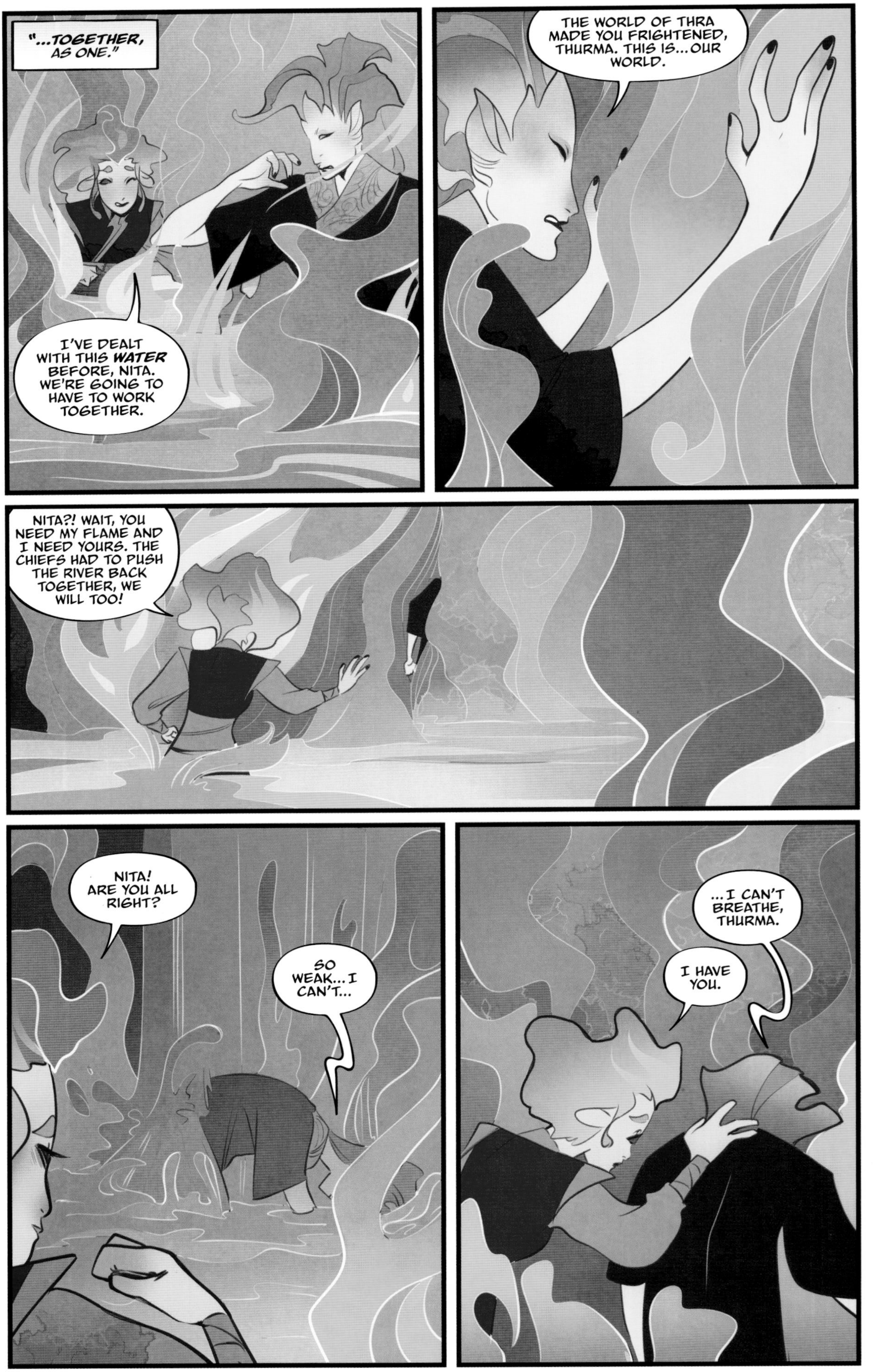
"...TOGETHER, AS ONE."
I'VE DEALT WITH THIS WATER BEFORE, NITA. WE'RE GOING TO HAVE TO WORK TOGETHER.
THE WORLD OF THRA MADE YOU FRIGHTENED, THURMA. THIS IS...OUR WORLD.
NITA?! WAIT, YOU NEED MY FLAME AND I NEED YOURS. THE CHIEFS HAD TO PUSH THE RIVER BACK TOGETHER, WE WILL TOO!
NITA! ARE YOU ALL RIGHT?
SO WEAK... I CAN'T...
...I CAN'T BREATHE, THURMA.
I HAVE YOU.

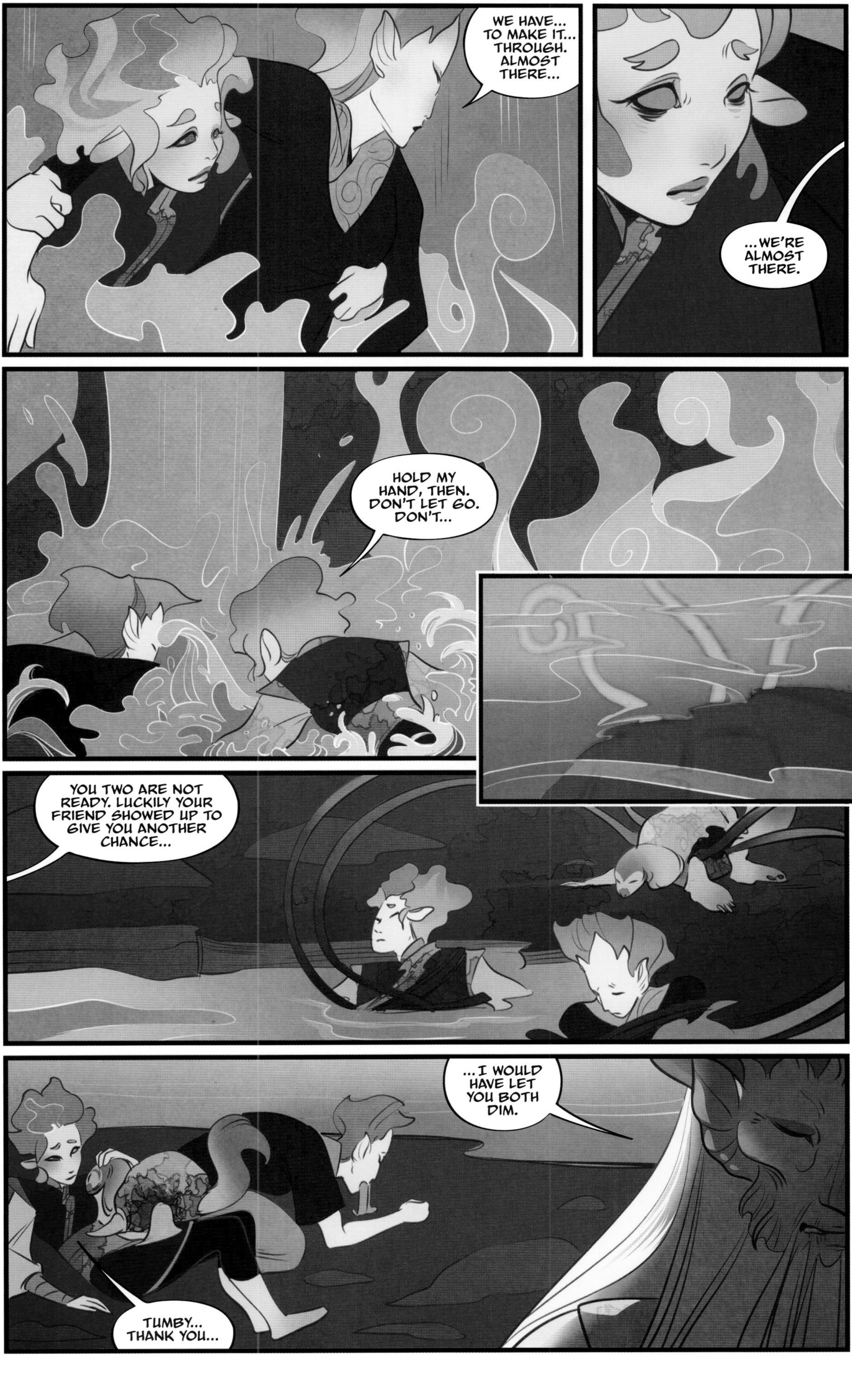
WE HAVE... TO MAKE IT... THROUGH. ALMOST THERE...
...WE'RE ALMOST THERE.
HOLD MY HAND, THEN. DON'T LET GO. DON'T...
YOU TWO ARE NOT READY. LUCKILY YOUR FRIEND SHOWED UP TO GIVE YOU ANOTHER CHANCE...
...I WOULD HAVE LET YOU BOTH DIM.
TUMBY... THANK YOU...

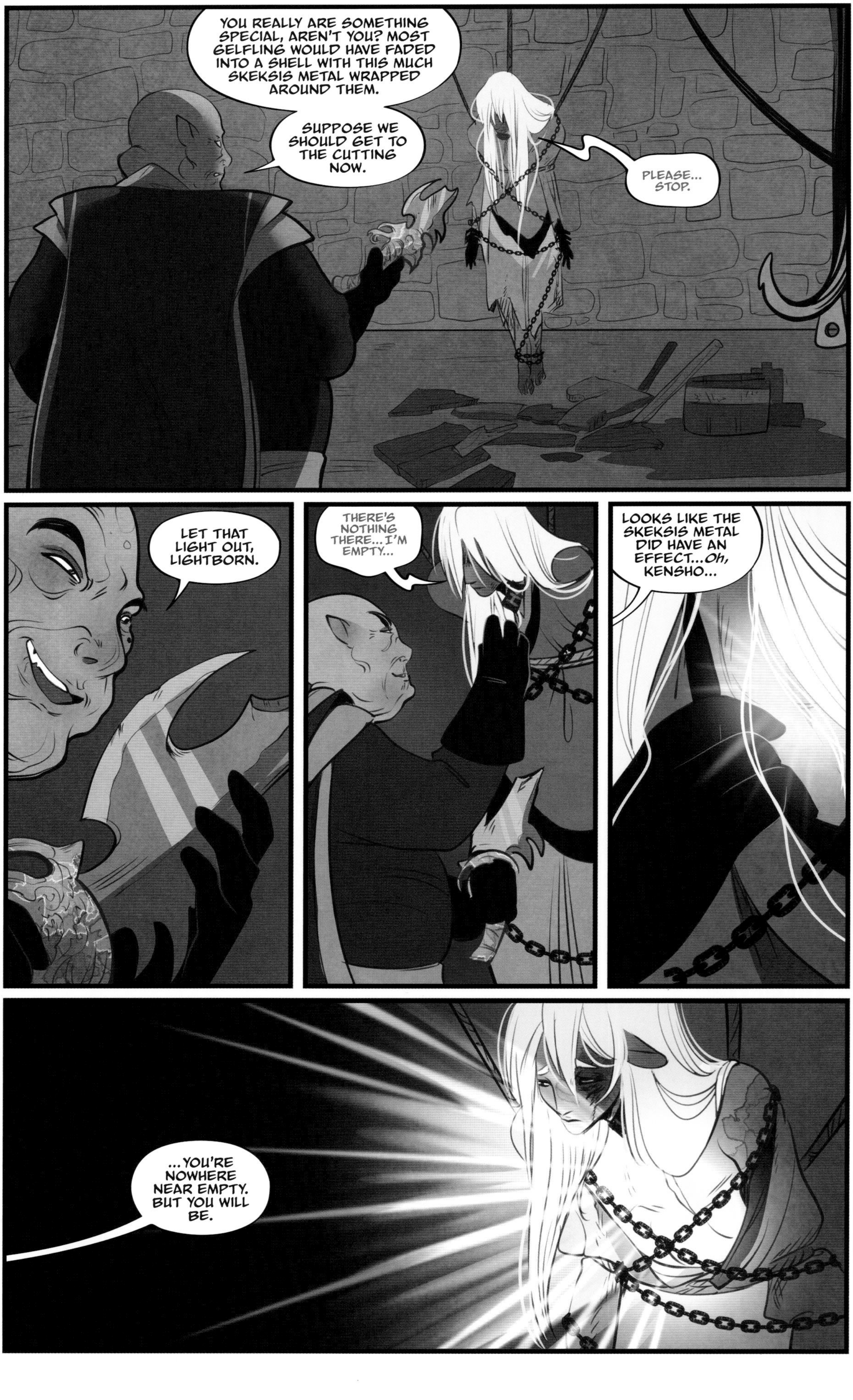
YOU REALLY ARE SOMETHING SPECIAL, AREN'T YOU? MOST GELFLING WOULD HAVE FADED INTO A SHELL WITH THIS MUCH SKEKSIS METAL WRAPPED AROUND THEM.
SUPPOSE WE SHOULD GET TO THE CUTTING NOW.
PLEASE... STOP.
LET THAT LIGHT OUT, LIGHTBORN.
THERE'S NOTHING THERE... I'M EMPTY...
LOOKS LIKE THE SKEKSIS METAL DID HAVE AN EFFECT... Oh, KENSHO...
...YOU'RE NOWHERE NEAR EMPTY. BUT YOU WILL BE.

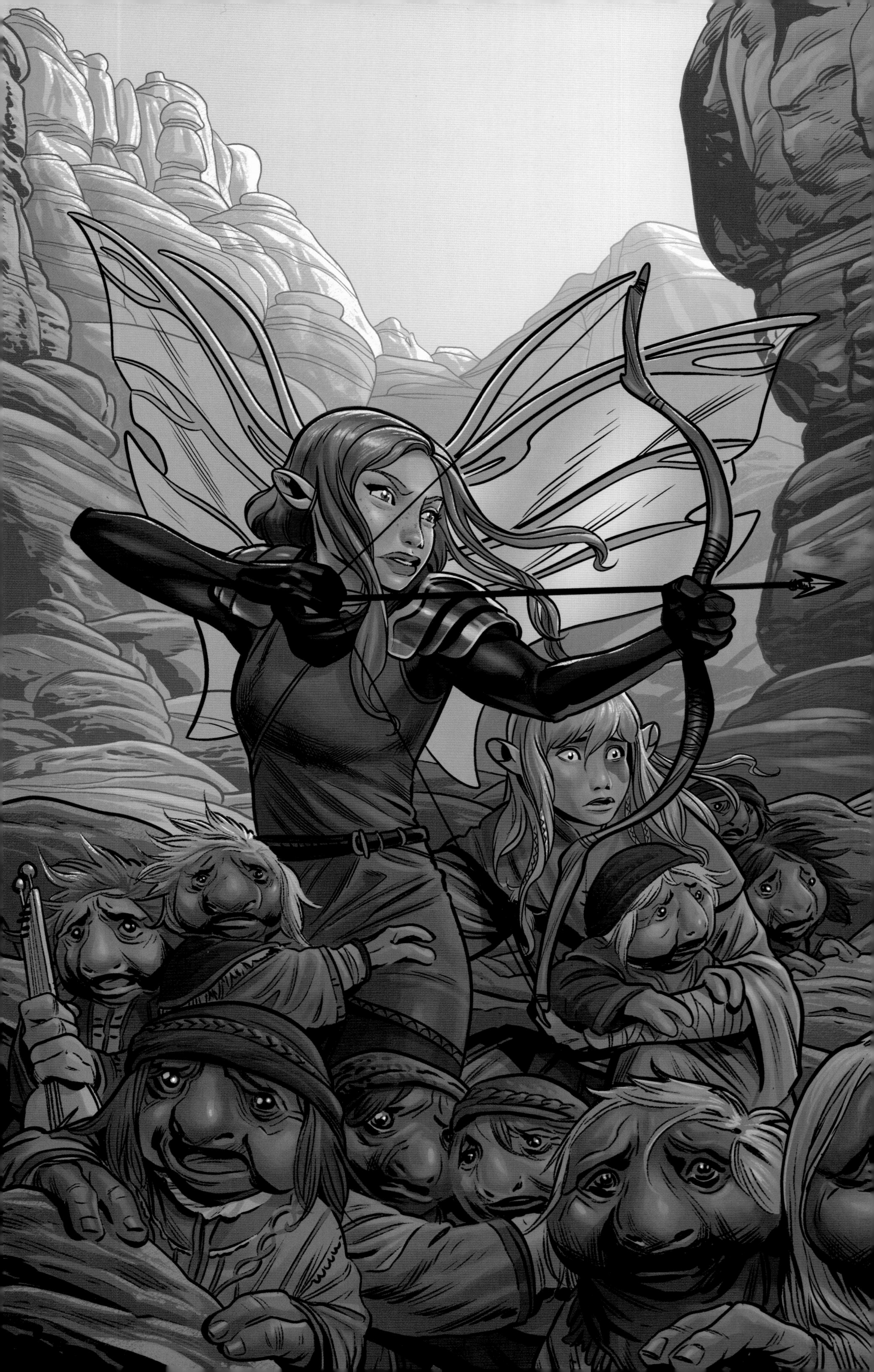

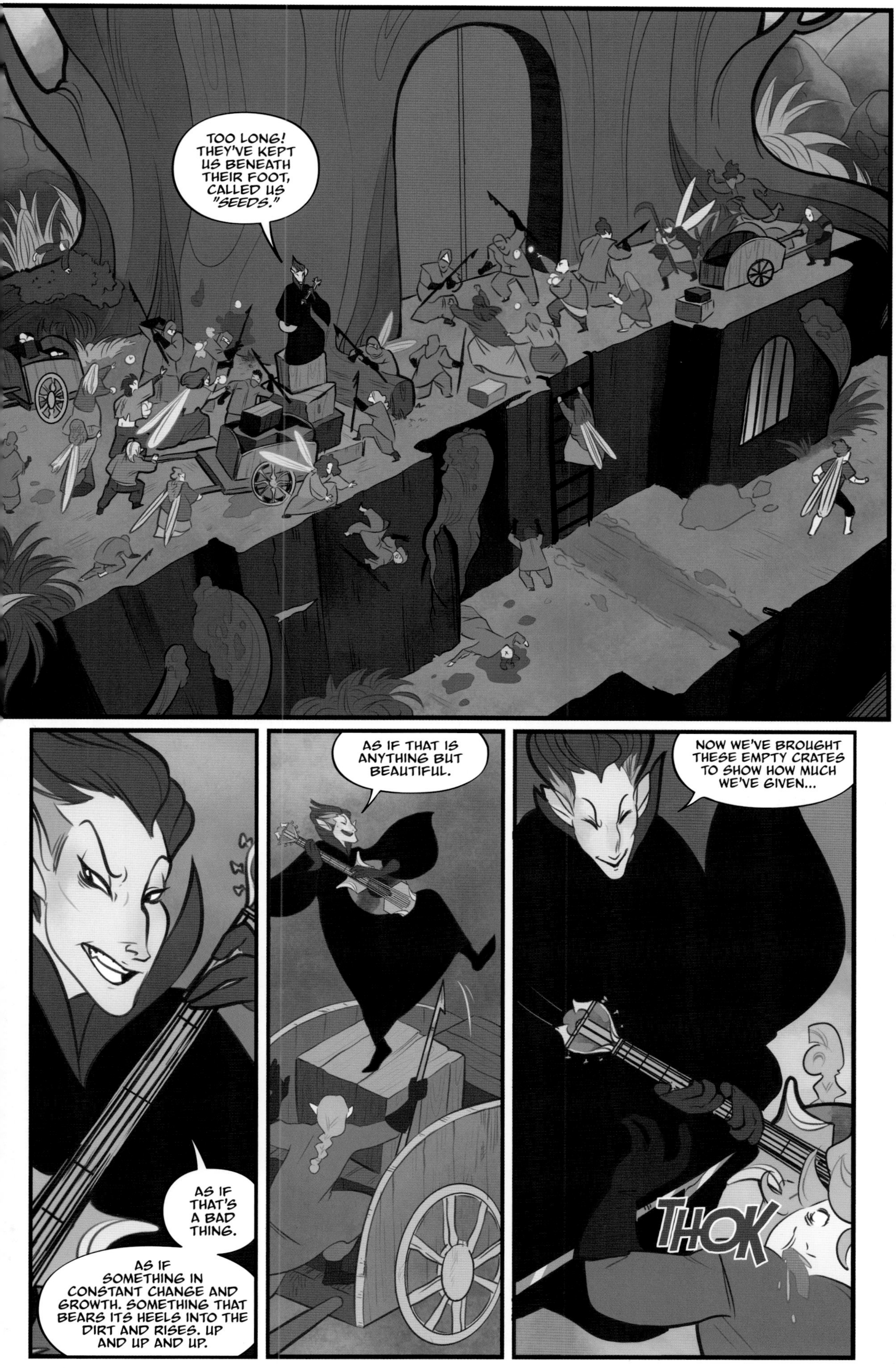
TOO LONG! THEY'VE KEPT US BENEATH THEIR FOOT, CALLED US "SEEDS."
AS IF THAT'S A BAD THING.
AS IF SOMETHING IN CONSTANT CHANGE AND GROWTH. SOMETHING THAT BEARS ITS HEELS INTO THE DIRT AND RISES. UP AND UP AND UP.
AS IF THAT IS ANYTHING BUT BEAUTIFUL.
NOW WE'VE BROUGHT THESE EMPTY CRATES TO SHOW HOW MUCH WE'VE GIVEN...
THOK

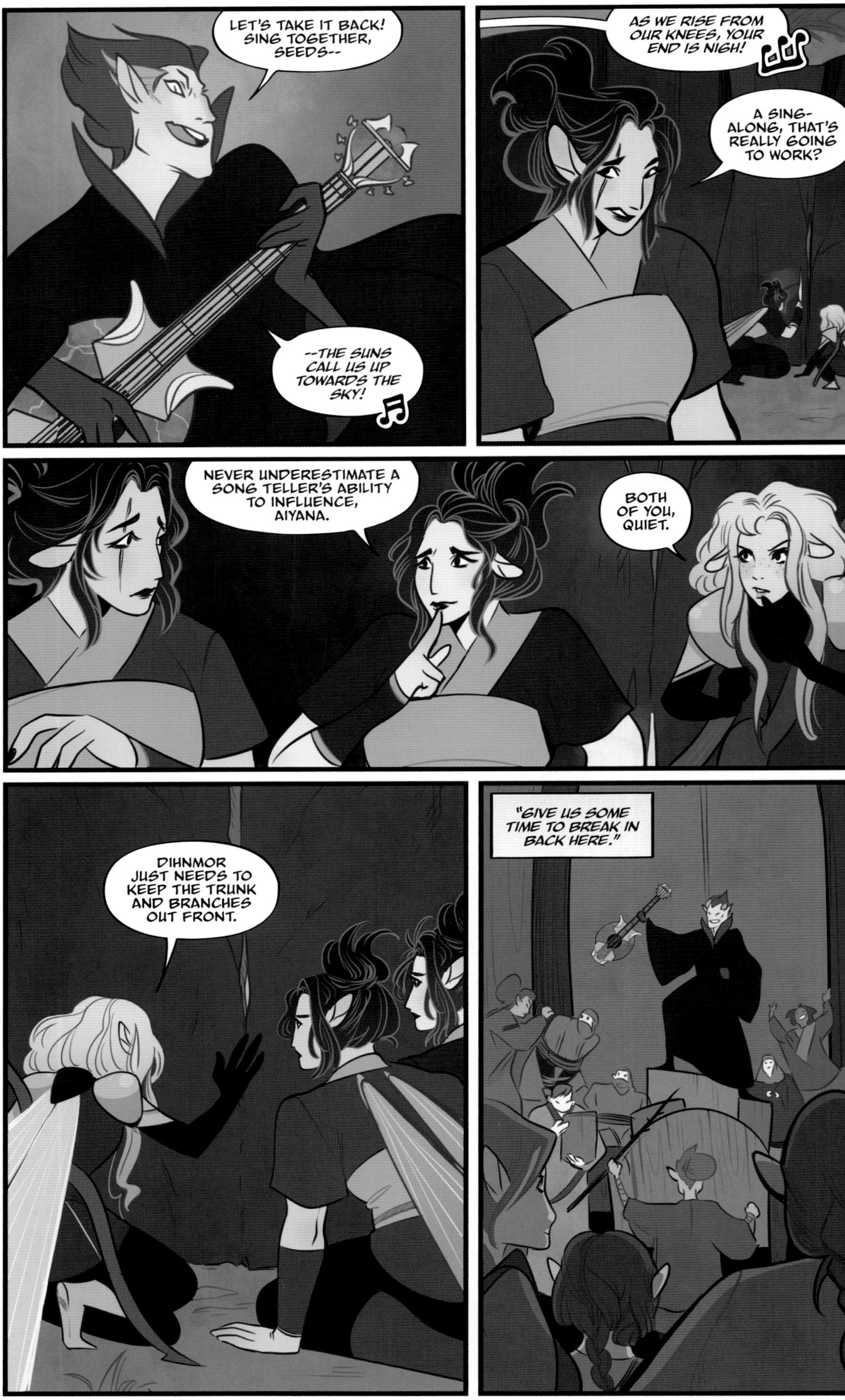
LET'S TAKE IT BACK! SING TOGETHER, SEEDS--
--THE SUNS CALL US UP TOWARDS THE SKY!
AS WE RISE FROM OUR KNEES, YOUR END IS NIGH!
A SING-ALONG, THAT'S REALLY GOING TO WORK?
NEVER UNDERESTIMATE A SONG TELLER'S ABILITY TO INFLUENCE, AIYANA.
BOTH OF YOU, QUIET.
DIHNMOR JUST NEEDS TO KEEP THE TRUNK AND BRANCHES OUT FRONT.
"GIVE US SOME TIME TO BREAK IN BACK HERE."

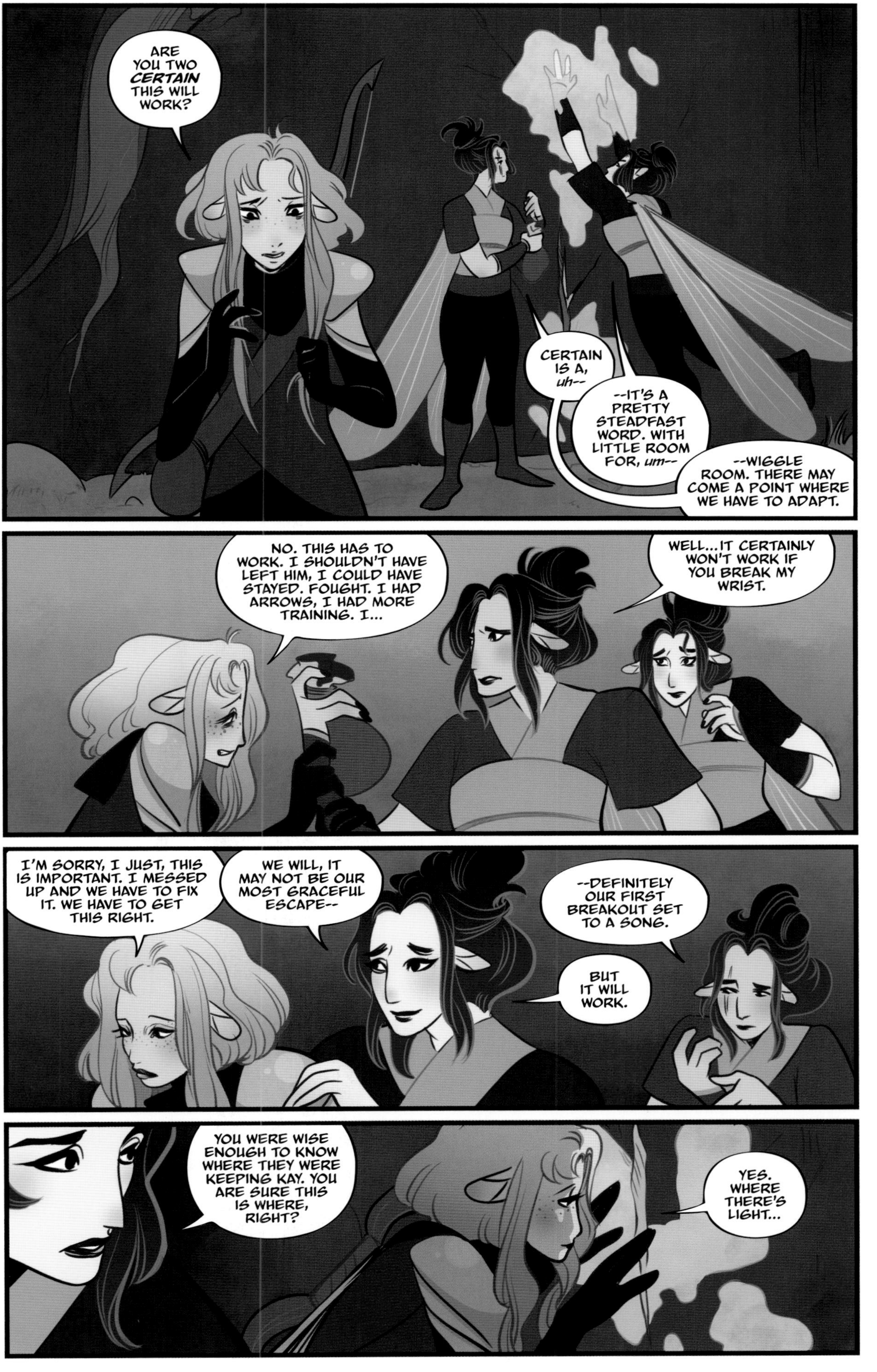
ARE YOU TWO CERTAIN THIS WILL WORK?
CERTAIN IS A, uh--
--IT'S A PRETTY STEADFAST WORD. WITH LITTLE ROOM FOR, um--
--WIGGLE ROOM. THERE MAY COME A POINT WHERE WE HAVE TO ADAPT.
NO. THIS HAS TO WORK. I SHOULDN'T HAVE LEFT HIM, I COULD HAVE STAYED. FOUGHT. I HAD ARROWS, I HAD MORE TRAINING. I...
WELL...IT CERTAINLY WON'T WORK IF YOU BREAK MY WRIST.
I'M SORRY, I JUST, THIS IS IMPORTANT. I MESSED UP AND WE HAVE TO FIX IT. WE HAVE TO GET THIS RIGHT.
WE WILL, IT MAY NOT BE OUR MOST GRACEFUL ESCAPE--
--DEFINITELY OUR FIRST BREAKOUT SET TO A SONG.
BUT IT WILL WORK.
YOU WERE WISE ENOUGH TO KNOW WHERE THEY WERE KEEPING KAY. YOU ARE SURE THIS IS WHERE, RIGHT?
YES. WHERE THERE'S LIGHT...

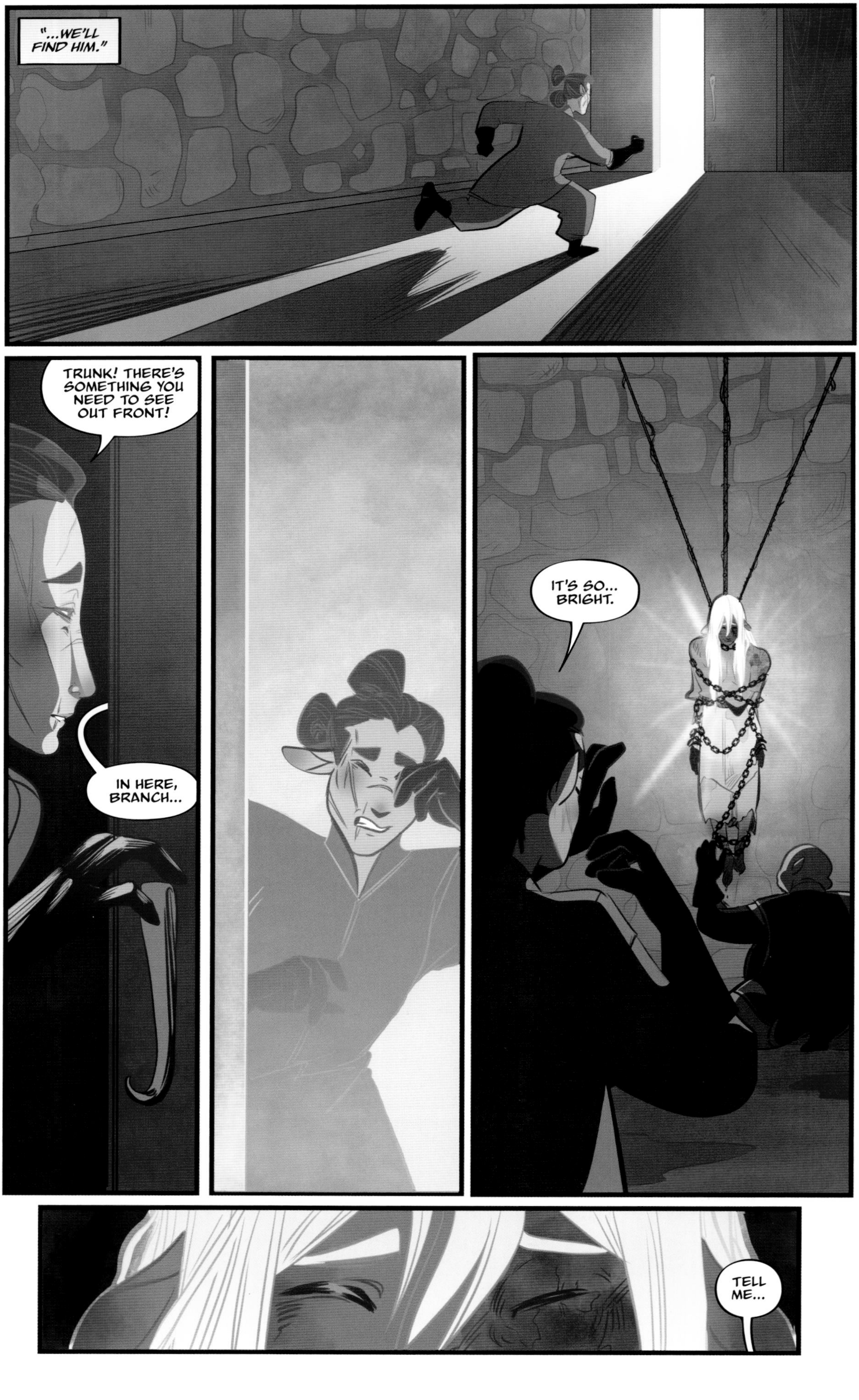
"...WE'LL FIND HIM."
TRUNK! THERE'S SOMETHING YOU NEED TO SEE OUT FRONT!
IN HERE, BRANCH...
IT'S SO... BRIGHT.
TELL ME...

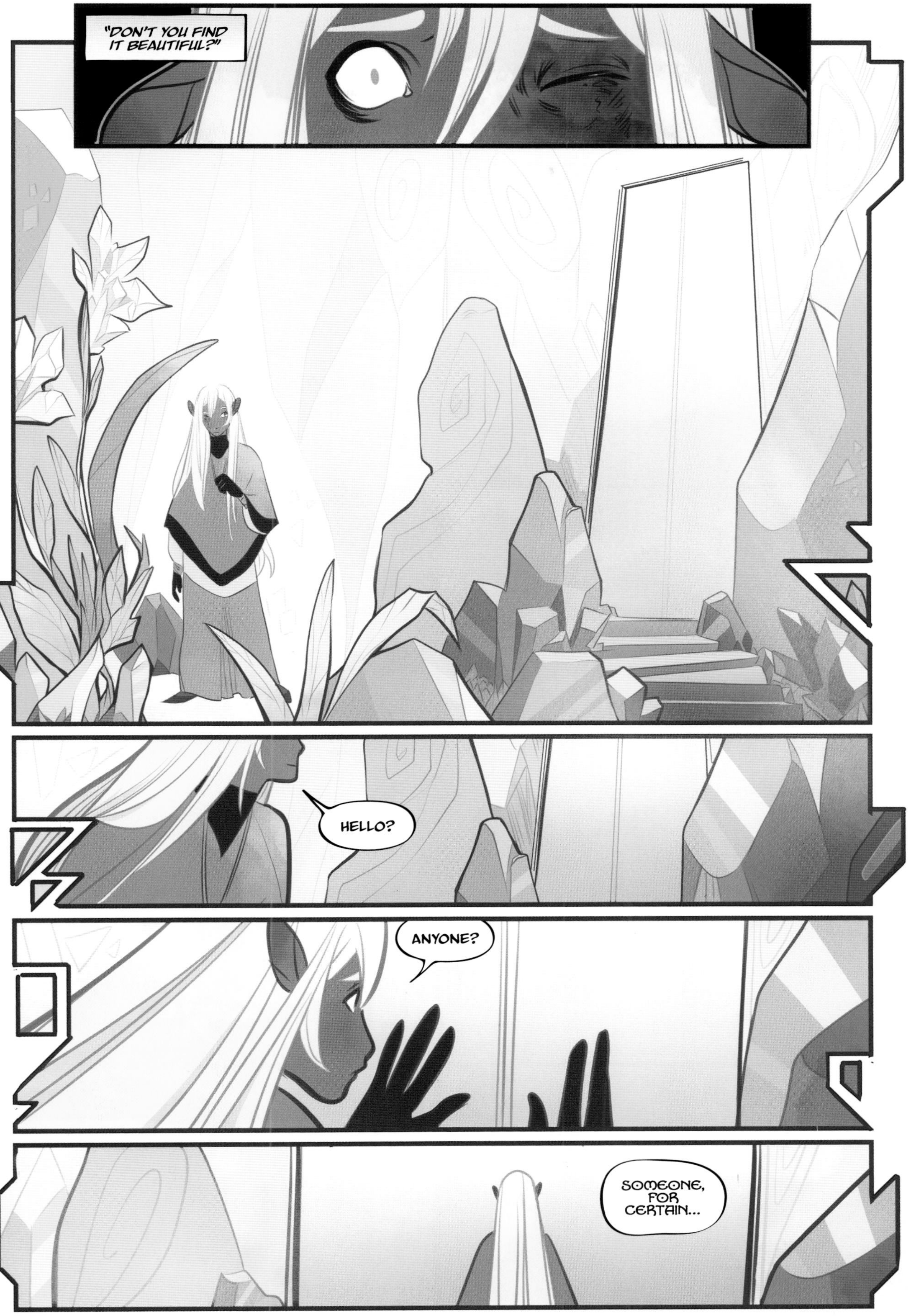
"DON'T YOU FIND IT BEAUTIFUL?"
HELLO?
ANYONE?
SOMEONE, FOR CERTAIN...

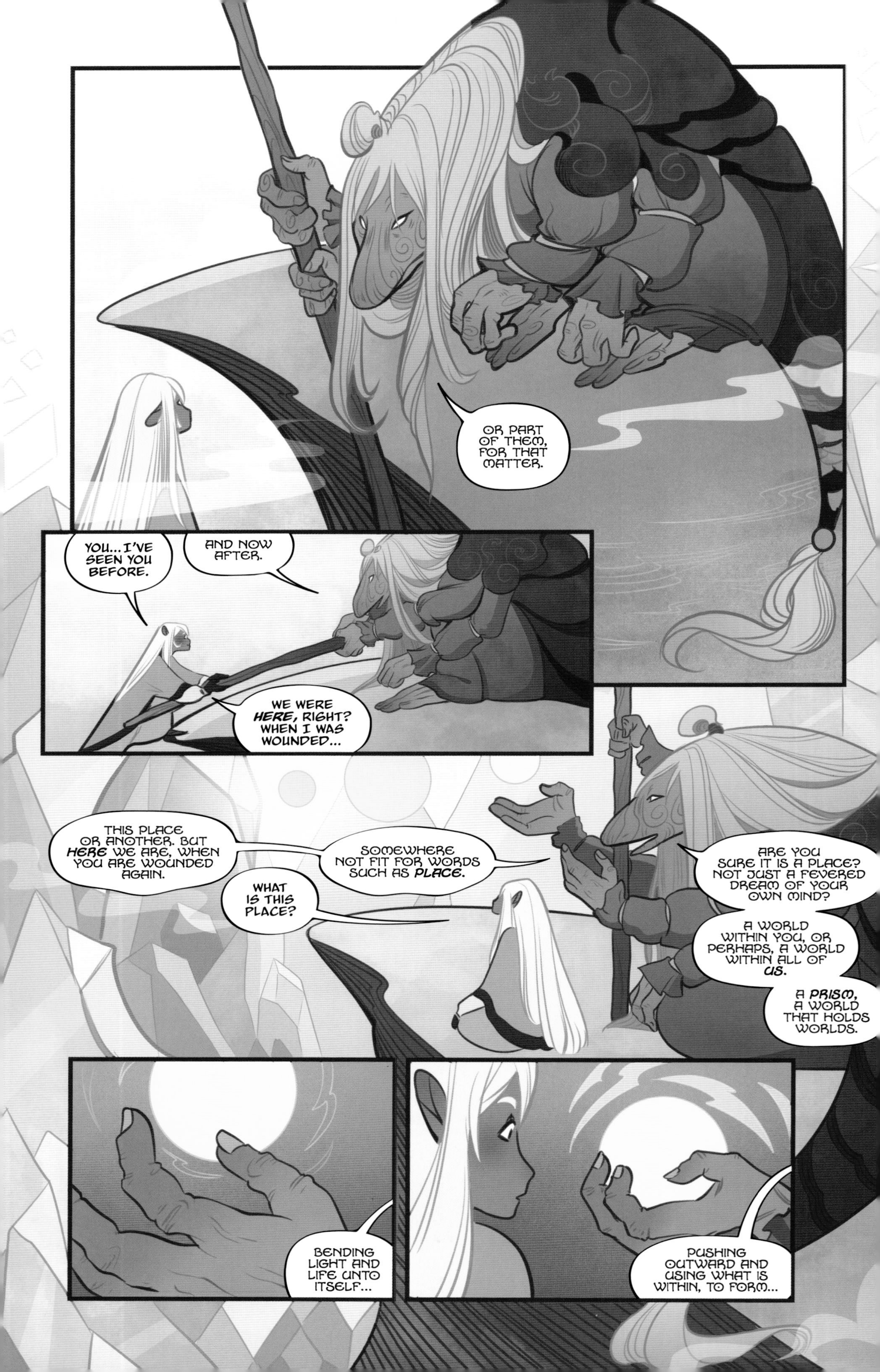
OR PART OF THEM, FOR THAT MATTER.
YOU...I'VE SEEN YOU BEFORE.
AND NOW AFTER.
WE WERE HERE, RIGHT? WHEN I WAS WOUNDED...
THIS PLACE OR ANOTHER. BUT HERE WE ARE, WHEN YOU ARE WOUNDED AGAIN.
WHAT IS THIS PLACE?
SOMEWHERE NOT FIT FOR WORDS SUCH AS PLACE.
ARE YOU SURE IT IS A PLACE? NOT JUST A FEVERED DREAM OF YOUR OWN MIND?
A WORLD WITHIN YOU, OR PERHAPS, A WORLD WITHIN ALL OF US.
A PRISM, A WORLD THAT HOLDS WORLDS.
BENDING LIGHT AND LIFE UNTO ITSELF...
PUSHING OUTWARD AND USING WHAT IS WITHIN, TO FORM...

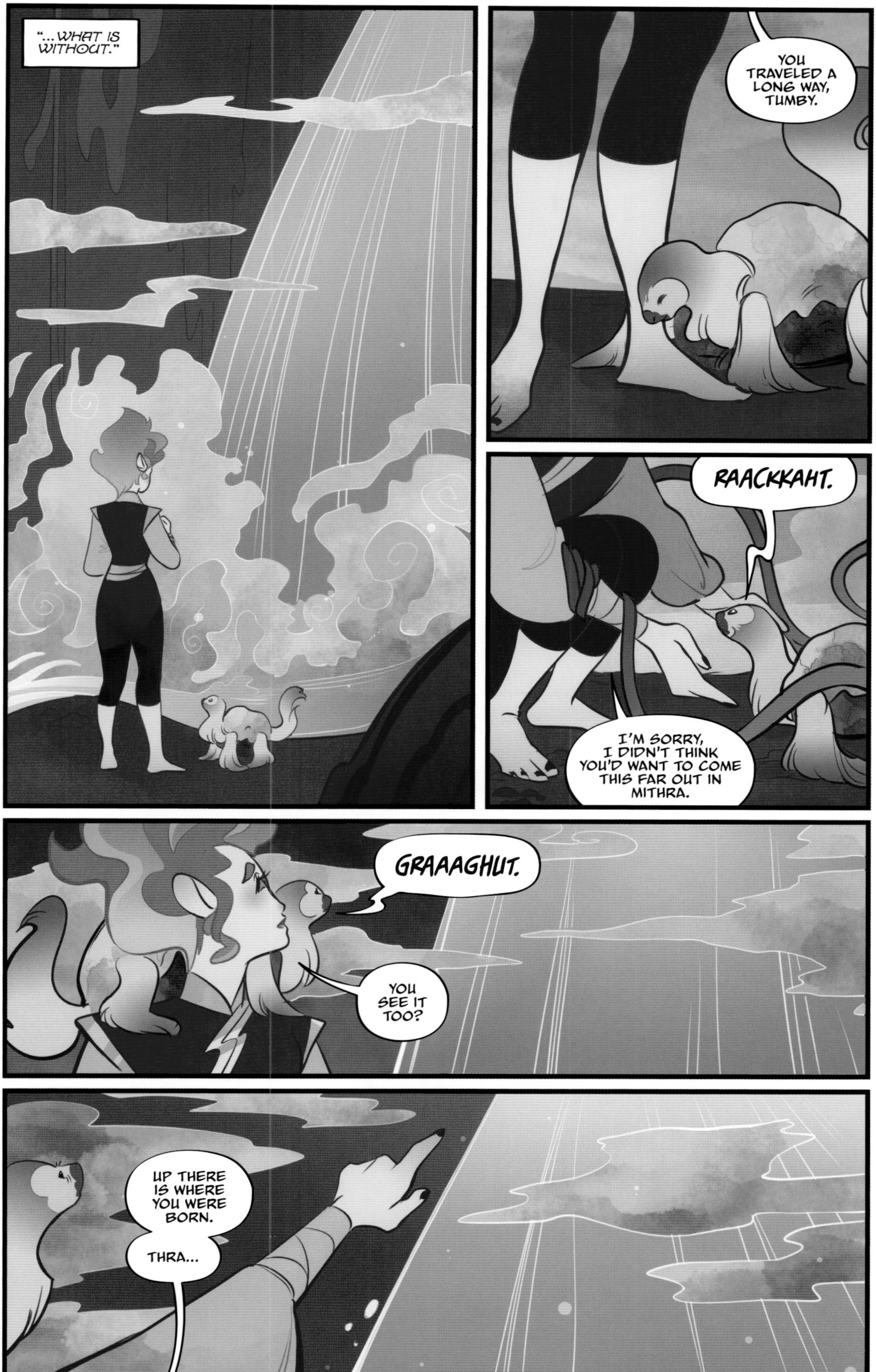
"...WHAT IS WITHOUT."
YOU TRAVELED A LONG WAY, TUMBY.
RAACKKAHT.
I'M SORRY, I DIDN'T THINK YOU'D WANT TO COME THIS FAR OUT IN MITHRA.
GRAAAGHUT.
YOU SEE IT TOO?
UP THERE IS WHERE YOU WERE BORN.
THRA...

DO YOU MISS IT? I DIDN'T THINK I WOULD... I THOUGHT I HAD MY HOME HERE.

BUT I MAY NOT EVEN HAVE THAT ANYMORE.

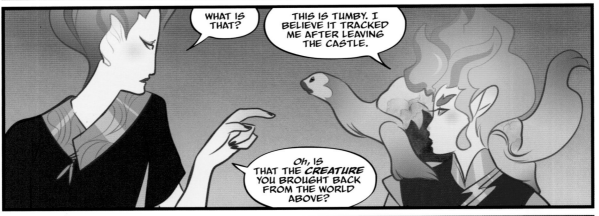

WHAT IS THAT?

THIS IS TUMBY. I BELIEVE IT TRACKED ME AFTER LEAVING THE CASTLE.

Oh, IS THAT THE *CREATURE* YOU BROUGHT BACK FROM THE WORLD ABOVE?

RARRRGHHHTZZ!

THAT MEANS, "YOU'RE WELCOME, I WAS GLAD TO SAVE YOUR LIFE."

I BELIEVE I WAS ALMOST THERE. I WILL ADMIT THOUGH...

THAT "BELIEF" ALMOST CAUSED YOU TO DIM?

IF WE'RE GOING TO GET THROUGH THIS, WE HAVE TO WORK AS ONE. JUST LIKE THOSE TRIBES THAT FIRST BUILT THE GLASS CASTLE.

THERE IS AN IRONY IN ENACTING A CEREMONY TO CHOOSE ONE LEADER INVOLVING MULTIPLE LEADERS WORKING TOGETHER.

NOT JUST WORKING TOGETHER, WORKING AS ONE. WHY DID YOU CHOOSE THE GLASS CASTLE?

IT WAS... IN A WAY, CHOSEN FOR ME. I'VE BEEN TOLD MY WHOLE LIFE I WAS DESTINED TO COMPLETE THIS TASK. IT MADE ME BELIEVE THAT I WAS BELIEVED IN.

IT WON'T BE CHATTER AND TALK THAT GRANTS YOU A THRONE...

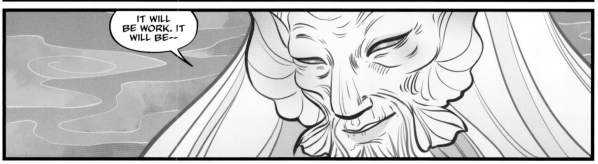

IT WILL BE WORK. IT WILL BE--

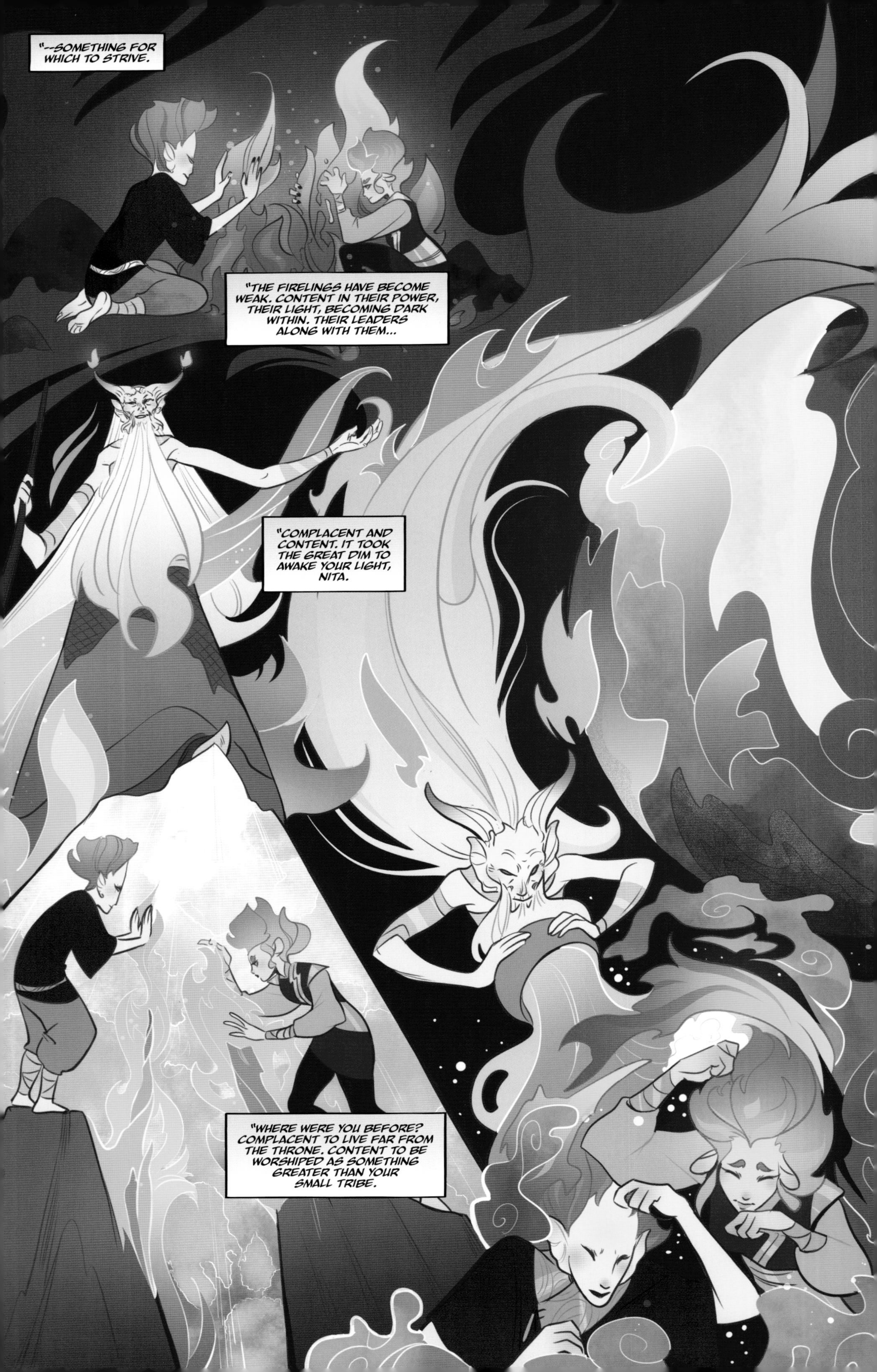
"--SOMETHING FOR WHICH TO STRIVE.
"THE FIRELINGS HAVE BECOME WEAK. CONTENT IN THEIR POWER, THEIR LIGHT, BECOMING DARK WITHIN. THEIR LEADERS ALONG WITH THEM...
"COMPLACENT AND CONTENT. IT TOOK THE GREAT DIM TO AWAKE YOUR LIGHT, NITA.
"WHERE WERE YOU BEFORE? COMPLACENT TO LIVE FAR FROM THE THRONE. CONTENT TO BE WORSHIPED AS SOMETHING GREATER THAN YOUR SMALL TRIBE.

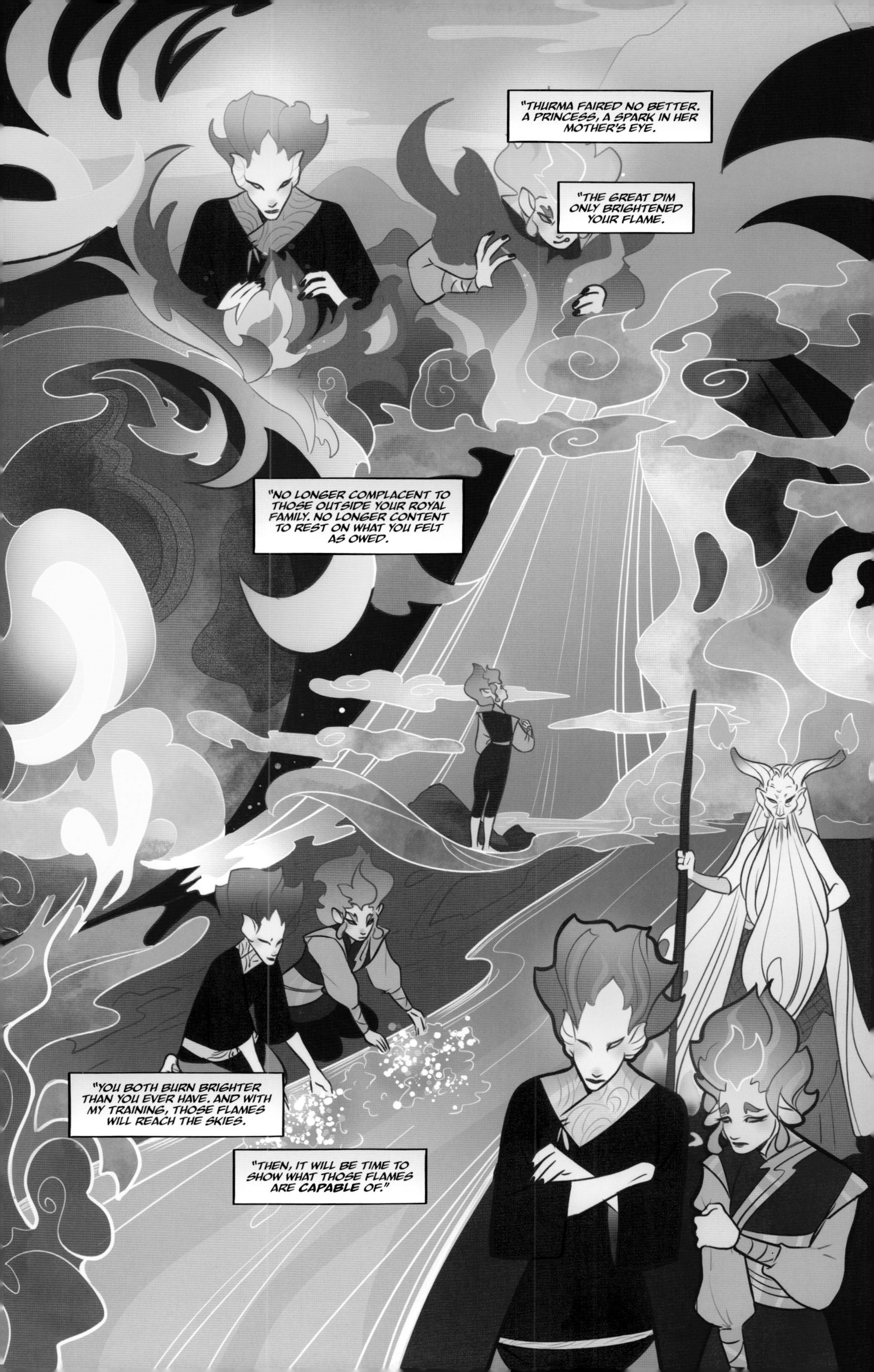
"THURMA FAIRED NO BETTER. A PRINCESS, A SPARK IN HER MOTHER'S EYE.
"THE GREAT DIM ONLY BRIGHTENED YOUR FLAME.
"NO LONGER COMPLACENT TO THOSE OUTSIDE YOUR ROYAL FAMILY. NO LONGER CONTENT TO REST ON WHAT YOU FELT AS OWED.
"YOU BOTH BURN BRIGHTER THAN YOU EVER HAVE. AND WITH MY TRAINING, THOSE FLAMES WILL REACH THE SKIES.
"THEN, IT WILL BE TIME TO SHOW WHAT THOSE FLAMES ARE CAPABLE OF."

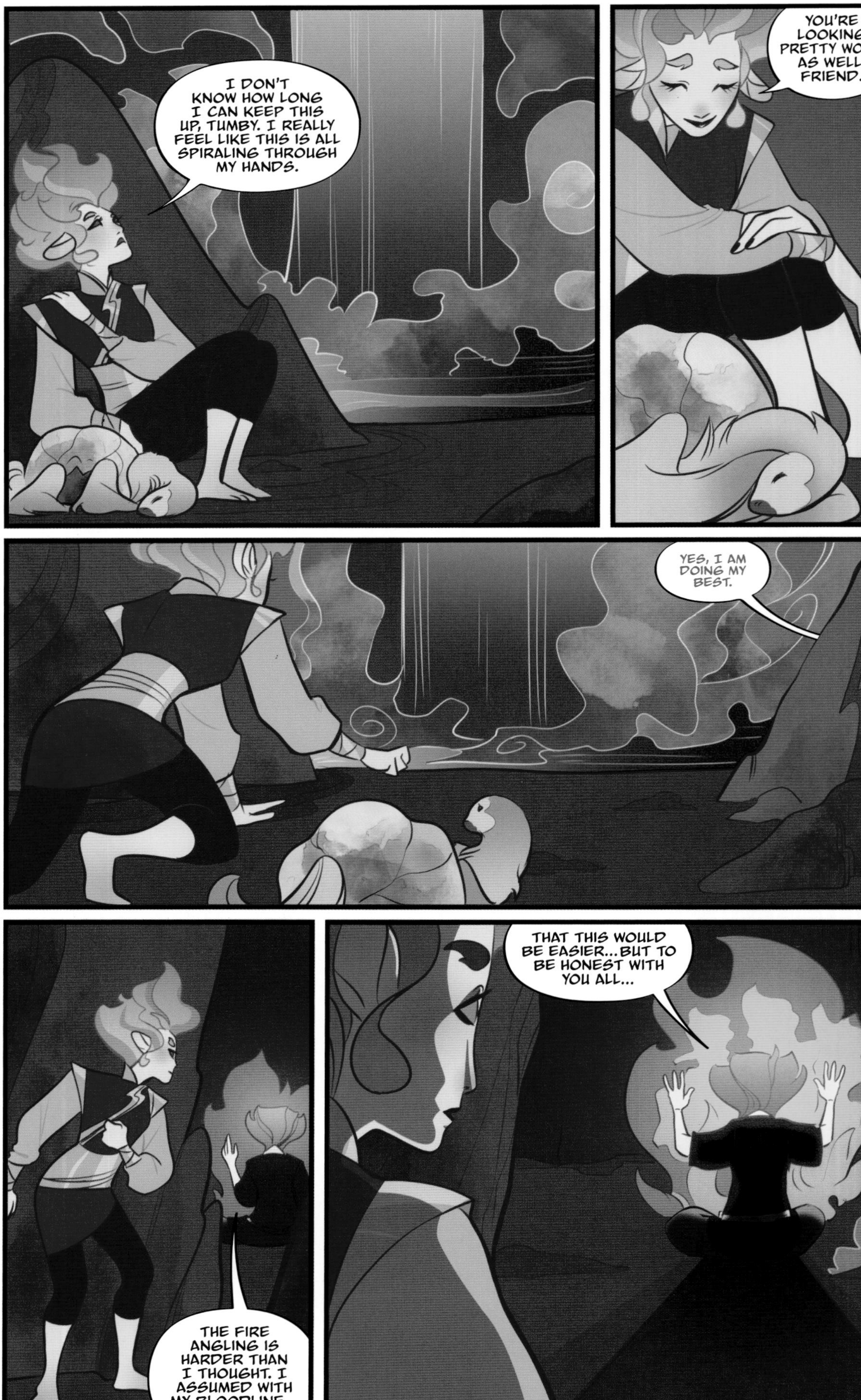
I DON'T KNOW HOW LONG I CAN KEEP THIS UP, TUMBY. I REALLY FEEL LIKE THIS IS ALL SPIRALING THROUGH MY HANDS.
YOU'RE LOOKING PRETTY WORN AS WELL, FRIEND.
YES, I AM DOING MY BEST.
THE FIRE ANGLING IS HARDER THAN I THOUGHT. I ASSUMED WITH MY BLOODLINE...
THAT THIS WOULD BE EASIER...BUT TO BE HONEST WITH YOU ALL...

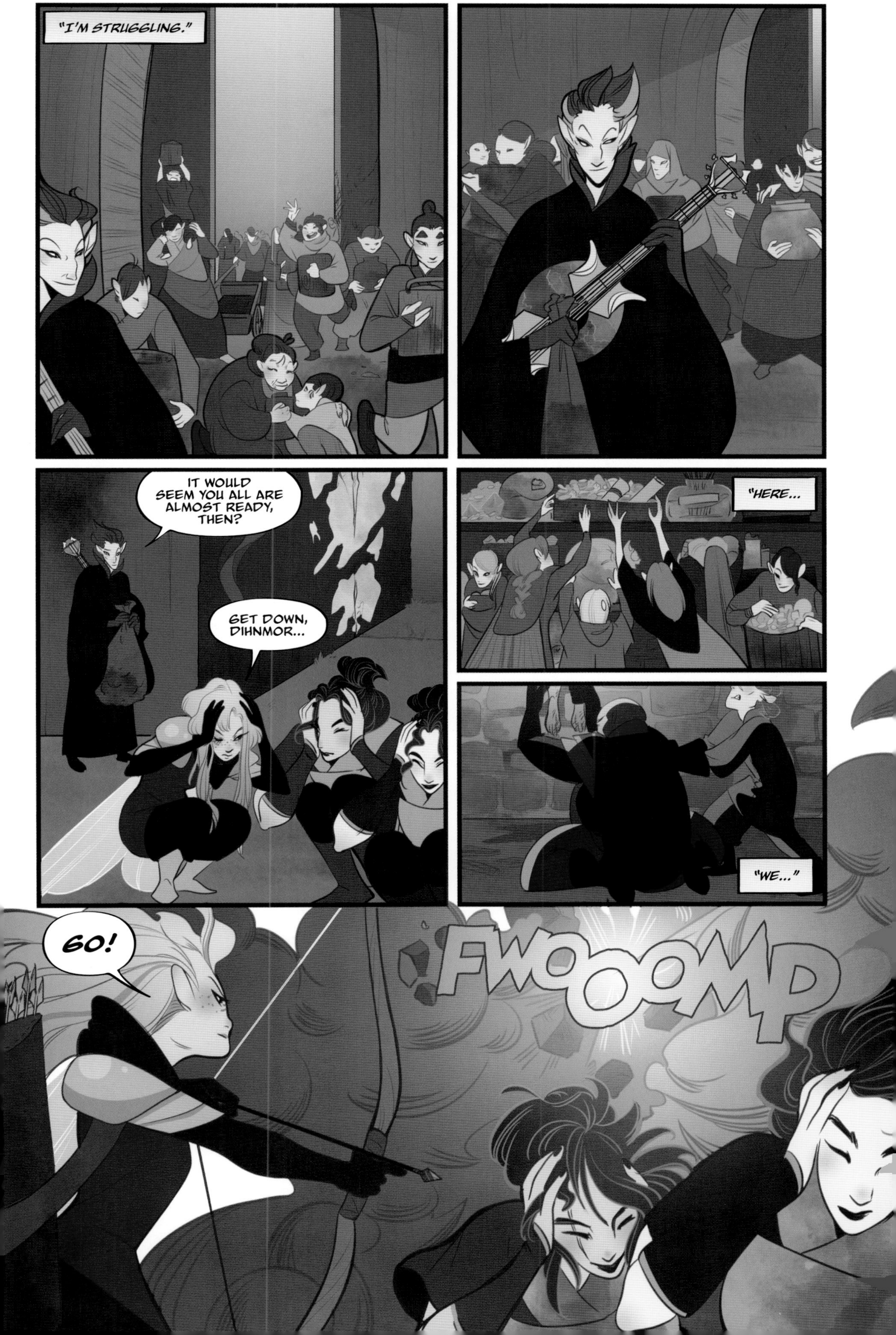
"I'M STRUGGLING."
IT WOULD SEEM YOU ALL ARE ALMOST READY, THEN?
GET DOWN, DIHNMOR...
"HERE...
"WE..."
GO!
FWOOOMP

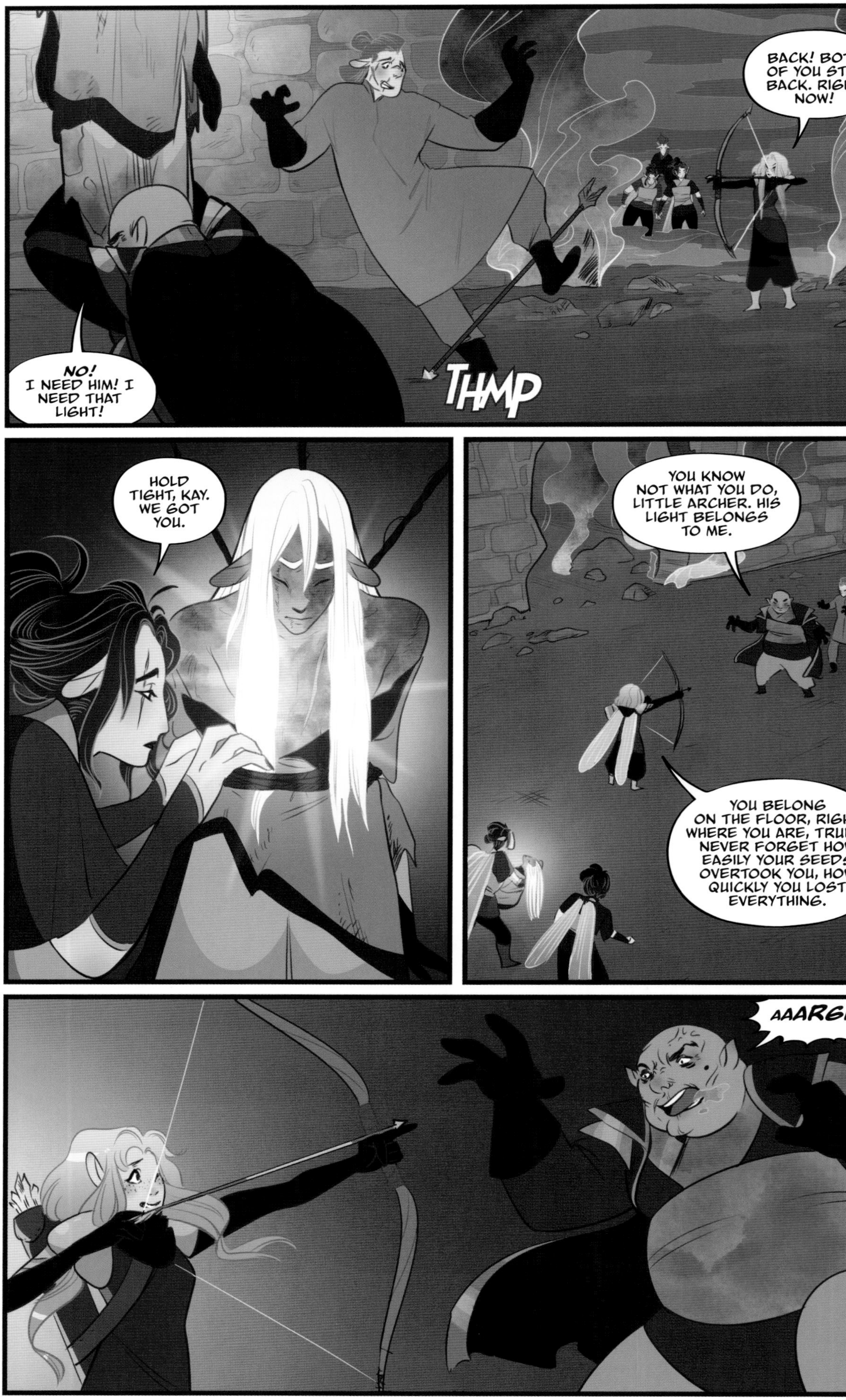
BACK! BOTH OF YOU STAY BACK. RIGHT NOW!
NO! I NEED HIM! I NEED THAT LIGHT!
THMP
HOLD TIGHT, KAY. WE GOT YOU.
YOU KNOW NOT WHAT YOU DO, LITTLE ARCHER. HIS LIGHT BELONGS TO ME.
YOU BELONG ON THE FLOOR, RIGHT WHERE YOU ARE, TRUNK. NEVER FORGET HOW EASILY YOUR SEEDS OVERTOOK YOU, HOW QUICKLY YOU LOST EVERYTHING.
AAARGH!

BATHE ME IN YOUR LIGHT! LET ME BE REBORN!

NO, NO, WHAT IS HAPPENING? I SEE ONLY NOTHINGNESS... ONLY...

CRAK

...DARKNESS.

HURRY NOW, HASTE IS OUR GREATEST ALLY AT THE MOMENT.

IS KAY ALRIGHT?

WHAT IS THAT POURING FROM HIM?

I'M SURE IT WAS SOME TORTURE OF THE TRUNK.

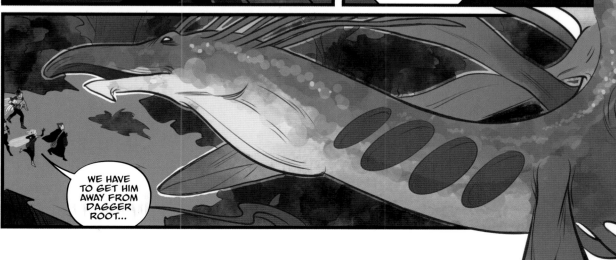

WE HAVE TO GET HIM AWAY FROM DAGGER ROOT...

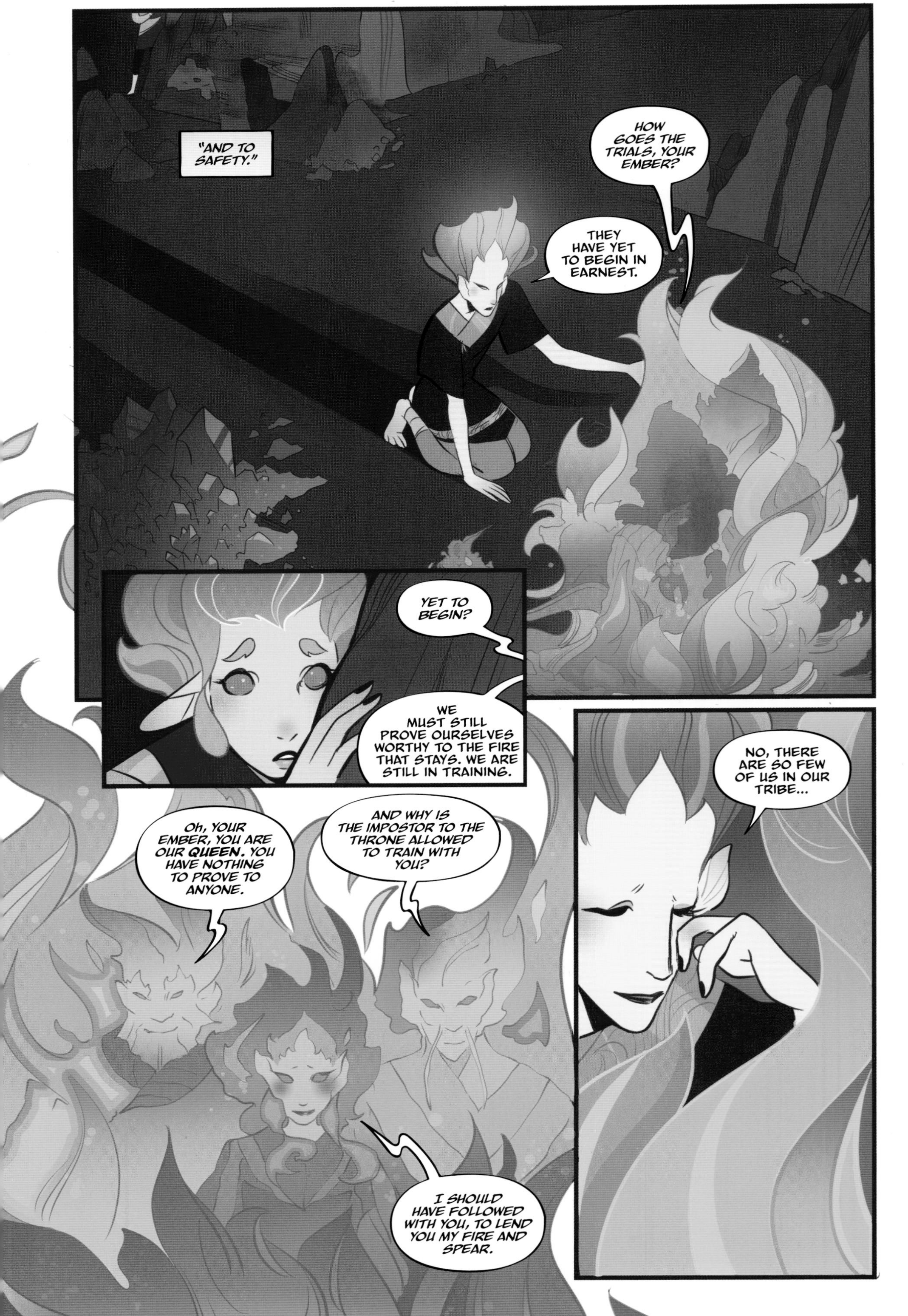
"AND TO SAFETY."
HOW GOES THE TRIALS, YOUR EMBER?
THEY HAVE YET TO BEGIN IN EARNEST.
YET TO BEGIN?
WE MUST STILL PROVE OURSELVES WORTHY TO THE FIRE THAT STAYS. WE ARE STILL IN TRAINING.
NO, THERE ARE SO FEW OF US IN OUR TRIBE...
Oh, YOUR EMBER, YOU ARE OUR **QUEEN**. YOU HAVE NOTHING TO PROVE TO ANYONE.
AND WHY IS THE IMPOSTOR TO THE THRONE ALLOWED TO TRAIN WITH YOU?
I SHOULD HAVE FOLLOWED WITH YOU, TO LEND YOU MY FIRE AND SPEAR.

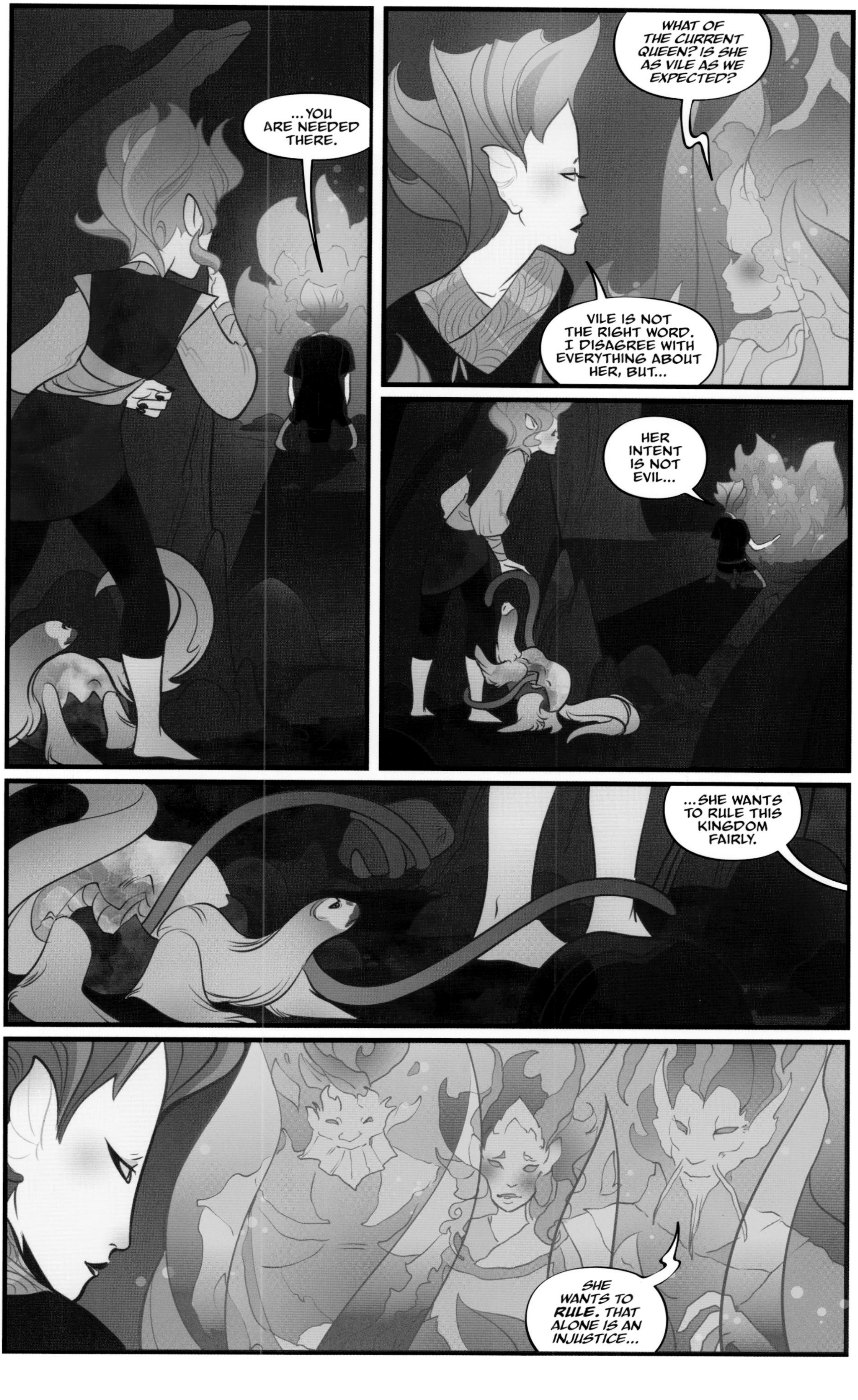
...YOU ARE NEEDED THERE.
WHAT OF THE CURRENT QUEEN? IS SHE AS VILE AS WE EXPECTED?
VILE IS NOT THE RIGHT WORD. I DISAGREE WITH EVERYTHING ABOUT HER, BUT...
HER INTENT IS NOT EVIL...
...SHE WANTS TO RULE THIS KINGDOM FAIRLY.
SHE WANTS TO RULE. THAT ALONE IS AN INJUSTICE...

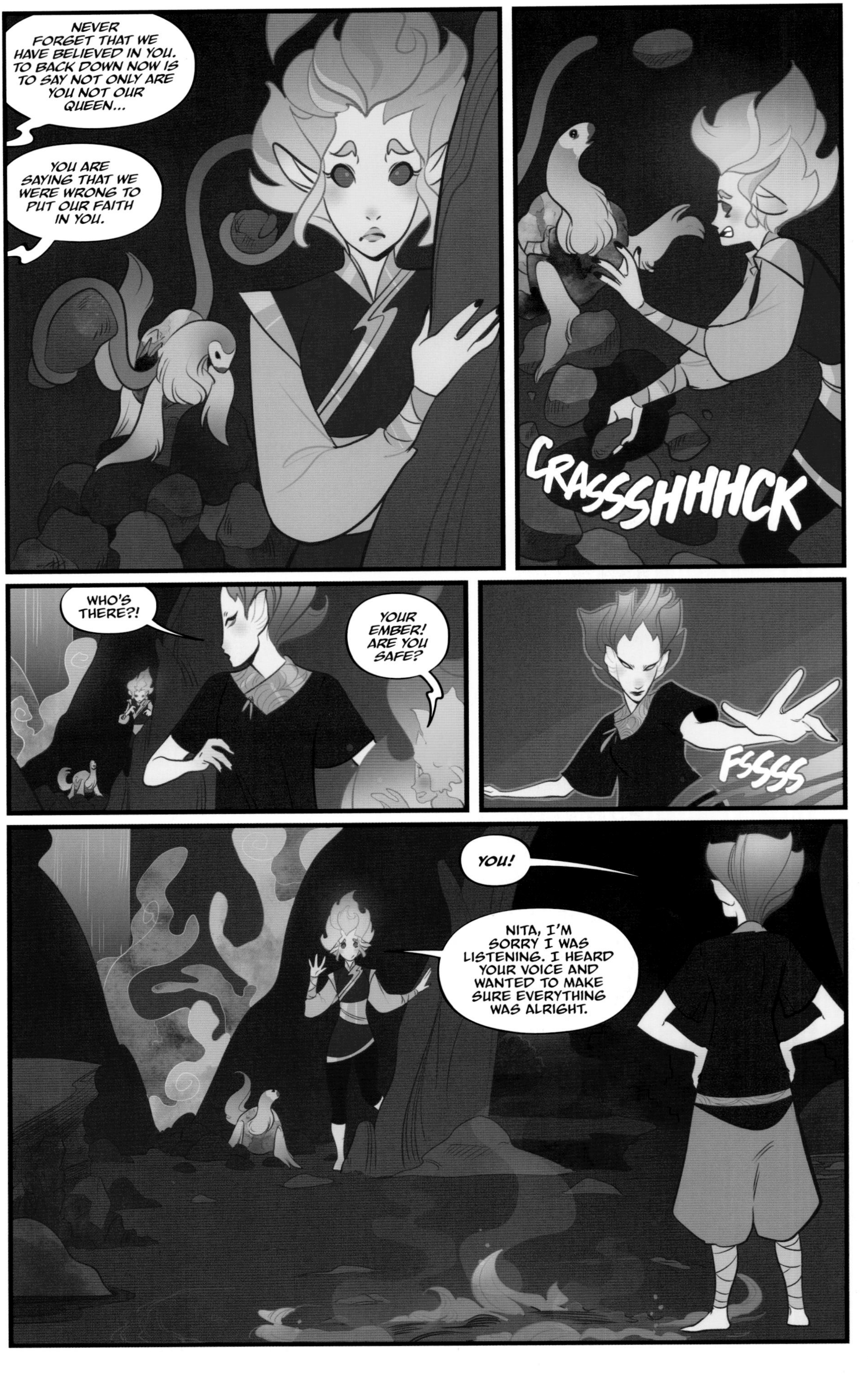

NEVER FORGET THAT WE HAVE BELIEVED IN YOU. TO BACK DOWN NOW IS TO SAY NOT ONLY ARE YOU NOT OUR QUEEN...
YOU ARE SAYING THAT WE WERE WRONG TO PUT OUR FAITH IN YOU.
CRASSSHHHCK
WHO'S THERE?!
YOUR EMBER! ARE YOU SAFE?
FSSSS
YOU!
NITA, I'M SORRY I WAS LISTENING. I HEARD YOUR VOICE AND WANTED TO MAKE SURE EVERYTHING WAS ALRIGHT.

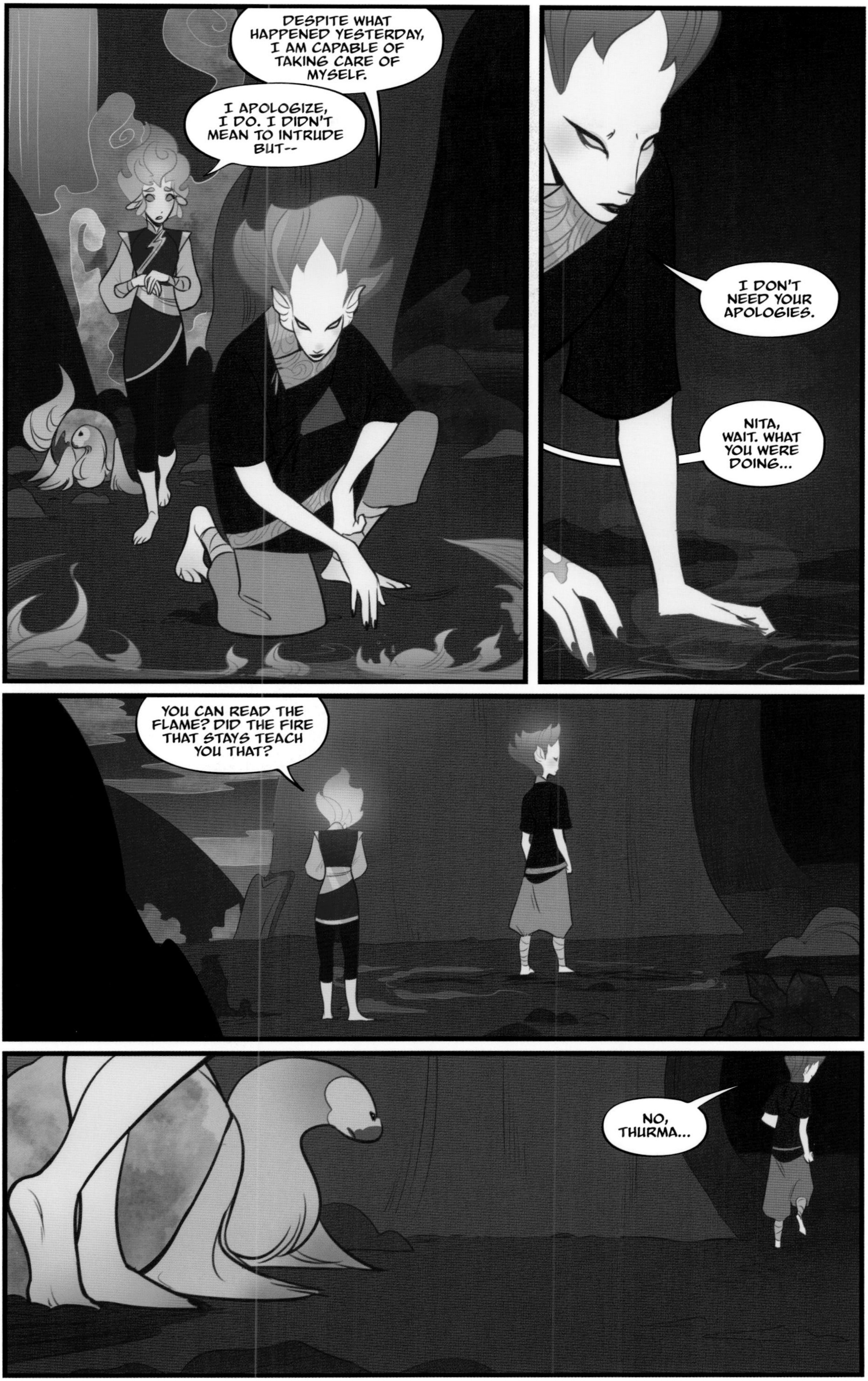
DESPITE WHAT HAPPENED YESTERDAY, I AM CAPABLE OF TAKING CARE OF MYSELF.
I APOLOGIZE, I DO. I DIDN'T MEAN TO INTRUDE BUT--
I DON'T NEED YOUR APOLOGIES.
NITA, WAIT. WHAT YOU WERE DOING...
YOU CAN READ THE FLAME? DID THE FIRE THAT STAYS TEACH YOU THAT?
NO, THURMA...

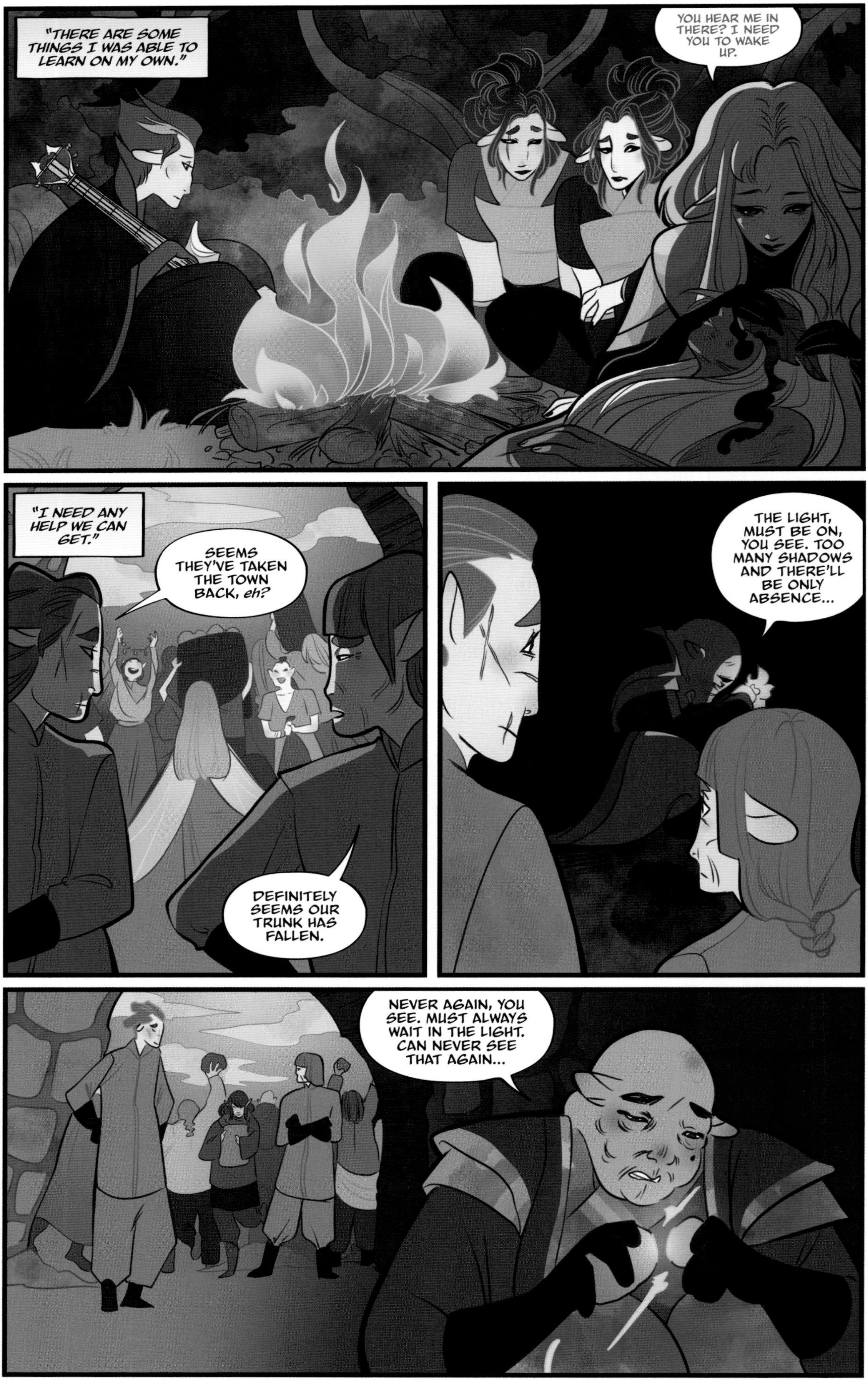
"THERE ARE SOME THINGS I WAS ABLE TO LEARN ON MY OWN."
YOU HEAR ME IN THERE? I NEED YOU TO WAKE UP.
"I NEED ANY HELP WE CAN GET."
SEEMS THEY'VE TAKEN THE TOWN BACK, *eh?*
DEFINITELY SEEMS OUR TRUNK HAS FALLEN.
THE LIGHT, MUST BE ON, YOU SEE. TOO MANY SHADOWS AND THERE'LL BE ONLY ABSENCE...
NEVER AGAIN, YOU SEE. MUST ALWAYS WAIT IN THE LIGHT. CAN NEVER SEE THAT AGAIN...

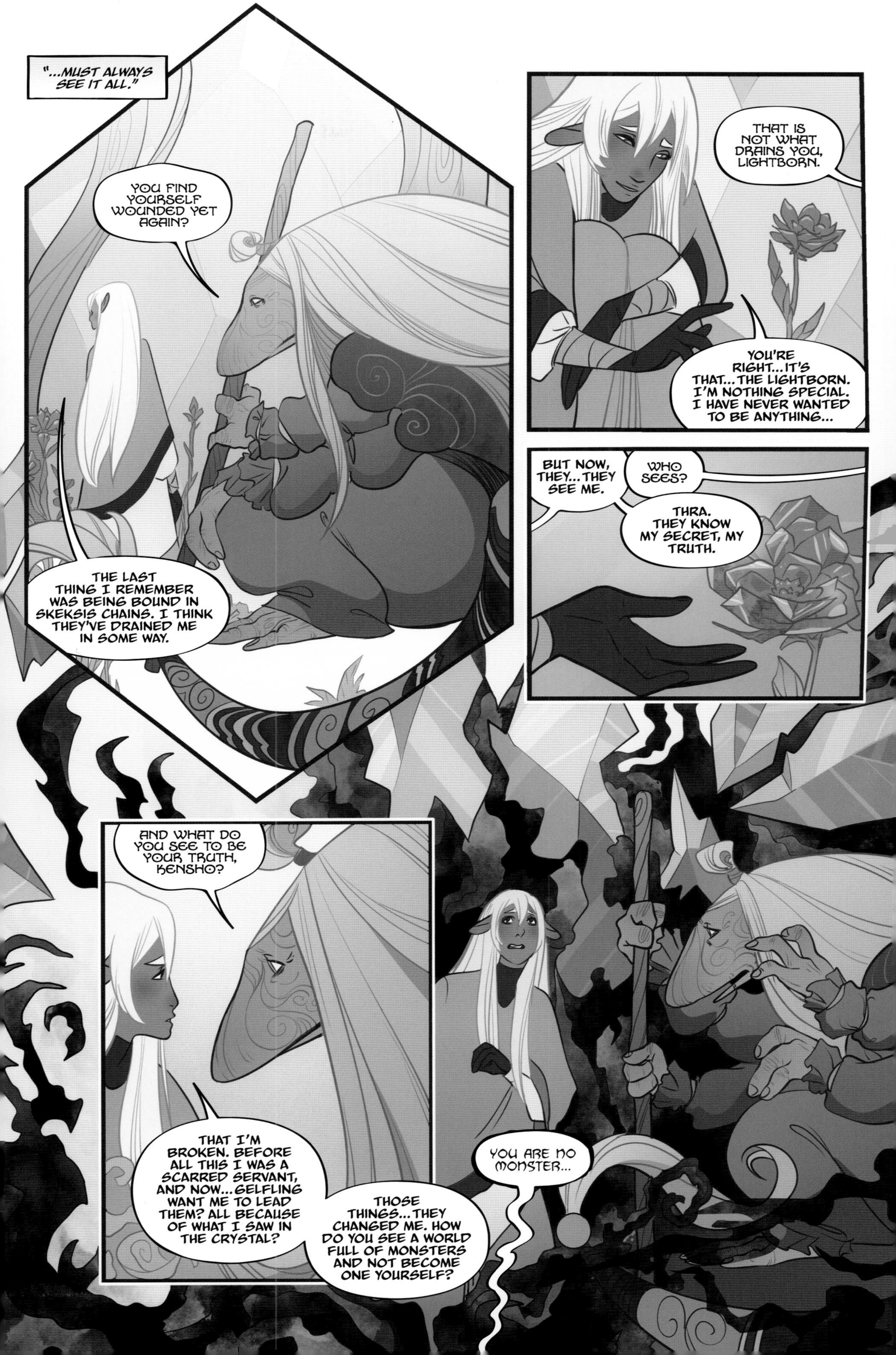
"...MUST ALWAYS SEE IT ALL."
YOU FIND YOURSELF WOUNDED YET AGAIN?
THE LAST THING I REMEMBER WAS BEING BOUND IN SKEKSIS CHAINS. I THINK THEY'VE DRAINED ME IN SOME WAY.
THAT IS NOT WHAT DRAINS YOU, LIGHTBORN.
YOU'RE RIGHT...IT'S THAT...THE LIGHTBORN. I'M NOTHING SPECIAL. I HAVE NEVER WANTED TO BE ANYTHING...
BUT NOW, THEY...THEY SEE ME.
WHO SEES?
THRA. THEY KNOW MY SECRET, MY TRUTH.
AND WHAT DO YOU SEE TO BE YOUR TRUTH, KENSHO?
THAT I'M BROKEN. BEFORE ALL THIS I WAS A SCARRED SERVANT, AND NOW...GELFLING WANT ME TO LEAD THEM? ALL BECAUSE OF WHAT I SAW IN THE CRYSTAL?
THOSE THINGS...THEY CHANGED ME. HOW DO YOU SEE A WORLD FULL OF MONSTERS AND NOT BECOME ONE YOURSELF?
YOU ARE NO MONSTER...

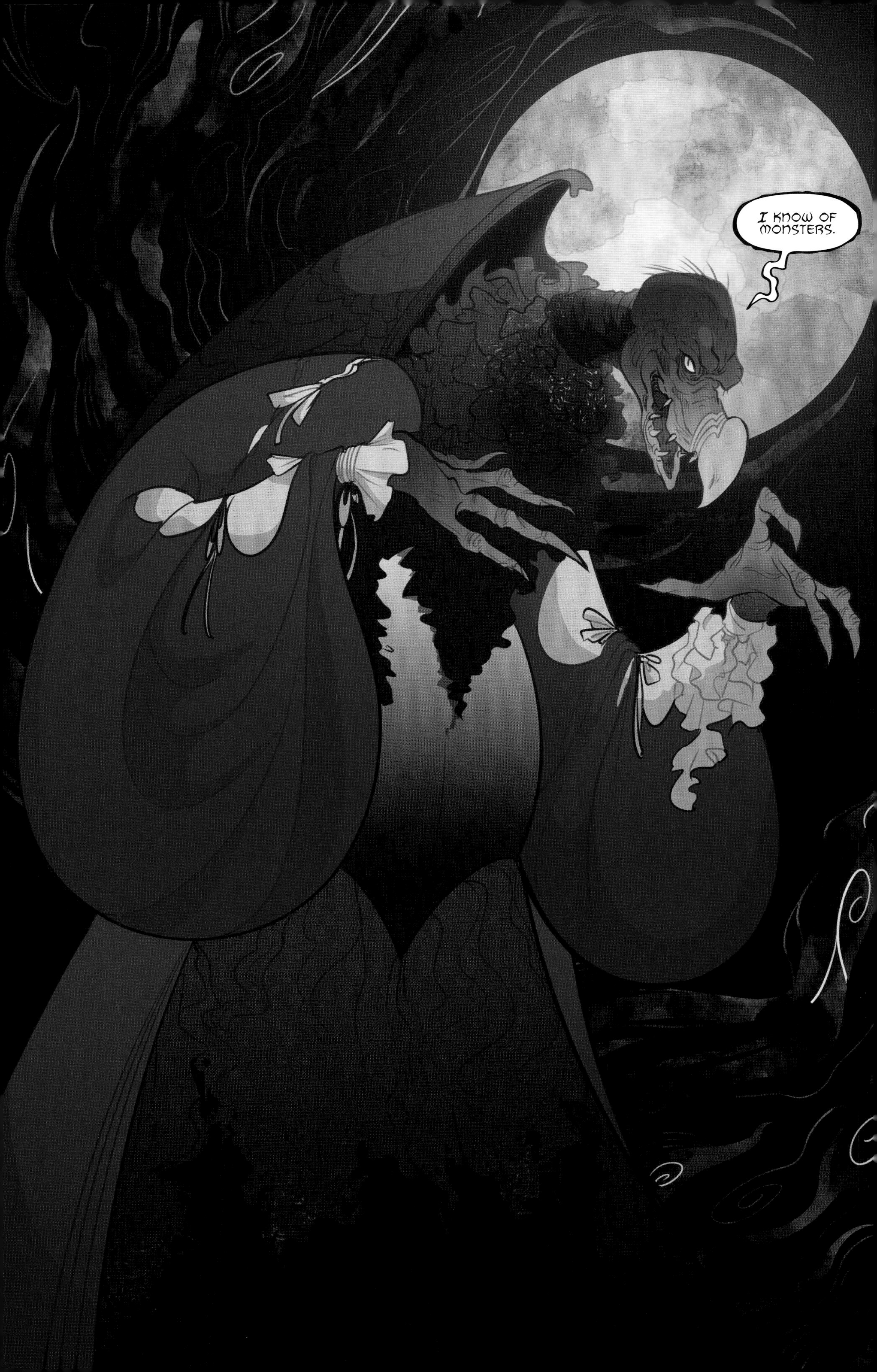
I KNOW OF MONSTERS.

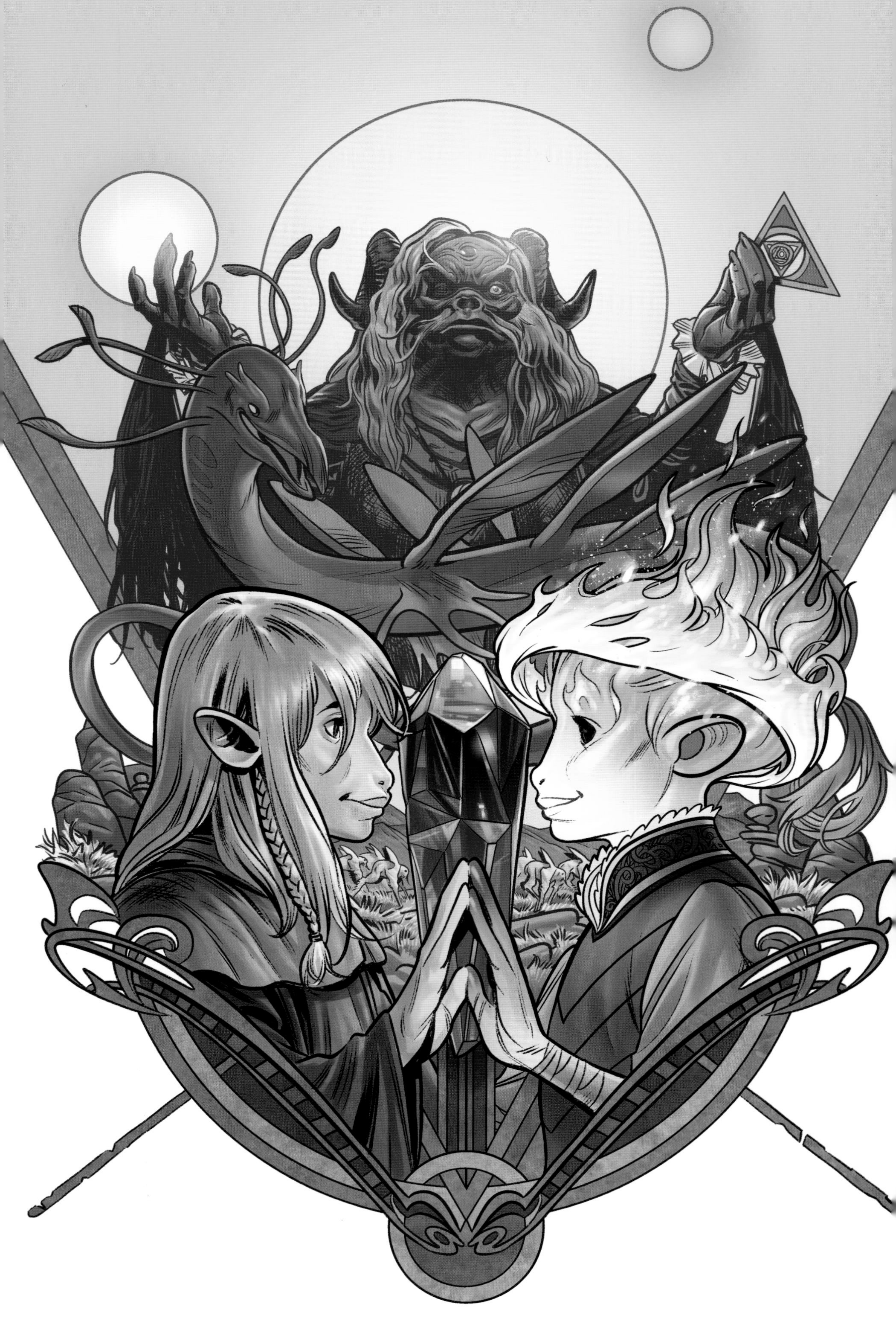

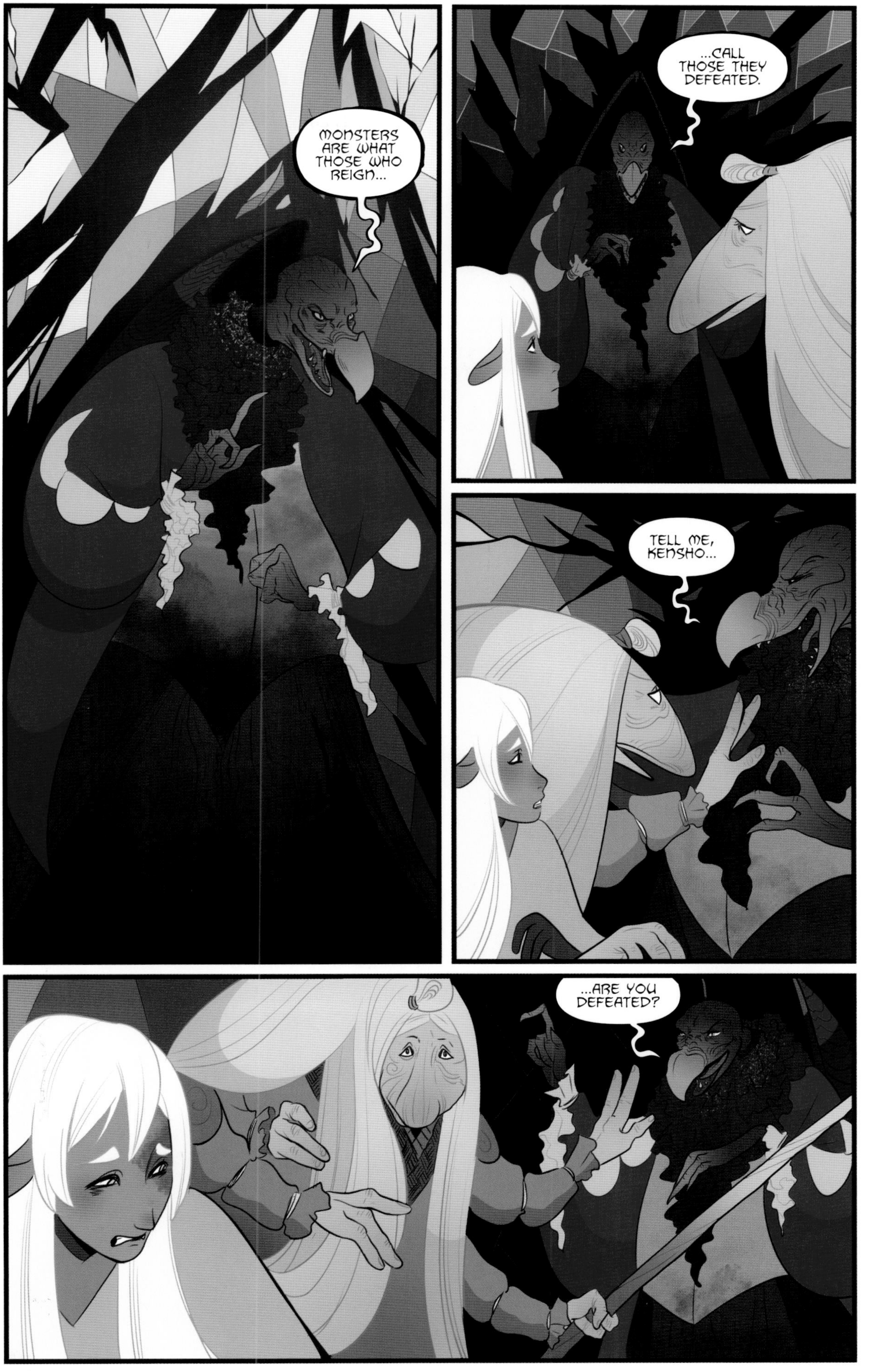
MONSTERS ARE WHAT THOSE WHO REIGN...
...CALL THOSE THEY DEFEATED.
TELL ME, KENSHO...
...ARE YOU DEFEATED?

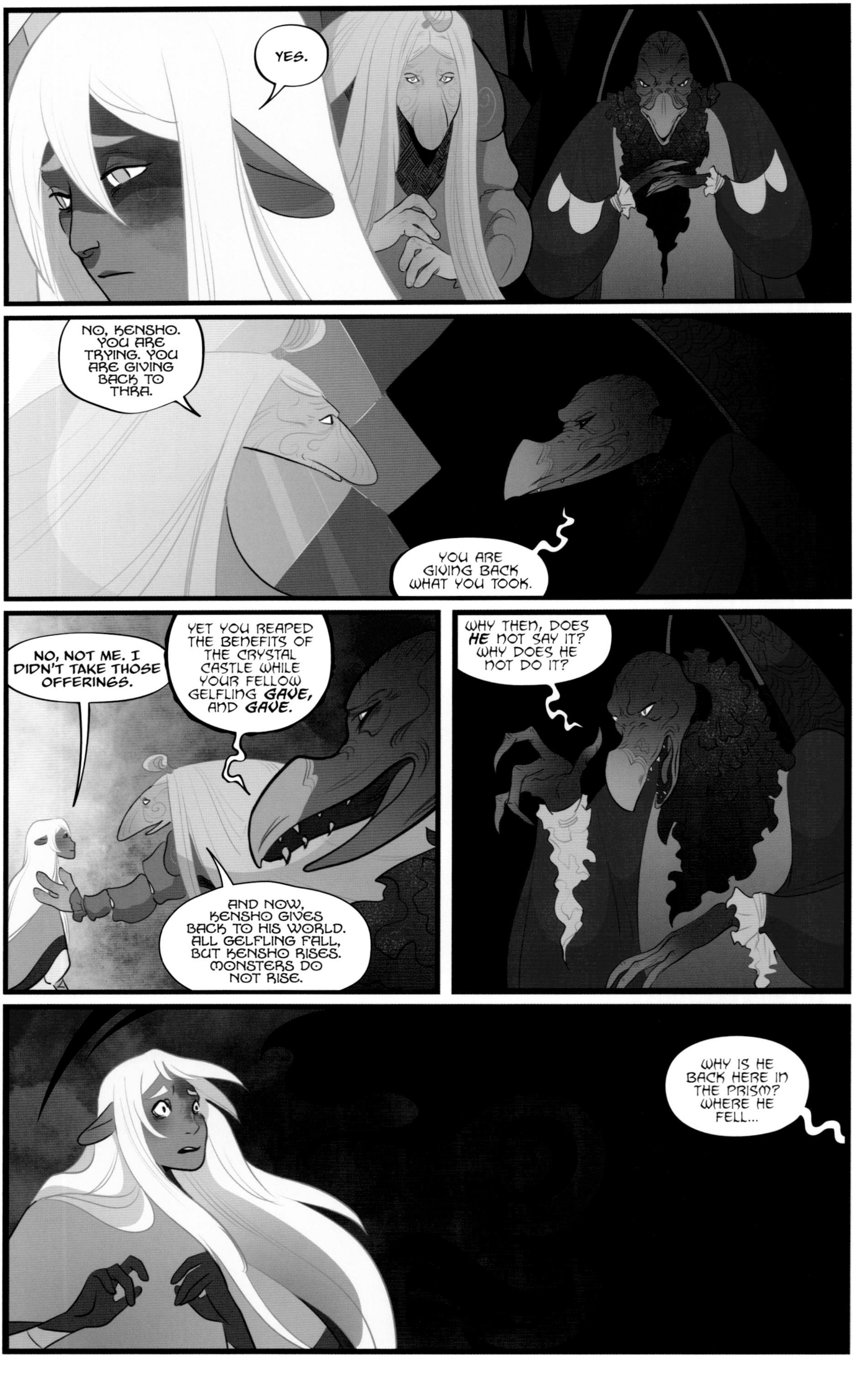
YES.
NO, KENSHO. YOU ARE TRYING. YOU ARE GIVING BACK TO THRA.
YOU ARE GIVING BACK WHAT YOU TOOK.
NO, NOT ME. I DIDN'T TAKE THOSE OFFERINGS.
YET YOU REAPED THE BENEFITS OF THE CRYSTAL CASTLE WHILE YOUR FELLOW GELFLING GAVE, AND GAVE.
AND NOW, KENSHO GIVES BACK TO HIS WORLD. ALL GELFLING FALL, BUT KENSHO RISES. MONSTERS DO NOT RISE.
WHY THEN, DOES HE NOT SAY IT? WHY DOES HE NOT DO IT?
WHY IS HE BACK HERE IN THE PRISM? WHERE HE FELL...

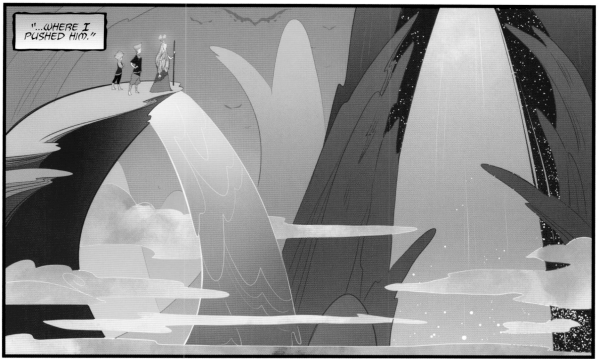

"...WHERE I PUSHED HIM."

FIRELINGS HAVE FORGOTTEN HOW **CONSTANT** OUR FLAME IS. HOW **BRIGHT** IT CAN BURN.

"EVEN IN THE FACE OF EXTINGUISH."

IT SEEMS YOU TWO ARE DIFFERENT. YOUR IDEA OF TRYING TO BREACH THE WATERFALL FROM ABOVE IS ADMIRABLE.

BUT TO DO THAT...

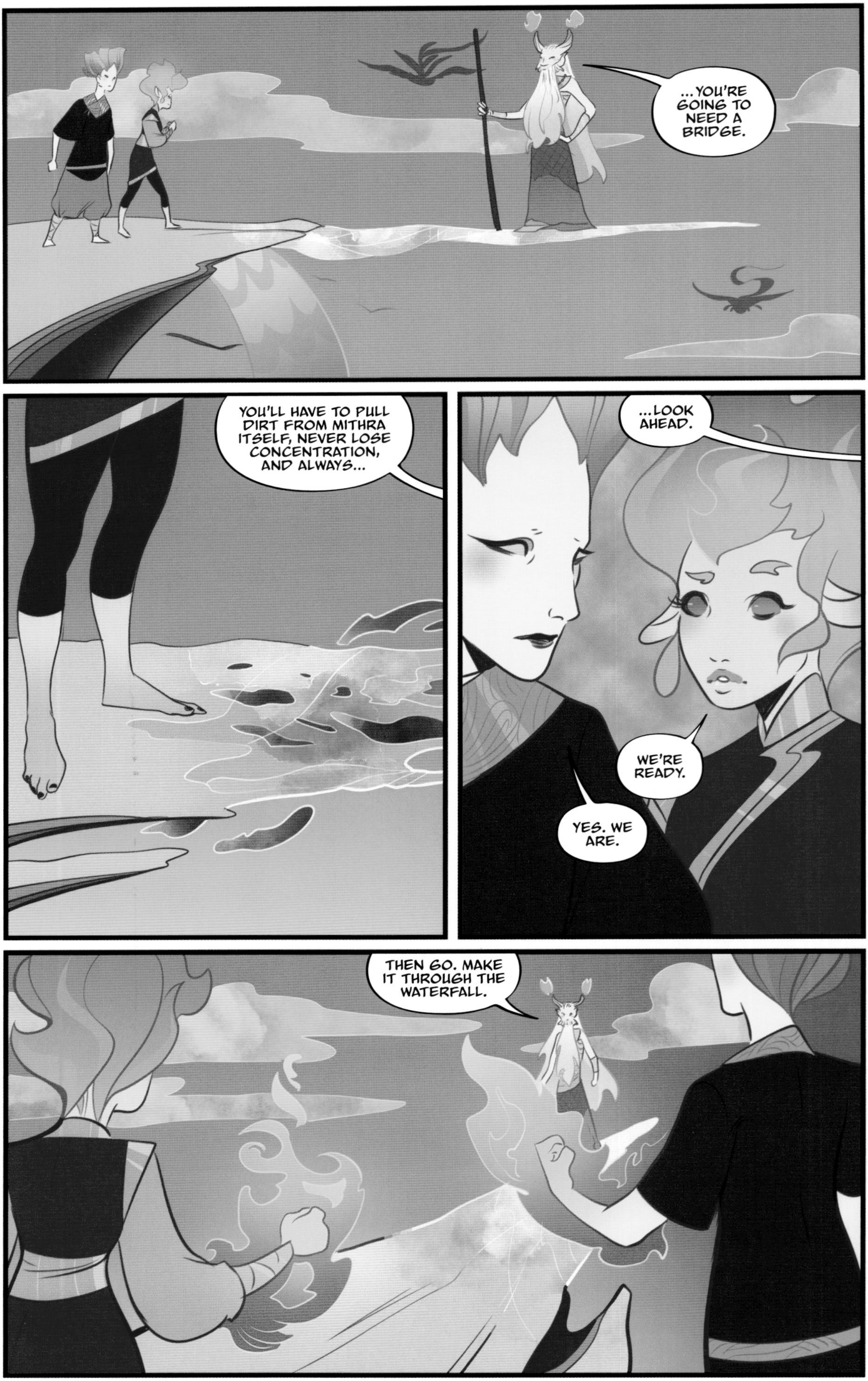
...YOU'RE GOING TO NEED A BRIDGE.
YOU'LL HAVE TO PULL DIRT FROM MITHRA ITSELF, NEVER LOSE CONCENTRATION, AND ALWAYS...
...LOOK AHEAD.
WE'RE READY.
YES. WE ARE.
THEN GO. MAKE IT THROUGH THE WATERFALL.

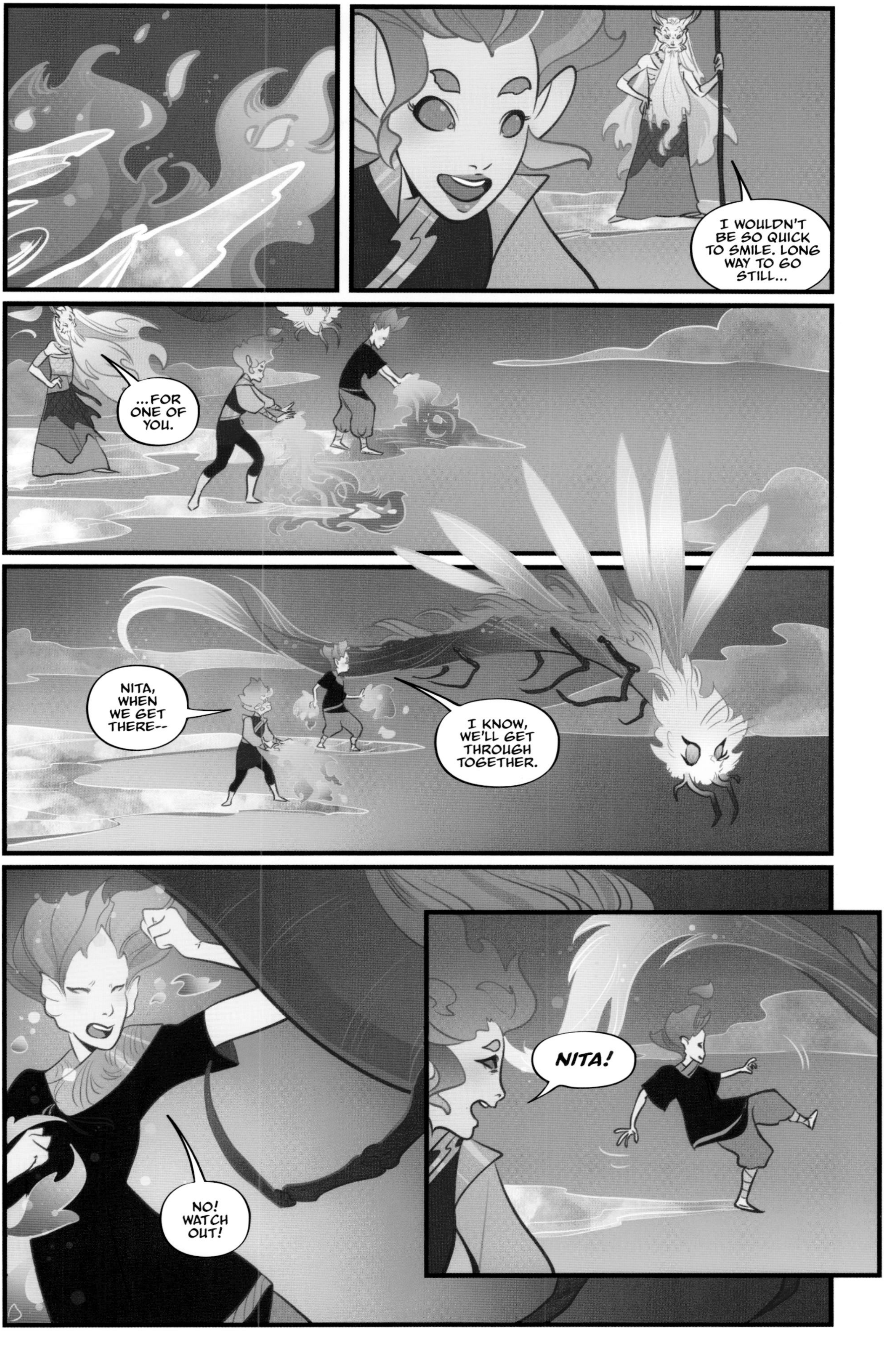
I WOULDN'T BE SO QUICK TO SMILE. LONG WAY TO GO STILL...
...FOR ONE OF YOU.
NITA, WHEN WE GET THERE--
I KNOW, WE'LL GET THROUGH TOGETHER.
NO! WATCH OUT!
NITA!

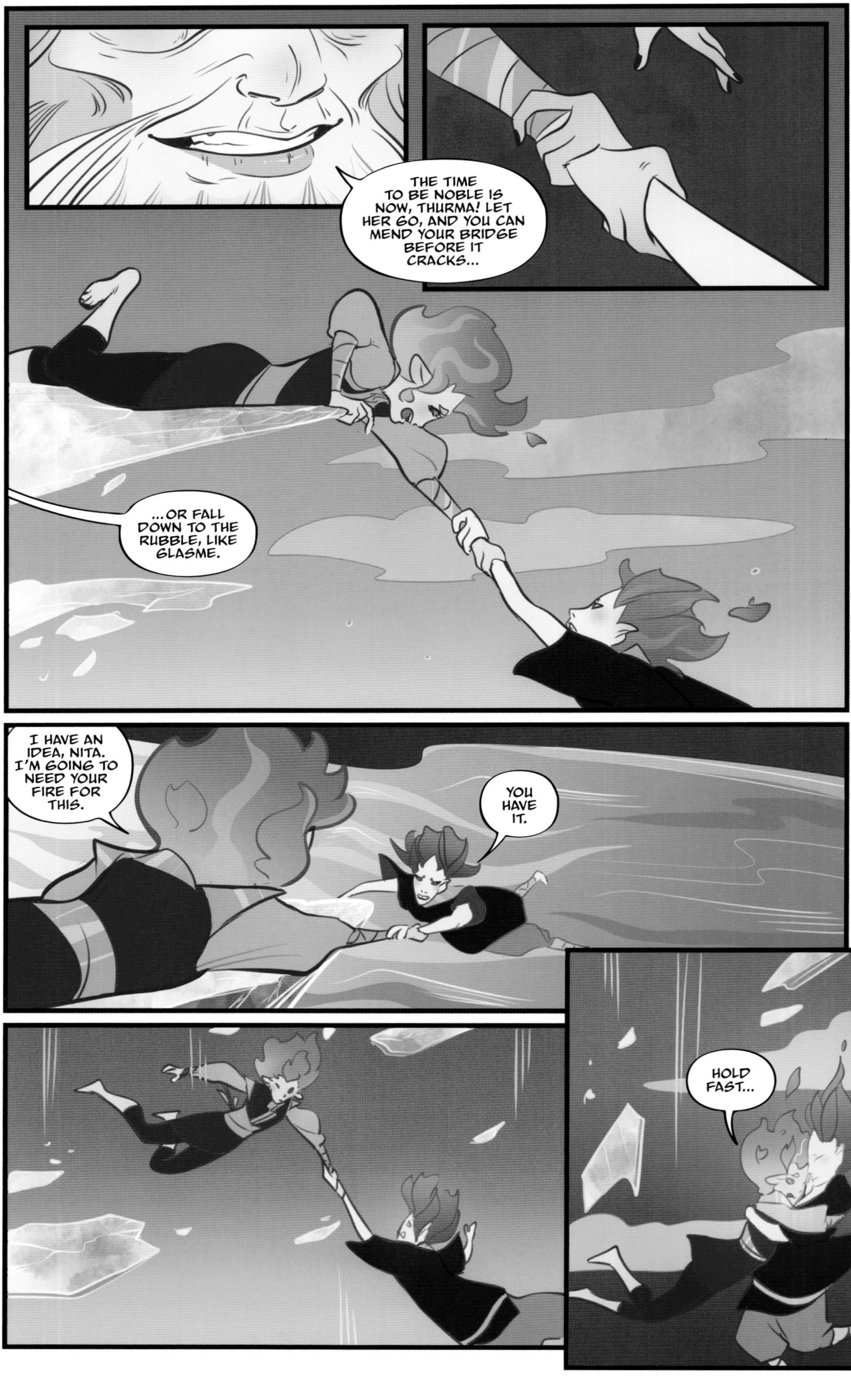
THE TIME TO BE NOBLE IS NOW, THURMA! LET HER GO, AND YOU CAN MEND YOUR BRIDGE BEFORE IT CRACKS...
...OR FALL DOWN TO THE RUBBLE, LIKE GLASME.
I HAVE AN IDEA, NITA. I'M GOING TO NEED YOUR FIRE FOR THIS.
YOU HAVE IT.
HOLD FAST...

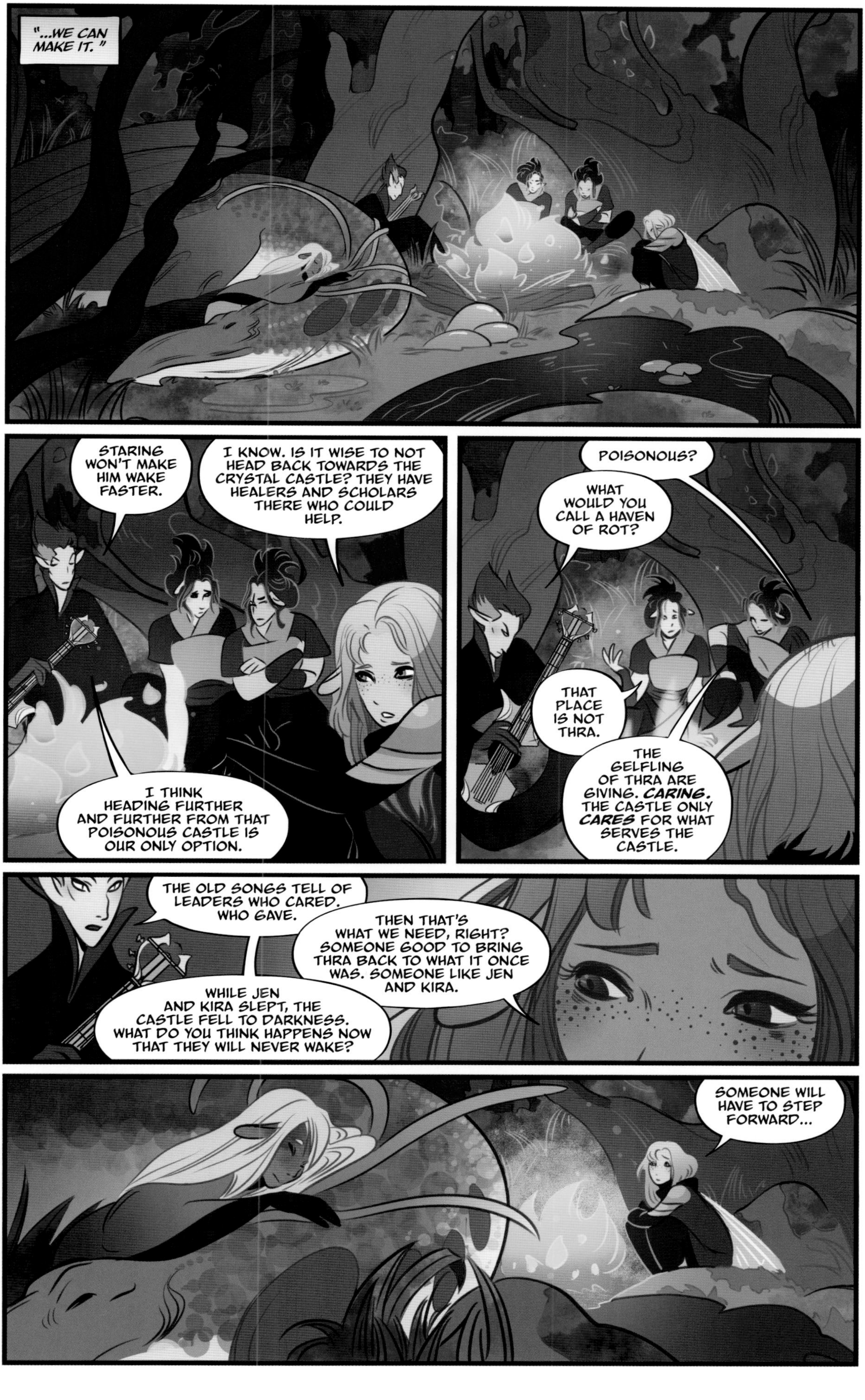
"...WE CAN MAKE IT."
STARING WON'T MAKE HIM WAKE FASTER.
I KNOW. IS IT WISE TO NOT HEAD BACK TOWARDS THE CRYSTAL CASTLE? THEY HAVE HEALERS AND SCHOLARS THERE WHO COULD HELP.
I THINK HEADING FURTHER AND FURTHER FROM THAT POISONOUS CASTLE IS OUR ONLY OPTION.
POISONOUS?
WHAT WOULD YOU CALL A HAVEN OF ROT?
THAT PLACE IS NOT THRA.
THE GELFLING OF THRA ARE GIVING. CARING. THE CASTLE ONLY CARES FOR WHAT SERVES THE CASTLE.
THE OLD SONGS TELL OF LEADERS WHO CARED. WHO GAVE.
THEN THAT'S WHAT WE NEED, RIGHT? SOMEONE GOOD TO BRING THRA BACK TO WHAT IT ONCE WAS. SOMEONE LIKE JEN AND KIRA.
WHILE JEN AND KIRA SLEPT, THE CASTLE FELL TO DARKNESS. WHAT DO YOU THINK HAPPENS NOW THAT THEY WILL NEVER WAKE?
SOMEONE WILL HAVE TO STEP FORWARD...

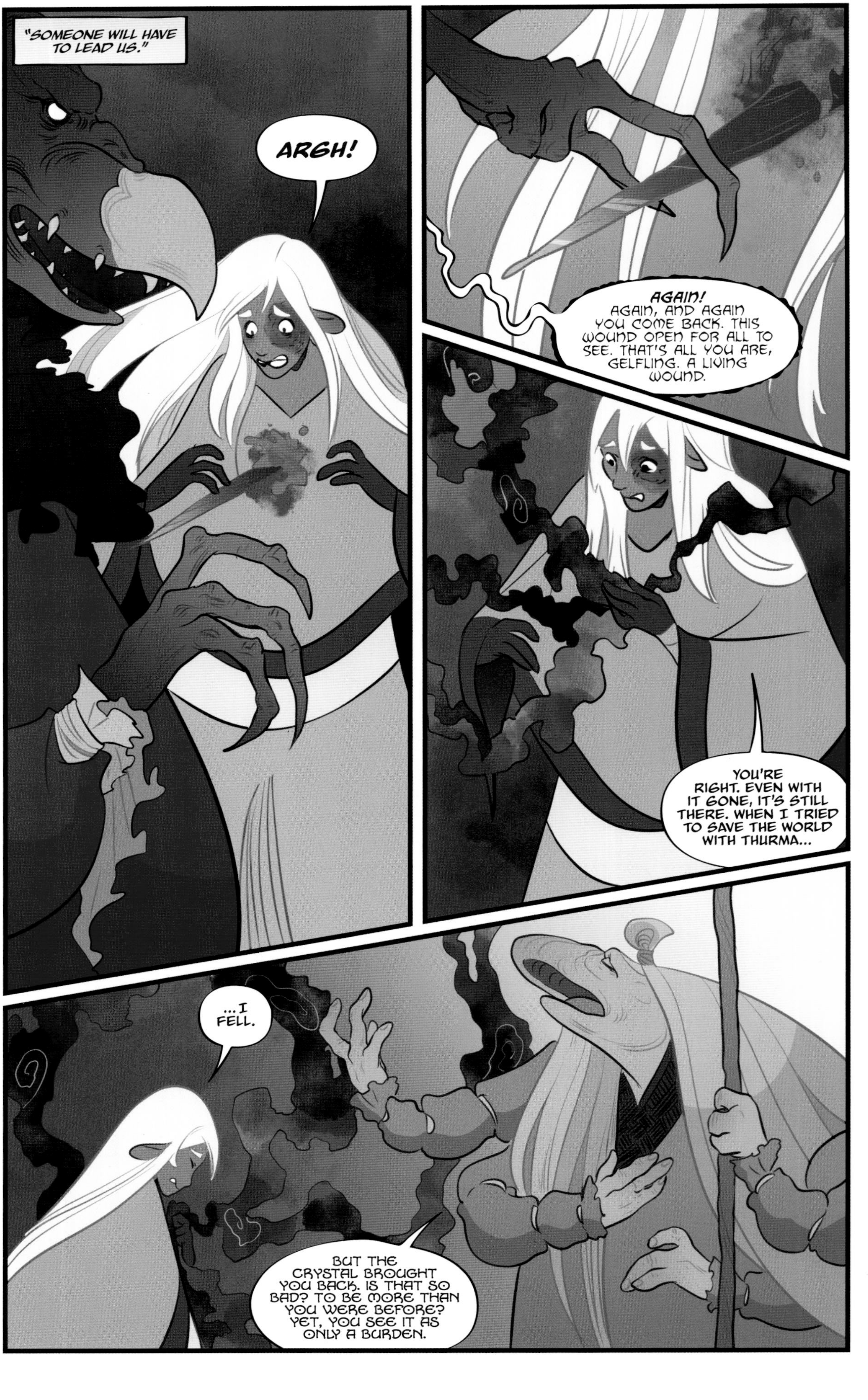
"SOMEONE WILL HAVE TO LEAD US."
ARGH!
AGAIN! AGAIN, AND AGAIN YOU COME BACK. THIS WOUND OPEN FOR ALL TO SEE. THAT'S ALL YOU ARE, GELFLING. A LIVING WOUND.
YOU'RE RIGHT. EVEN WITH IT GONE, IT'S STILL THERE. WHEN I TRIED TO SAVE THE WORLD WITH THURMA...
...I FELL.
BUT THE CRYSTAL BROUGHT YOU BACK. IS THAT SO BAD? TO BE MORE THAN YOU WERE BEFORE? YET, YOU SEE IT AS ONLY A BURDEN.

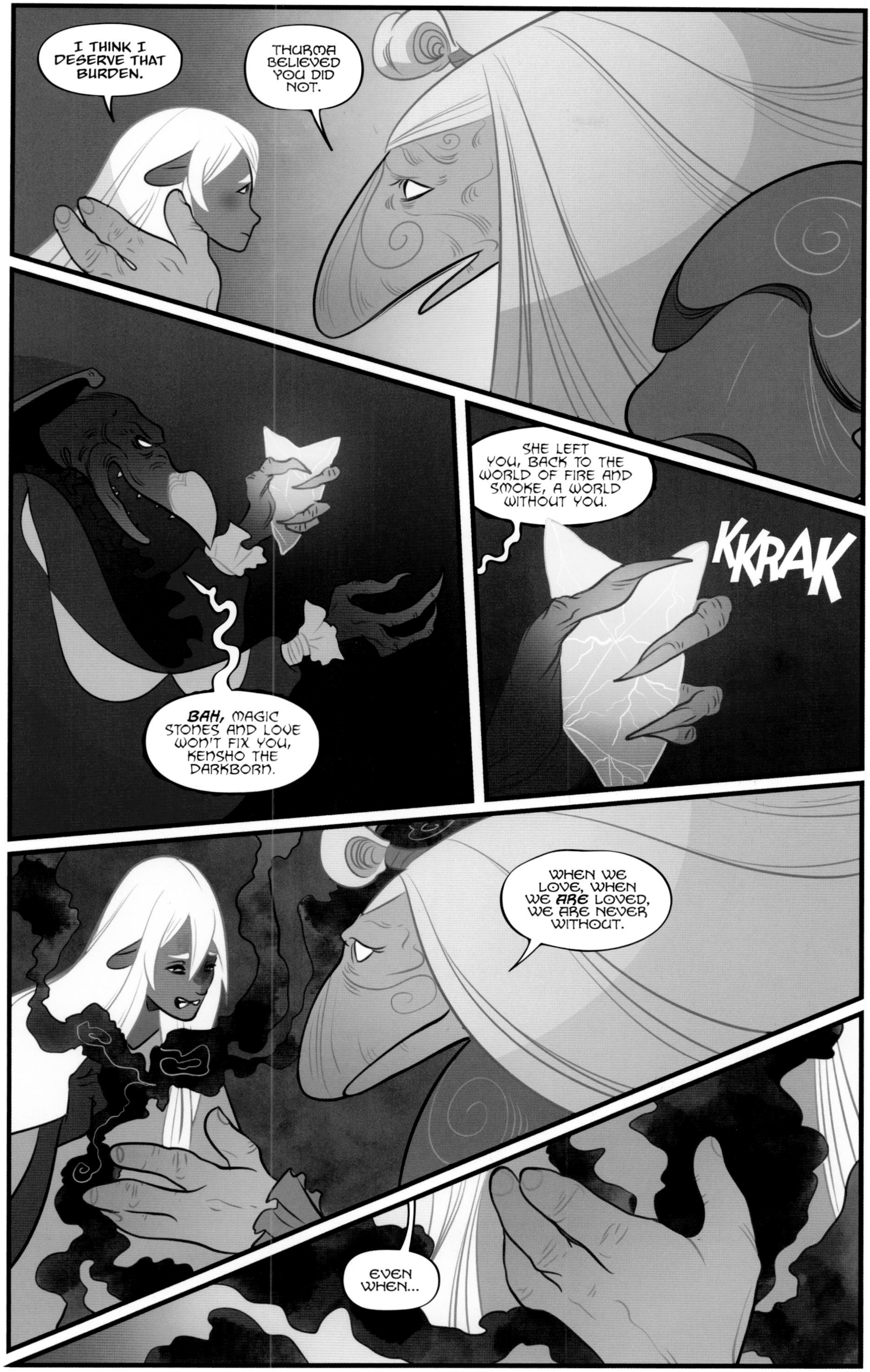
I THINK I DESERVE THAT BURDEN.
THURMA BELIEVED YOU DID NOT.
BAH, MAGIC STONES AND LOVE WON'T FIX YOU, KENSHO THE DARKBORN.
SHE LEFT YOU, BACK TO THE WORLD OF FIRE AND SMOKE, A WORLD WITHOUT YOU.
KKRAK
WHEN WE LOVE, WHEN WE ARE LOVED, WE ARE NEVER WITHOUT.
EVEN WHEN...

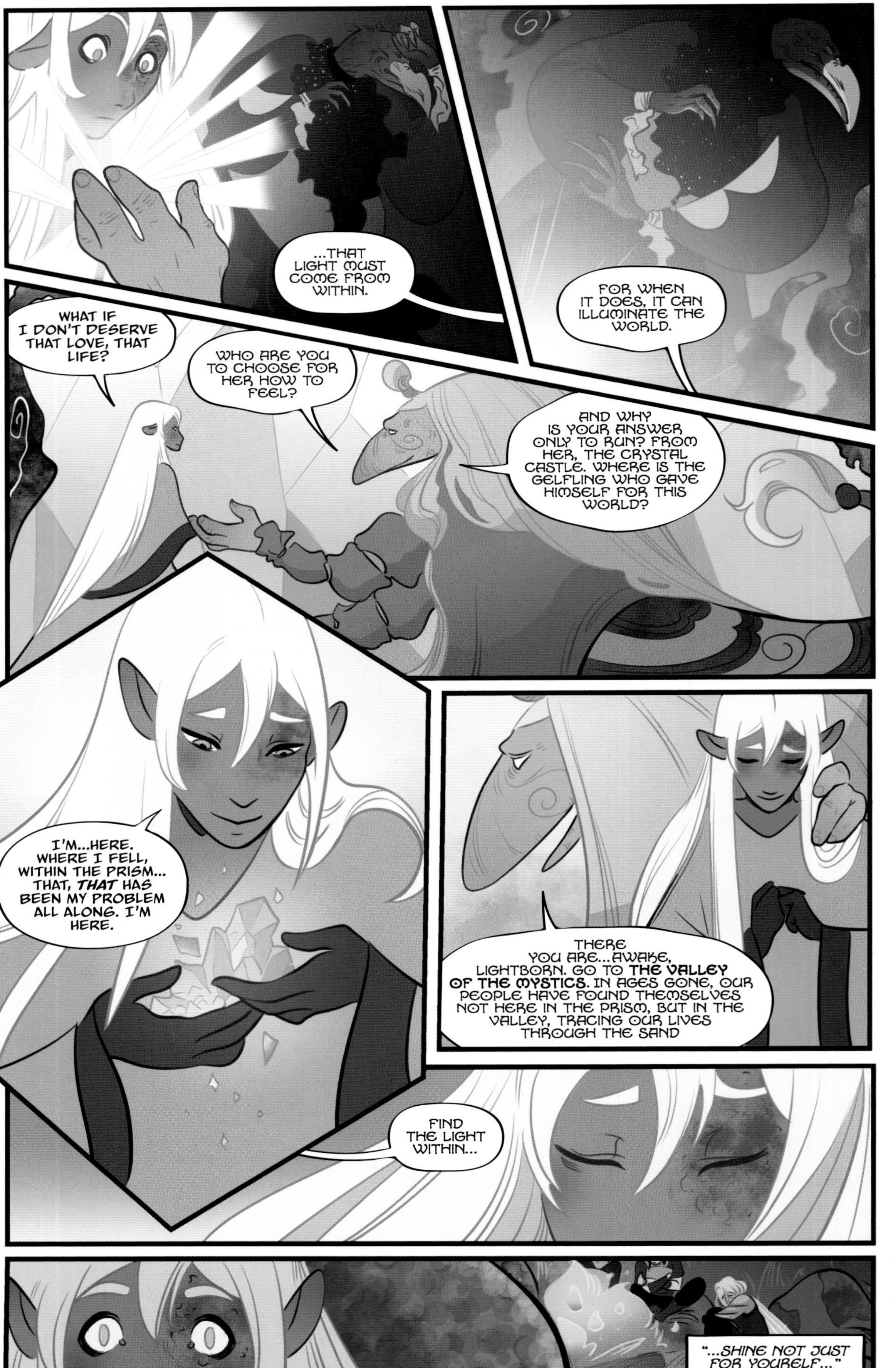
...THAT LIGHT MUST COME FROM WITHIN.
FOR WHEN IT DOES, IT CAN ILLUMINATE THE WORLD.
WHAT IF I DON'T DESERVE THAT LOVE, THAT LIFE?
WHO ARE YOU TO CHOOSE FOR HER HOW TO FEEL?
AND WHY IS YOUR ANSWER ONLY TO RUN? FROM HER, THE CRYSTAL CASTLE. WHERE IS THE GELFLING WHO GAVE HIMSELF FOR THIS WORLD?
I'M...HERE. WHERE I FELL, WITHIN THE PRISM... THAT, THAT HAS BEEN MY PROBLEM ALL ALONG. I'M HERE.
THERE YOU ARE...AWAKE, LIGHTBORN. GO TO THE VALLEY OF THE MYSTICS. IN AGES GONE, OUR PEOPLE HAVE FOUND THEMSELVES NOT HERE IN THE PRISM, BUT IN THE VALLEY, TRACING OUR LIVES THROUGH THE SAND
FIND THE LIGHT WITHIN...
"...SHINE NOT JUST FOR YOURELF..."

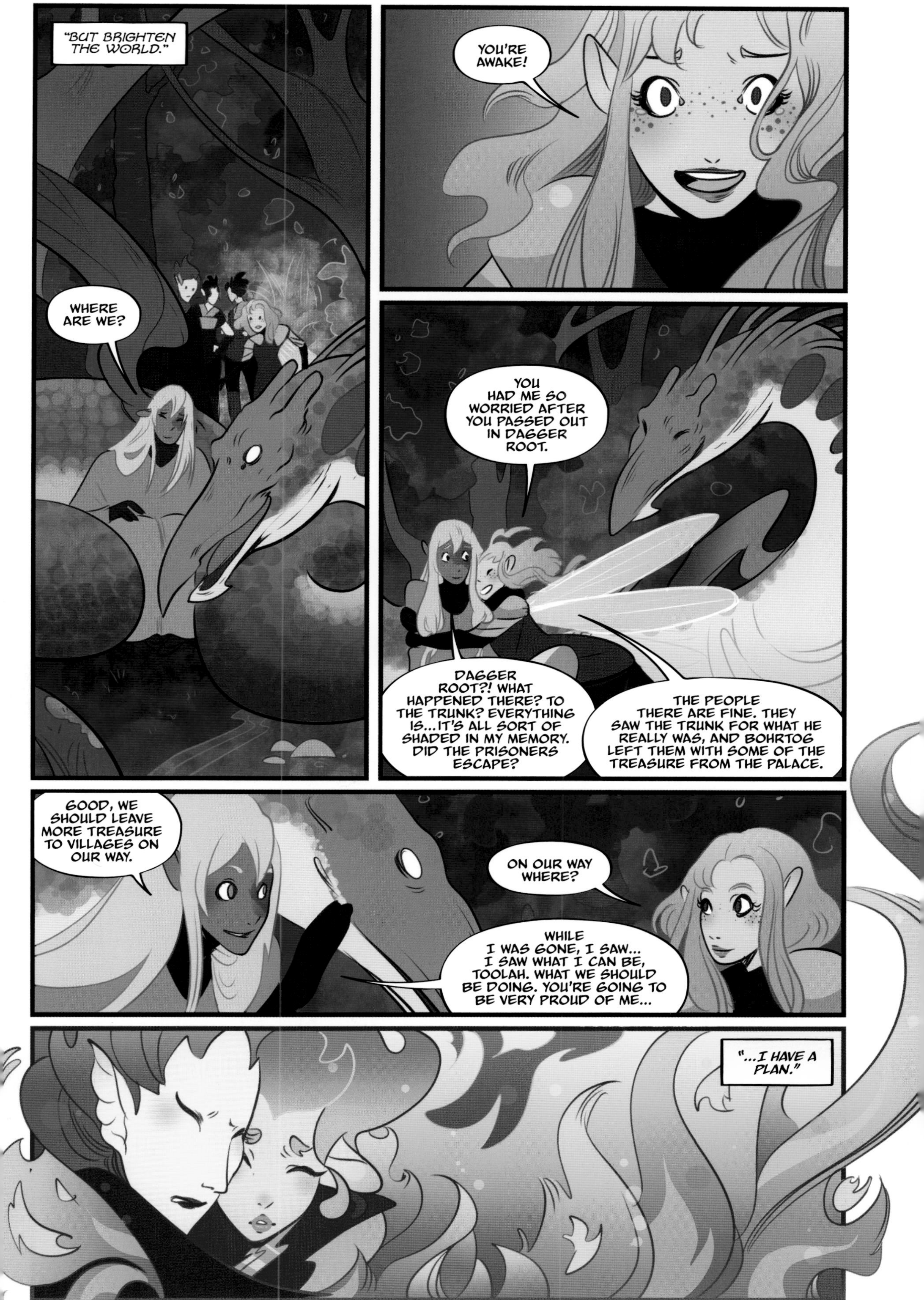
"BUT BRIGHTEN THE WORLD."
WHERE ARE WE?
YOU'RE AWAKE!
YOU HAD ME SO WORRIED AFTER YOU PASSED OUT IN DAGGER ROOT.
DAGGER ROOT?! WHAT HAPPENED THERE? TO THE TRUNK? EVERYTHING IS...IT'S ALL SORT OF SHADED IN MY MEMORY. DID THE PRISONERS ESCAPE?
THE PEOPLE THERE ARE FINE. THEY SAW THE TRUNK FOR WHAT HE REALLY WAS, AND BOHRTOG LEFT THEM WITH SOME OF THE TREASURE FROM THE PALACE.
GOOD, WE SHOULD LEAVE MORE TREASURE TO VILLAGES ON OUR WAY.
ON OUR WAY WHERE?
WHILE I WAS GONE, I SAW... I SAW WHAT I CAN BE, TOOLAH. WHAT WE SHOULD BE DOING. YOU'RE GOING TO BE VERY PROUD OF ME...
"...I HAVE A PLAN."

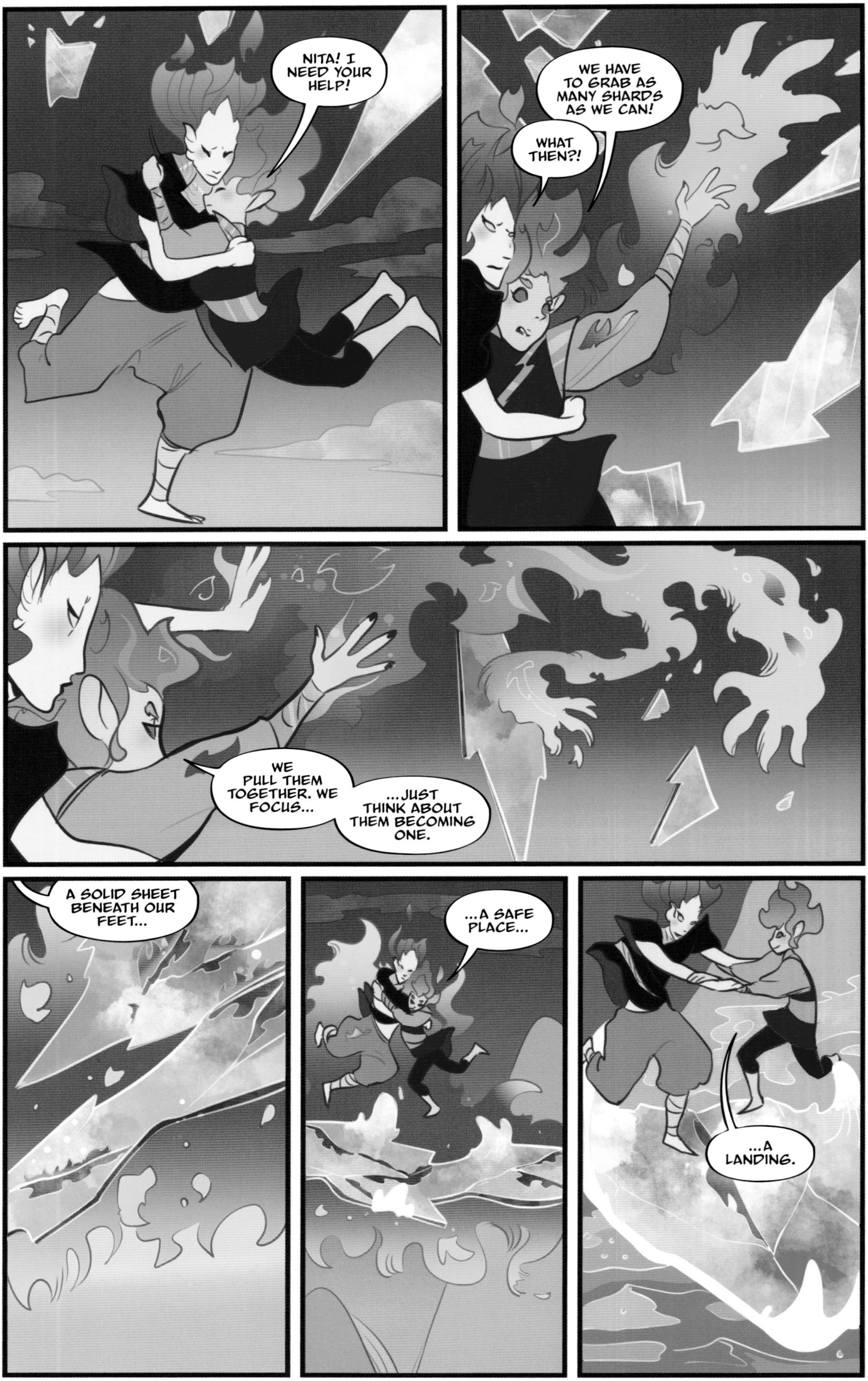
NITA! I NEED YOUR HELP!
WE HAVE TO GRAB AS MANY SHARDS AS WE CAN!
WHAT THEN?!
WE PULL THEM TOGETHER. WE FOCUS...
...JUST THINK ABOUT THEM BECOMING ONE.
A SOLID SHEET BENEATH OUR FEET...
...A SAFE PLACE...
...A LANDING.

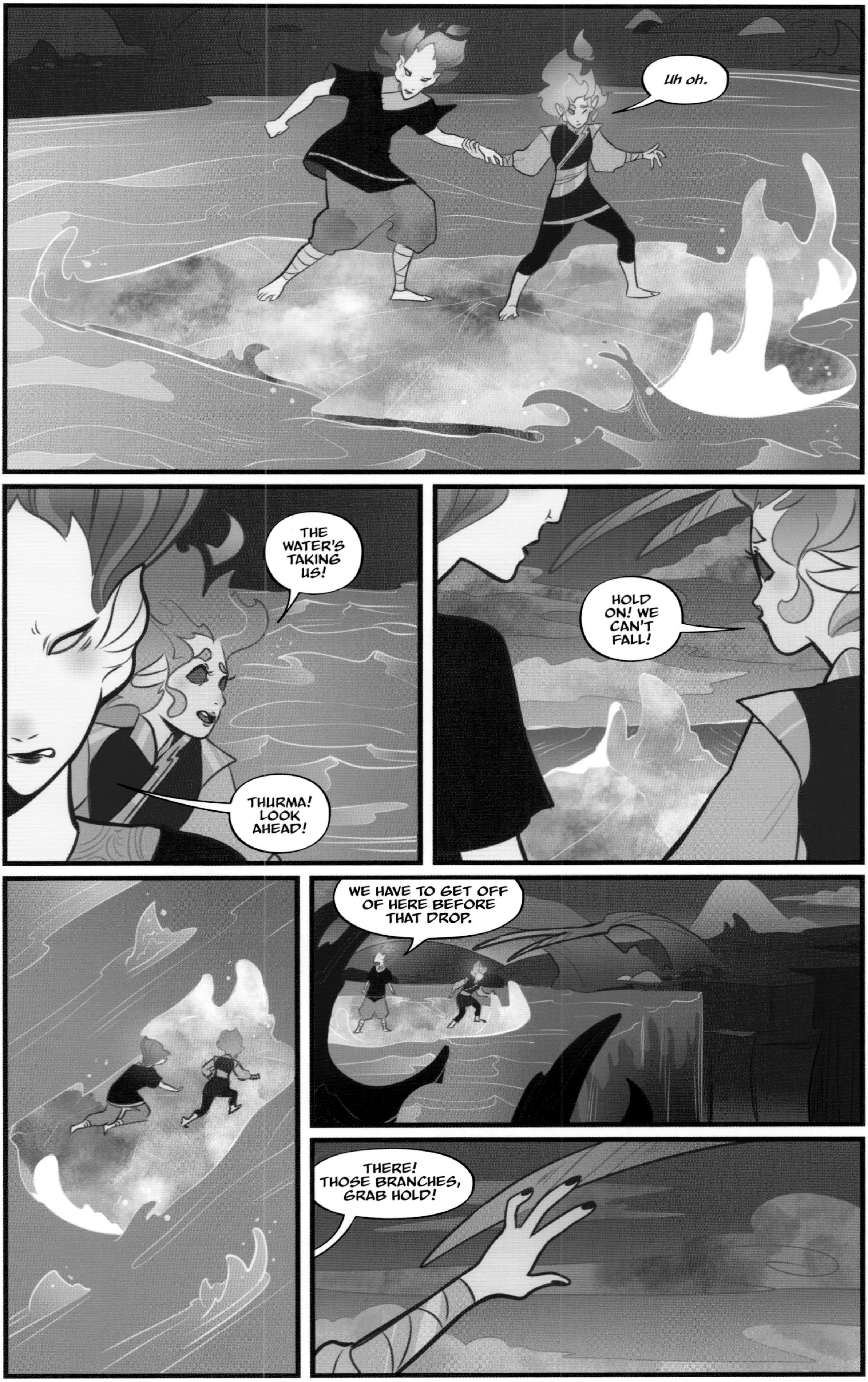
Uh oh.
THE WATER'S TAKING US!
THURMA! LOOK AHEAD!
HOLD ON! WE CAN'T FALL!
WE HAVE TO GET OFF OF HERE BEFORE THAT DROP.
THERE! THOSE BRANCHES, GRAB HOLD!

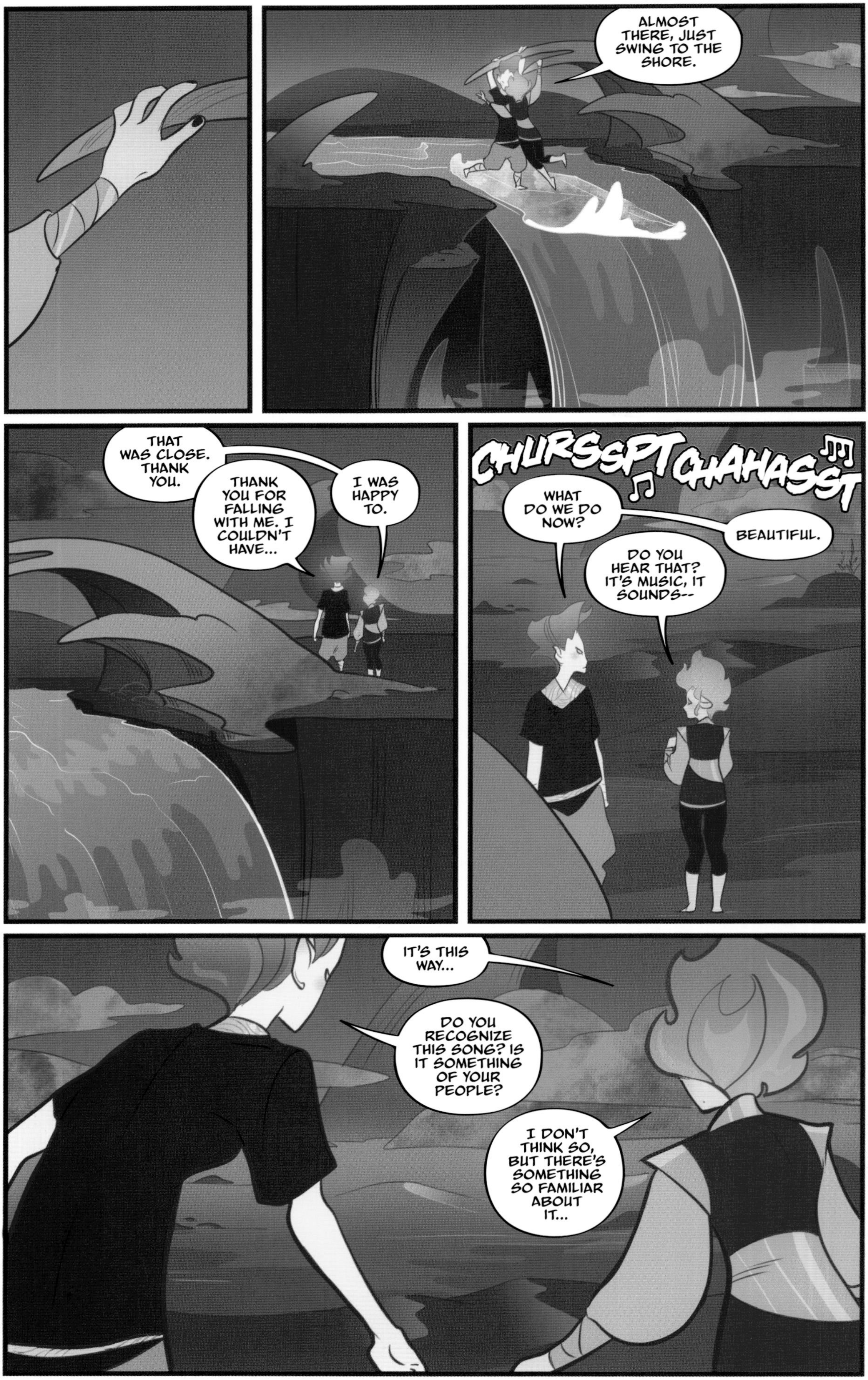
ALMOST THERE, JUST SWING TO THE SHORE.
THAT WAS CLOSE. THANK YOU.
I WAS HAPPY TO.
THANK YOU FOR FALLING WITH ME. I COULDN'T HAVE...
CHURSSPT CHAHASST
WHAT DO WE DO NOW?
BEAUTIFUL.
DO YOU HEAR THAT? IT'S MUSIC, IT SOUNDS--
IT'S THIS WAY...
DO YOU RECOGNIZE THIS SONG? IS IT SOMETHING OF YOUR PEOPLE?
I DON'T THINK SO, BUT THERE'S SOMETHING SO FAMILIAR ABOUT IT...

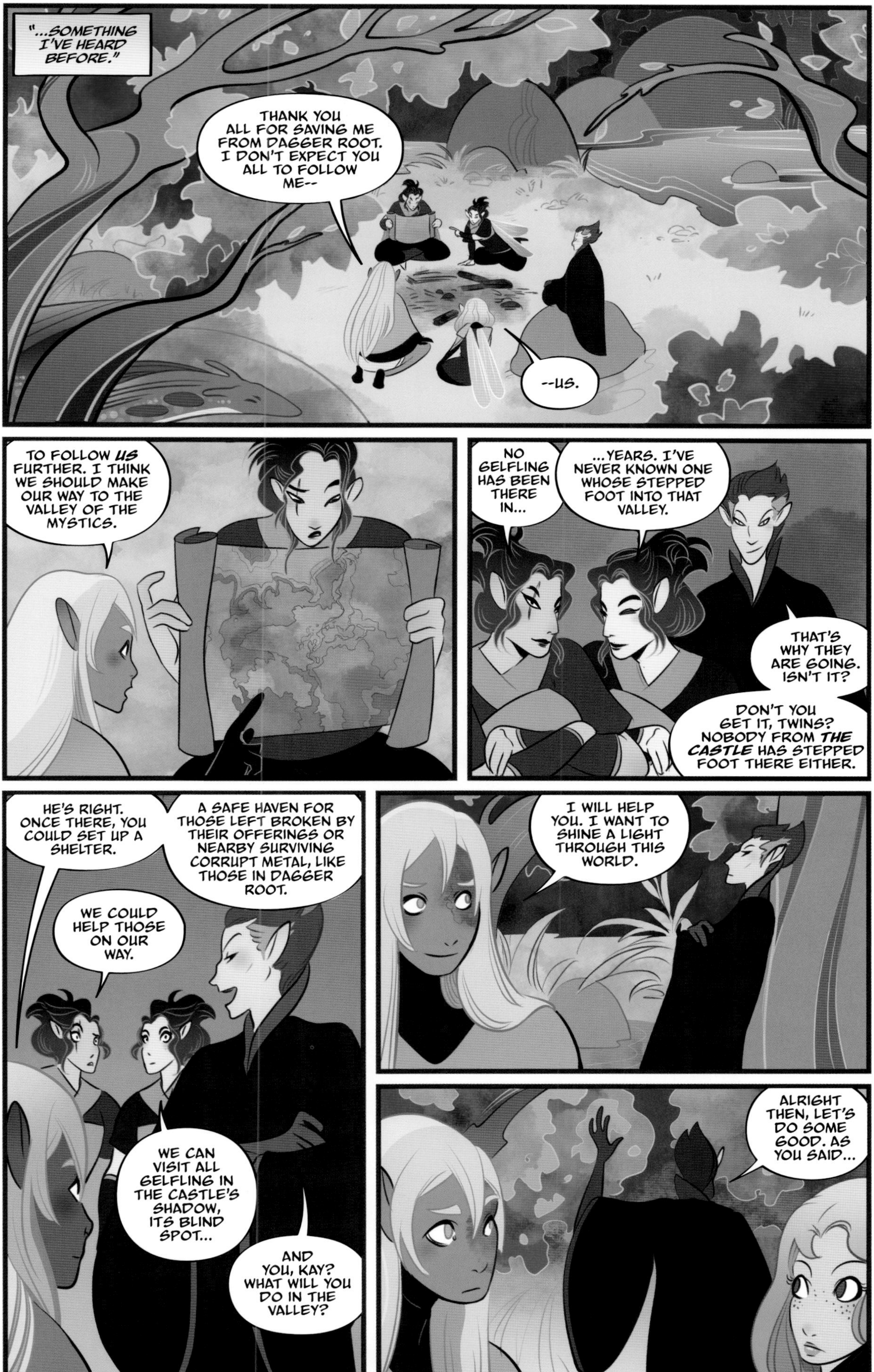
"...SOMETHING I'VE HEARD BEFORE."
THANK YOU ALL FOR SAVING ME FROM DAGGER ROOT. I DON'T EXPECT YOU ALL TO FOLLOW ME--
--US.
TO FOLLOW *US* FURTHER. I THINK WE SHOULD MAKE OUR WAY TO THE VALLEY OF THE MYSTICS.
NO GELFLING HAS BEEN THERE IN...
...YEARS. I'VE NEVER KNOWN ONE WHOSE STEPPED FOOT INTO THAT VALLEY.
THAT'S WHY THEY ARE GOING. ISN'T IT?
DON'T YOU GET IT, TWINS? NOBODY FROM *THE CASTLE* HAS STEPPED FOOT THERE EITHER.
HE'S RIGHT. ONCE THERE, YOU COULD SET UP A SHELTER.
A SAFE HAVEN FOR THOSE LEFT BROKEN BY THEIR OFFERINGS OR NEARBY SURVIVING CORRUPT METAL, LIKE THOSE IN DAGGER ROOT.
WE COULD HELP THOSE ON OUR WAY.
WE CAN VISIT ALL GELFLING IN THE CASTLE'S SHADOW, ITS BLIND SPOT...
AND YOU, KAY? WHAT WILL YOU DO IN THE VALLEY?
I WILL HELP YOU. I WANT TO SHINE A LIGHT THROUGH THIS WORLD.
ALRIGHT THEN, LET'S DO SOME GOOD. AS YOU SAID...

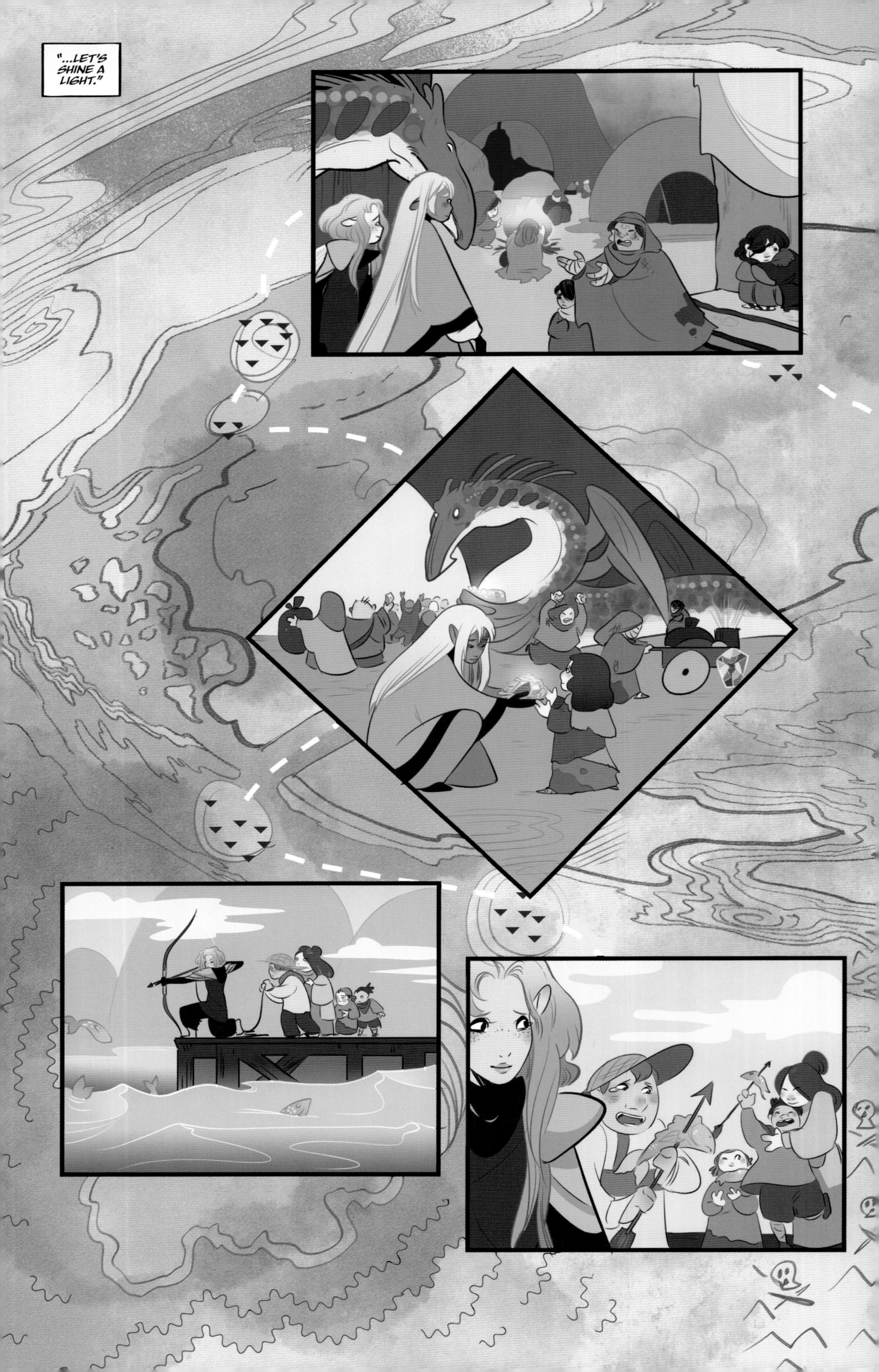
"...LET'S SHINE A LIGHT."

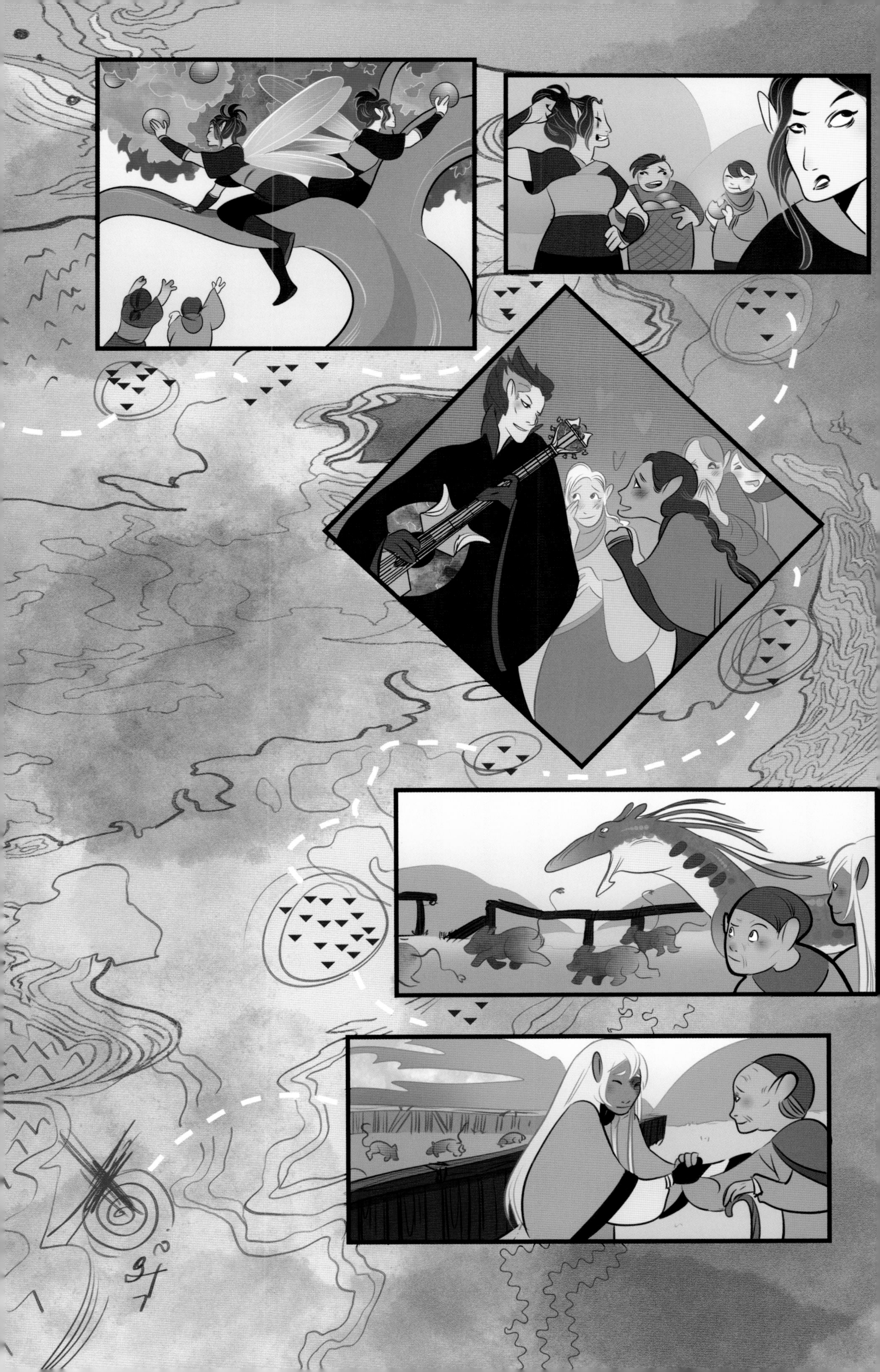

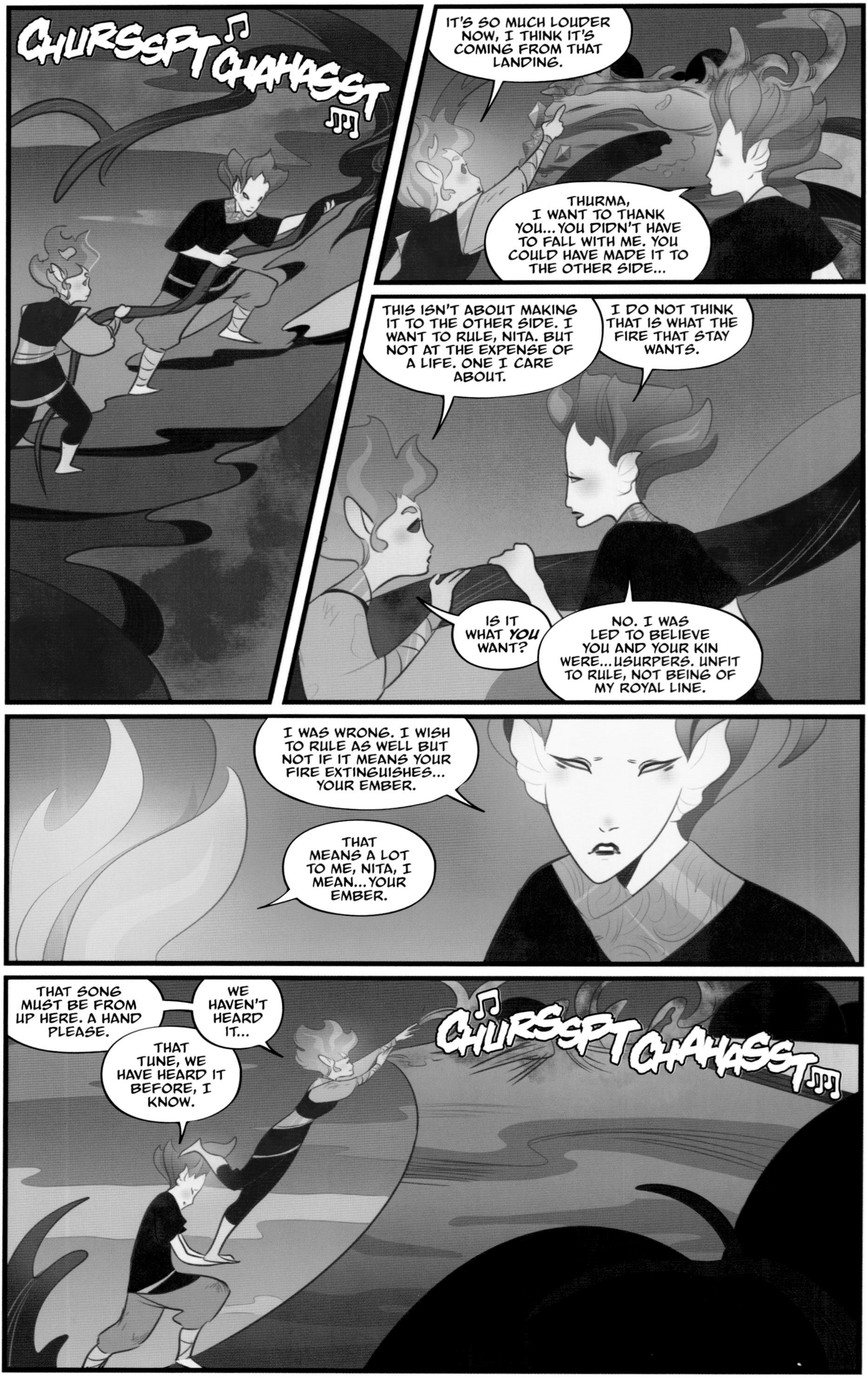
CHURSSPT CHAHASST
IT'S SO MUCH LOUDER NOW, I THINK IT'S COMING FROM THAT LANDING.
THURMA, I WANT TO THANK YOU...YOU DIDN'T HAVE TO FALL WITH ME. YOU COULD HAVE MADE IT TO THE OTHER SIDE...
THIS ISN'T ABOUT MAKING IT TO THE OTHER SIDE. I WANT TO RULE, NITA. BUT NOT AT THE EXPENSE OF A LIFE. ONE I CARE ABOUT.
I DO NOT THINK THAT IS WHAT THE FIRE THAT STAY WANTS.
IS IT WHAT *YOU* WANT?
NO. I WAS LED TO BELIEVE YOU AND YOUR KIN WERE...USURPERS. UNFIT TO RULE, NOT BEING OF MY ROYAL LINE.
I WAS WRONG. I WISH TO RULE AS WELL BUT NOT IF IT MEANS YOUR FIRE EXTINGUISHES... YOUR EMBER.
THAT MEANS A LOT TO ME, NITA, I MEAN...YOUR EMBER.
THAT SONG MUST BE FROM UP HERE. A HAND PLEASE.
WE HAVEN'T HEARD IT...
THAT TUNE, WE HAVE HEARD IT BEFORE, I KNOW.
CHURSSPT CHAHASST

...WE'VE FELT IT.

SWAHOR--

IS THAT ONE OF THOSE CREATURES?

THE FIRE THAT STAYS CALLED IT A FRAGOR.

IT'S SO SMALL...

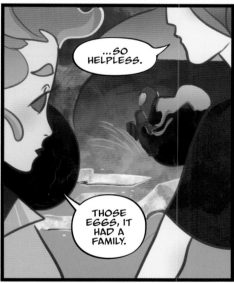

...SO HELPLESS.

THOSE EGGS, IT HAD A FAMILY.

THERE'S GLASS HERE.

DO YOU THINK THE FRAGOR SHATTERED THE GLASS AS THE OLDER ONE DID IN THE HALLOW?

I DON'T THINK SO, YOU HEARD ITS SONG AS WELL. MORE COMFORT AND BEAUTY THAN DESTRUCTION AND CHAOS.

IT WANTS US TO FOLLOW. I'M NOT SURE HOW...

ITS SONG, IT SPEAKS THROUGH ITS SONG...

CHURSSPT

CHAHASST

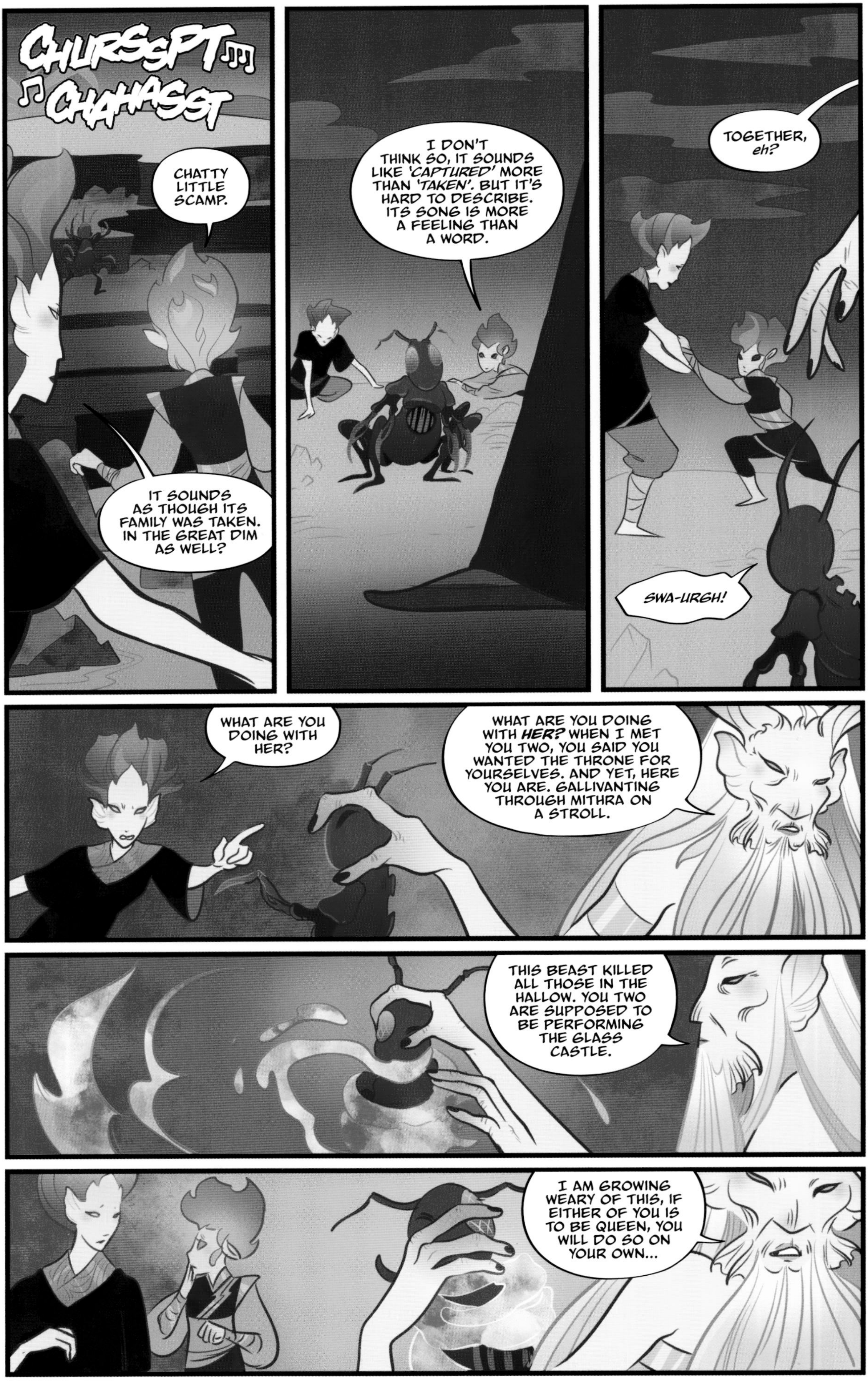
CHURSSPT
CHAHASST
CHATTY LITTLE SCAMP.
IT SOUNDS AS THOUGH ITS FAMILY WAS TAKEN. IN THE GREAT DIM AS WELL?
I DON'T THINK SO, IT SOUNDS LIKE 'CAPTURED' MORE THAN 'TAKEN'. BUT IT'S HARD TO DESCRIBE. ITS SONG IS MORE A FEELING THAN A WORD.
TOGETHER, eh?
SWA-URGH!
WHAT ARE YOU DOING WITH HER?
WHAT ARE YOU DOING WITH HER? WHEN I MET YOU TWO, YOU SAID YOU WANTED THE THRONE FOR YOURSELVES. AND YET, HERE YOU ARE. GALLIVANTING THROUGH MITHRA ON A STROLL.
THIS BEAST KILLED ALL THOSE IN THE HALLOW. YOU TWO ARE SUPPOSED TO BE PERFORMING THE GLASS CASTLE.
I AM GROWING WEARY OF THIS, IF EITHER OF YOU IS TO BE QUEEN, YOU WILL DO SO ON YOUR OWN...

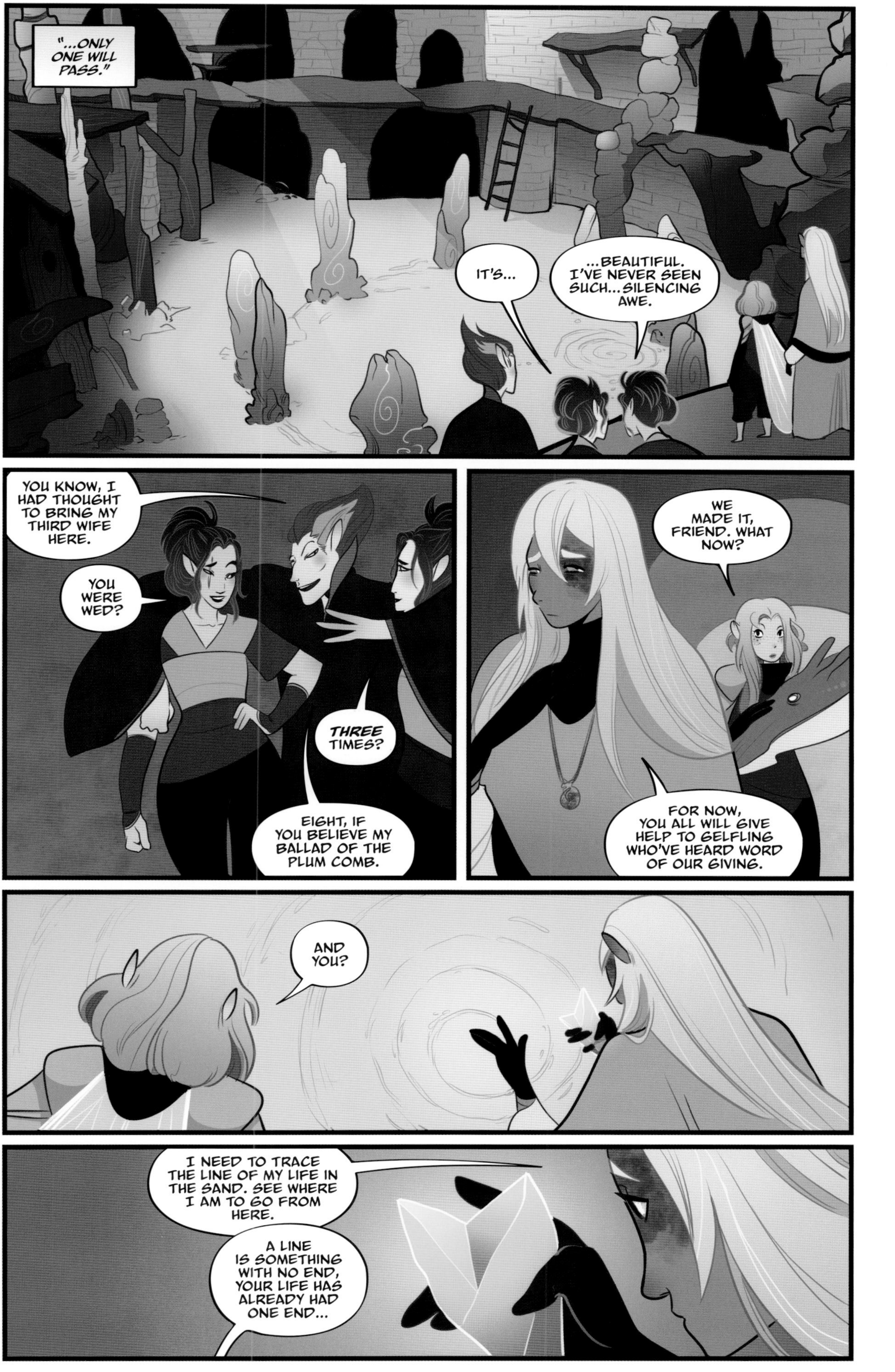
"...ONLY ONE WILL PASS."
IT'S...
...BEAUTIFUL. I'VE NEVER SEEN SUCH...SILENCING AWE.
YOU KNOW, I HAD THOUGHT TO BRING MY THIRD WIFE HERE.
YOU WERE WED?
THREE TIMES?
EIGHT, IF YOU BELIEVE MY BALLAD OF THE PLUM COMB.
WE MADE IT, FRIEND. WHAT NOW?
FOR NOW, YOU ALL WILL GIVE HELP TO GELFLING WHO'VE HEARD WORD OF OUR GIVING.
AND YOU?
I NEED TO TRACE THE LINE OF MY LIFE IN THE SAND. SEE WHERE I AM TO GO FROM HERE.
A LINE IS SOMETHING WITH NO END, YOUR LIFE HAS ALREADY HAD ONE END...

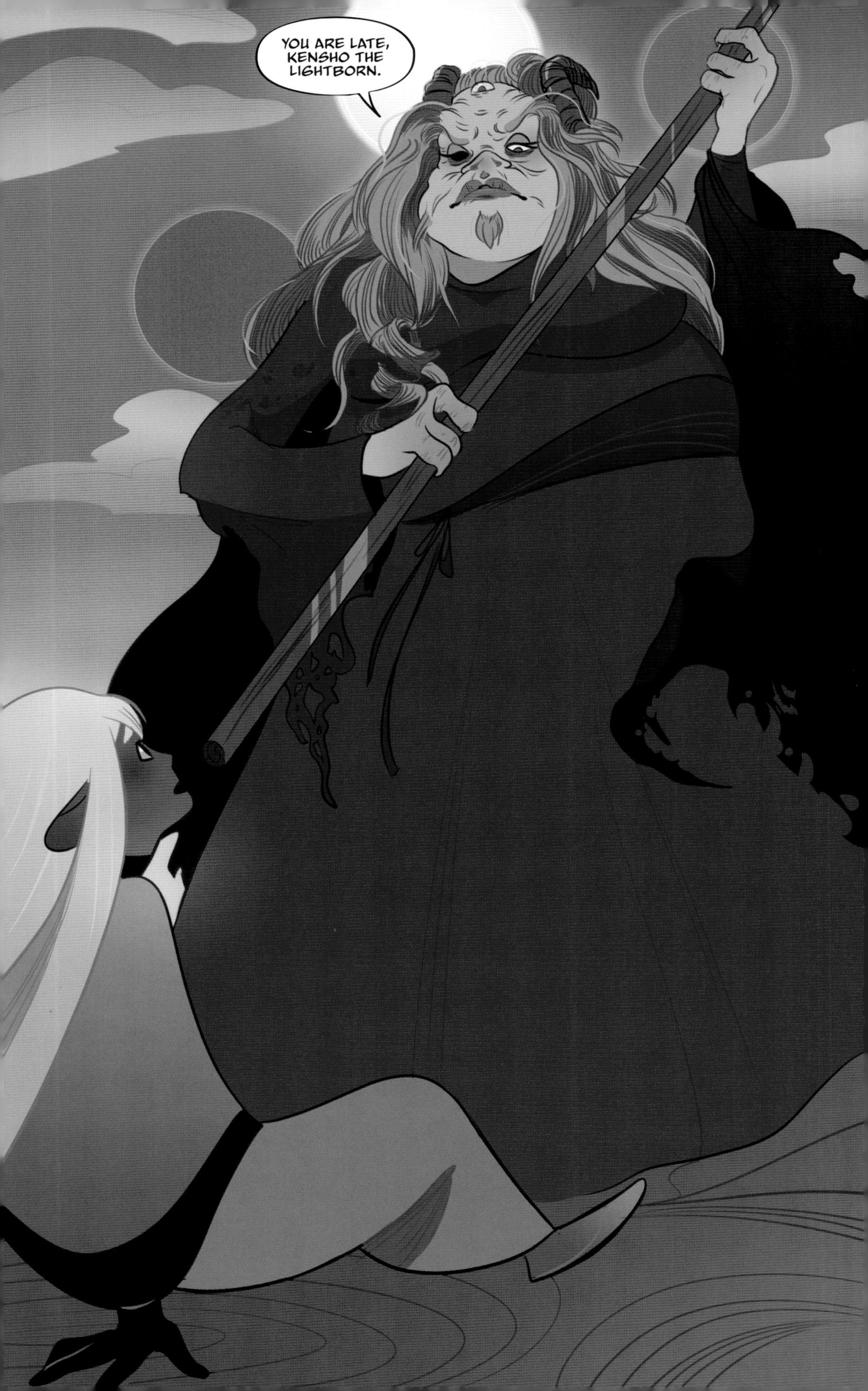
YOU ARE LATE, KENSHO THE LIGHTBORN.

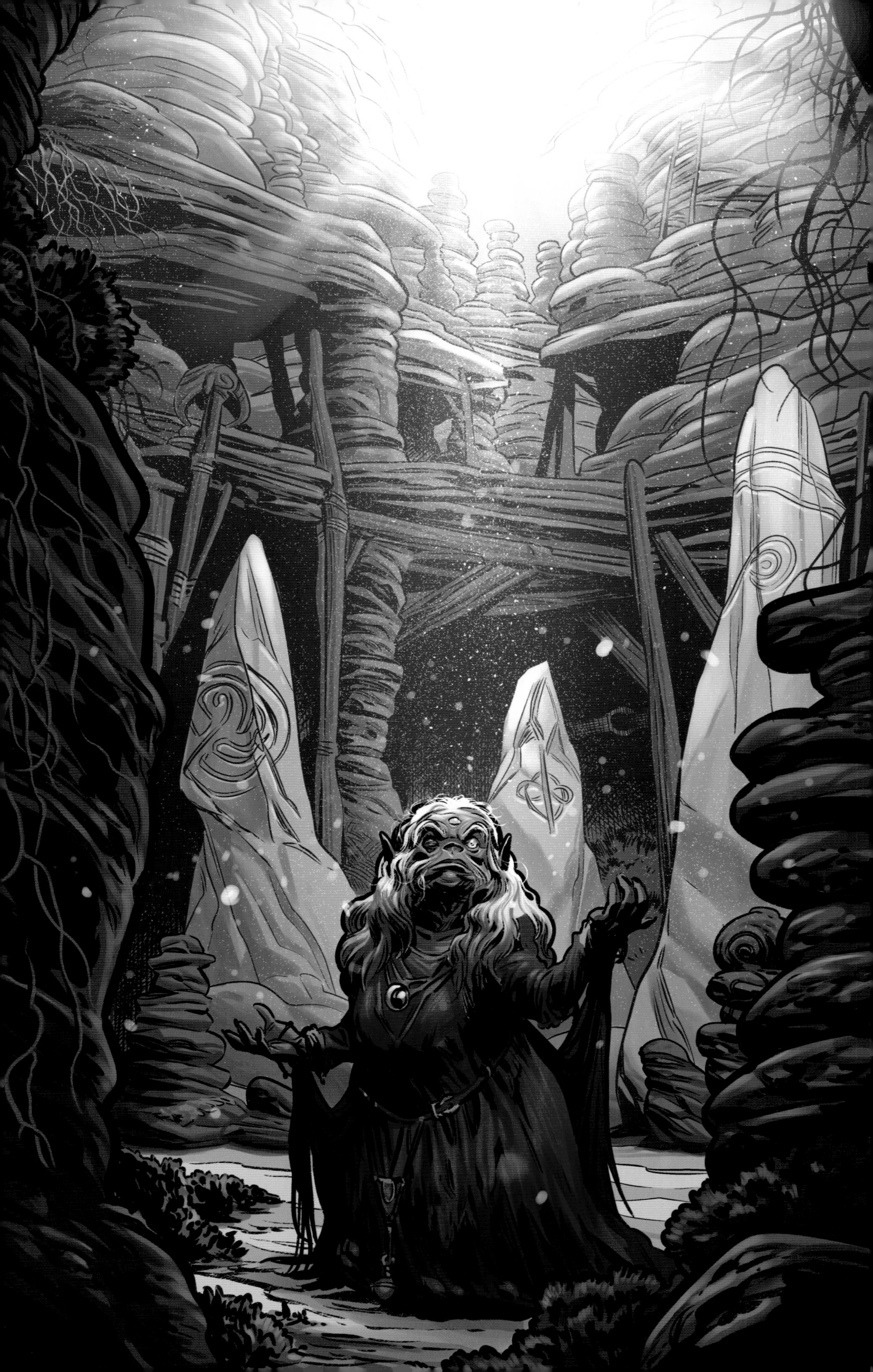

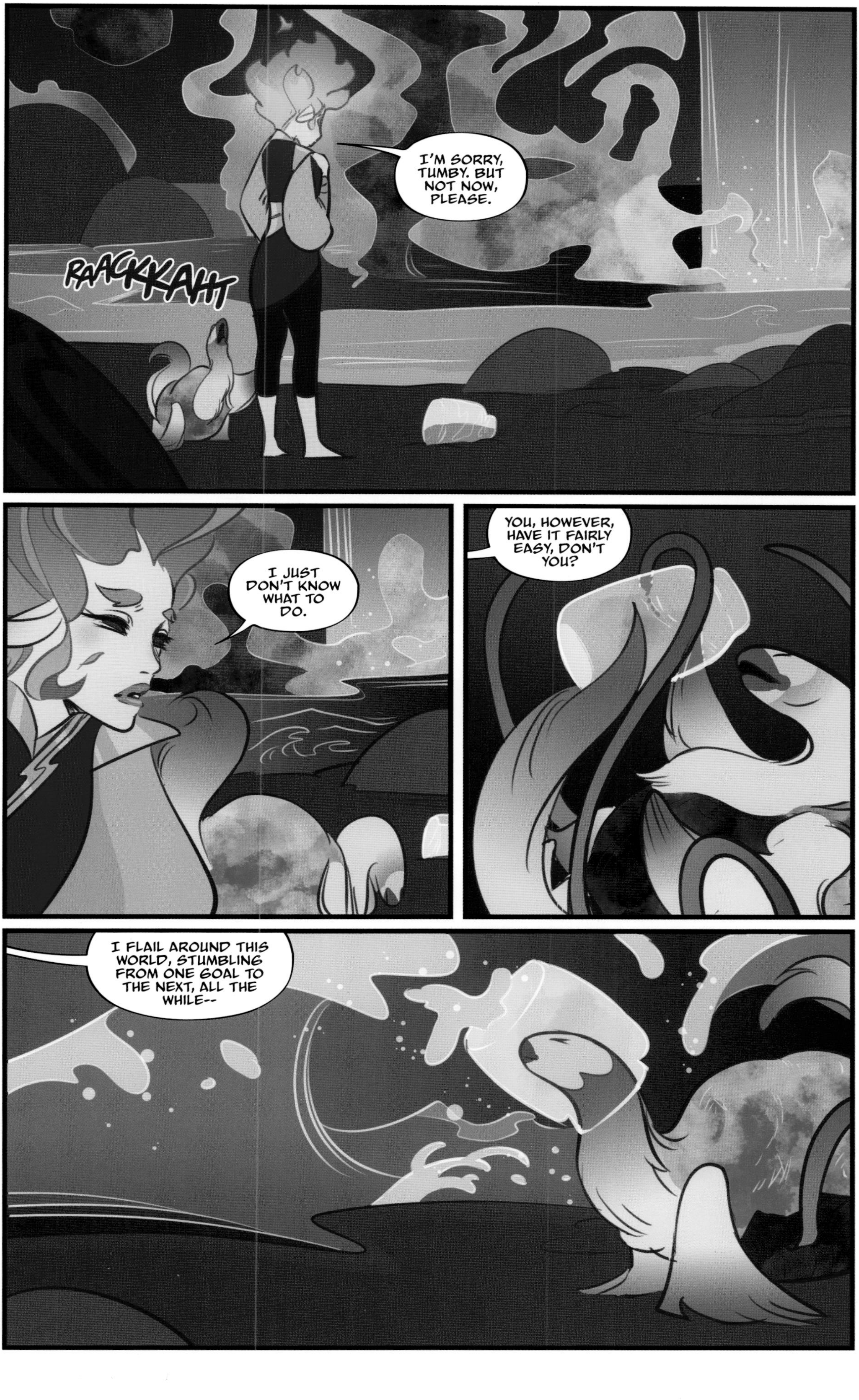
I'M SORRY, TUMBY. BUT NOT NOW, PLEASE.
RAACKKAHT
I JUST DON'T KNOW WHAT TO DO.
YOU, HOWEVER, HAVE IT FAIRLY EASY, DON'T YOU?
I FLAIL AROUND THIS WORLD, STUMBLING FROM ONE GOAL TO THE NEXT, ALL THE WHILE--

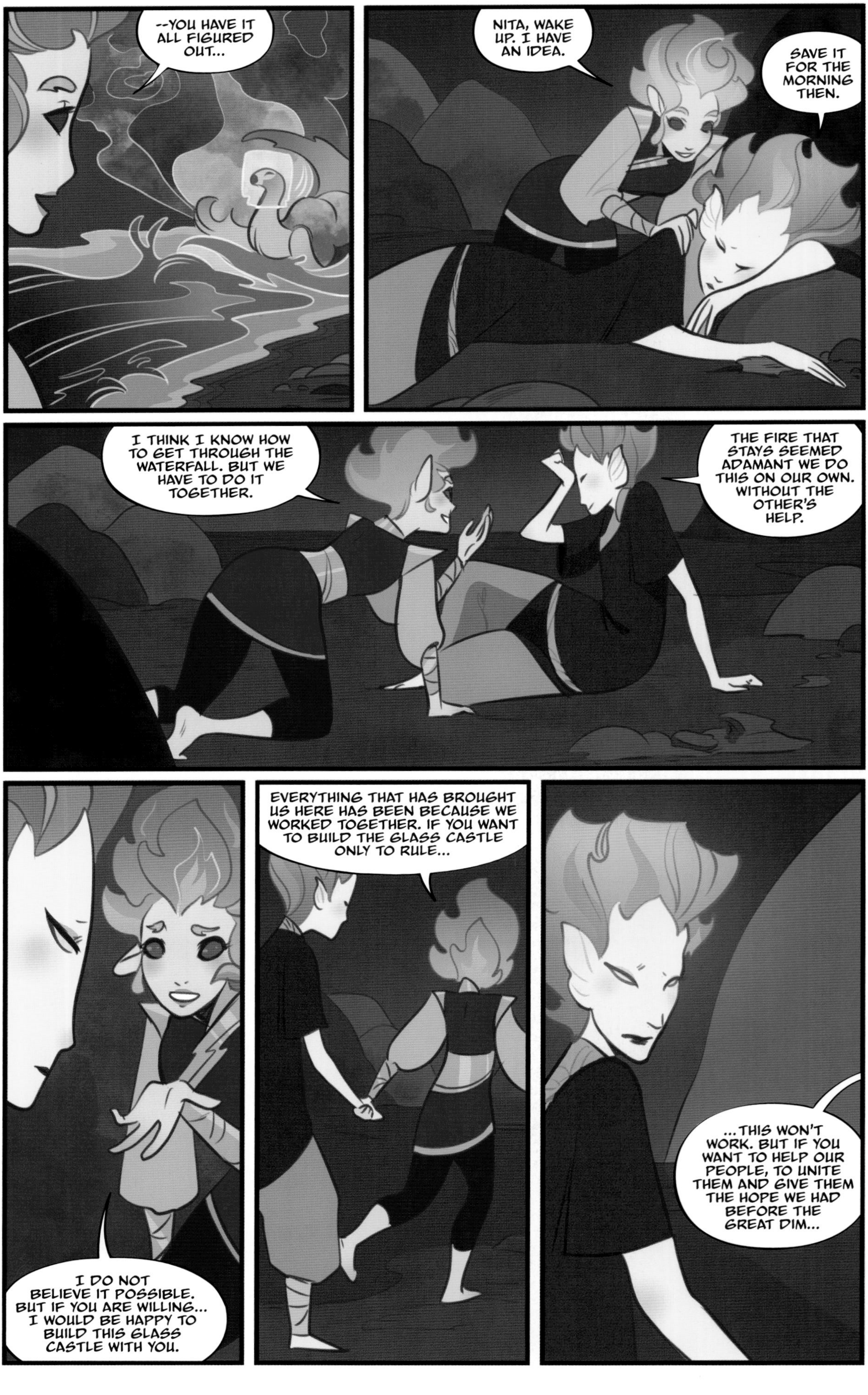
--YOU HAVE IT ALL FIGURED OUT...
NITA, WAKE UP. I HAVE AN IDEA.
SAVE IT FOR THE MORNING THEN.
I THINK I KNOW HOW TO GET THROUGH THE WATERFALL. BUT WE HAVE TO DO IT TOGETHER.
THE FIRE THAT STAYS SEEMED ADAMANT WE DO THIS ON OUR OWN. WITHOUT THE OTHER'S HELP.
I DO NOT BELIEVE IT POSSIBLE. BUT IF YOU ARE WILLING... I WOULD BE HAPPY TO BUILD THIS GLASS CASTLE WITH YOU.
EVERYTHING THAT HAS BROUGHT US HERE HAS BEEN BECAUSE WE WORKED TOGETHER. IF YOU WANT TO BUILD THE GLASS CASTLE ONLY TO RULE...
...THIS WON'T WORK. BUT IF YOU WANT TO HELP OUR PEOPLE, TO UNITE THEM AND GIVE THEM THE HOPE WE HAD BEFORE THE GREAT DIM...

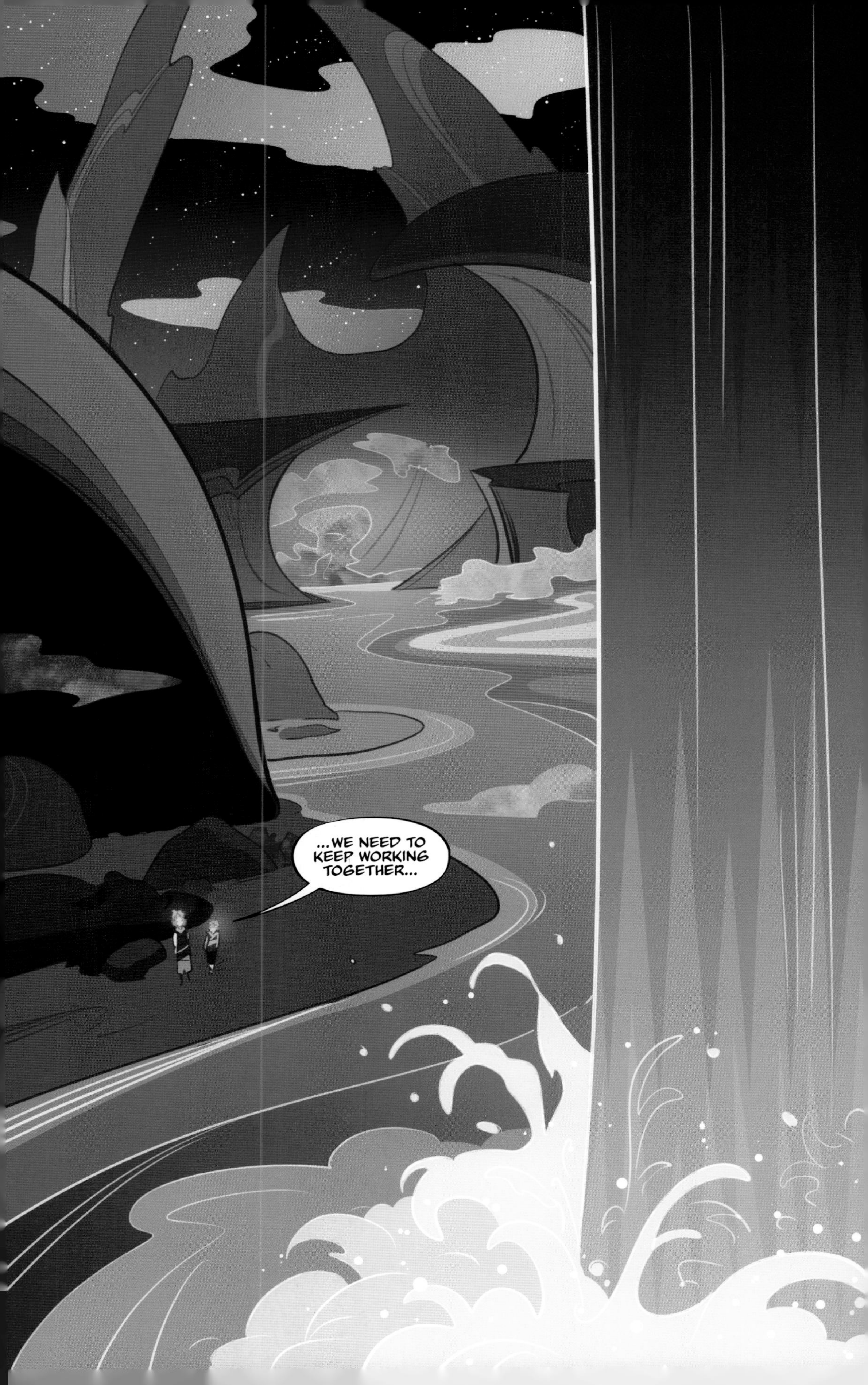
...WE NEED TO KEEP WORKING TOGETHER...

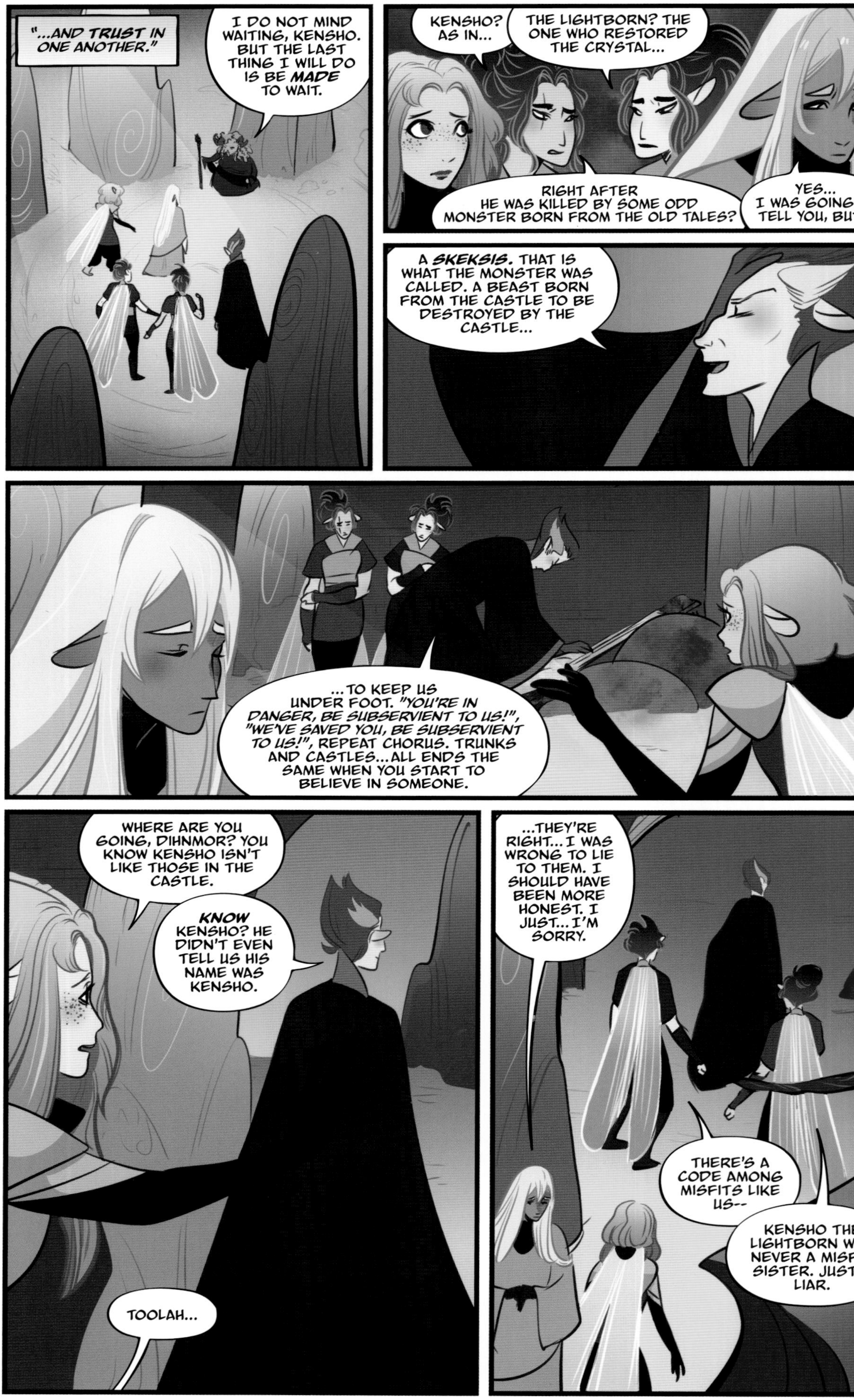
"...AND TRUST IN ONE ANOTHER."
I DO NOT MIND WAITING, KENSHO. BUT THE LAST THING I WILL DO IS BE MADE TO WAIT.
KENSHO? AS IN...
THE LIGHTBORN? THE ONE WHO RESTORED THE CRYSTAL...
RIGHT AFTER HE WAS KILLED BY SOME ODD MONSTER BORN FROM THE OLD TALES?
YES... I WAS GOING TO TELL YOU, BUT--
A SKEKSIS. THAT IS WHAT THE MONSTER WAS CALLED. A BEAST BORN FROM THE CASTLE TO BE DESTROYED BY THE CASTLE...
...TO KEEP US UNDER FOOT. "YOU'RE IN DANGER, BE SUBSERVIENT TO US!", "WE'VE SAVED YOU, BE SUBSERVIENT TO US!", REPEAT CHORUS. TRUNKS AND CASTLES...ALL ENDS THE SAME WHEN YOU START TO BELIEVE IN SOMEONE.
WHERE ARE YOU GOING, DIHNMOR? YOU KNOW KENSHO ISN'T LIKE THOSE IN THE CASTLE.
KNOW KENSHO? HE DIDN'T EVEN TELL US HIS NAME WAS KENSHO.
TOOLAH...
...THEY'RE RIGHT... I WAS WRONG TO LIE TO THEM. I SHOULD HAVE BEEN MORE HONEST. I JUST... I'M SORRY.
THERE'S A CODE AMONG MISFITS LIKE US--
KENSHO THE LIGHTBORN WAS NEVER A MISFIT, SISTER. JUST A LIAR.

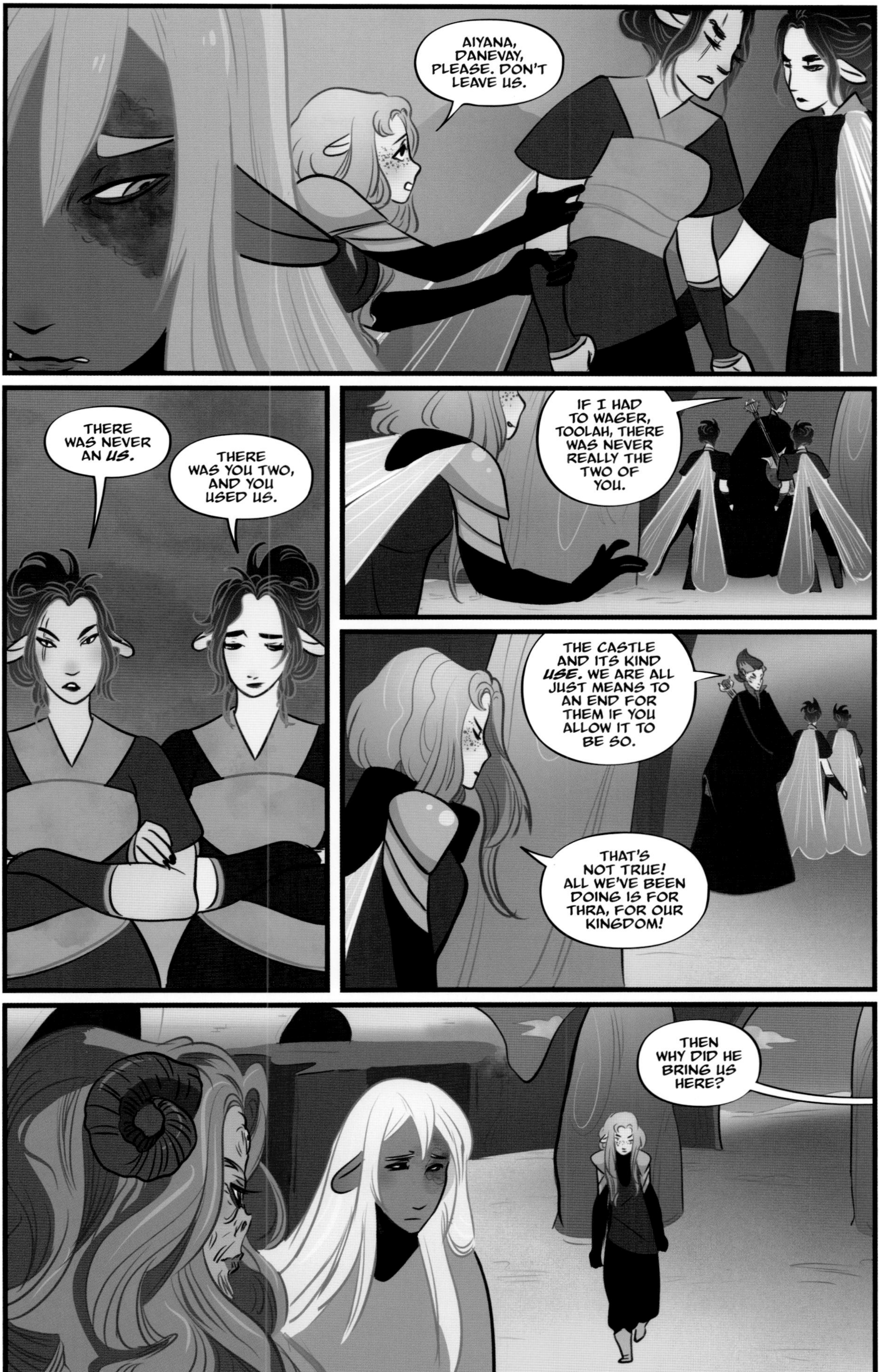
AIYANA, DANEVAY, PLEASE. DON'T LEAVE US.
THERE WAS NEVER AN *US.*
THERE WAS YOU TWO, AND YOU USED US.
IF I HAD TO WAGER, TOOLAH, THERE WAS NEVER REALLY THE TWO OF YOU.
THE CASTLE AND ITS KIND *USE.* WE ARE ALL JUST MEANS TO AN END FOR THEM IF YOU ALLOW IT TO BE SO.
THAT'S NOT TRUE! ALL WE'VE BEEN DOING IS FOR THRA, FOR OUR KINGDOM!
THEN WHY DID HE BRING US HERE?

TELL THEM, KENSHO. TELL THEM HOW YOU BROUGHT US HERE TO SET UP A SANCTUARY FOR GELFLING.

I DID... BUT I ALSO NEEDED--

NEEDED WHAT?!

I NEEDED TO FIX ME.

FIX YOU? WHAT DO YOU THINK WE WERE DOING? EVERYONE'S BROKEN, KENSHO.

BUT THE GOOD ONES DON'T SHATTER THEIR FRIENDS TO PUT THEMSELVES BACK TOGETHER.

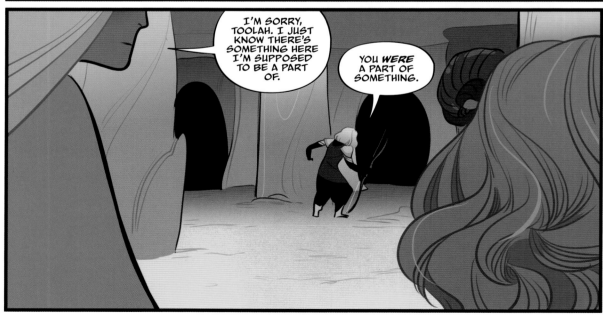

I'M SORRY, TOOLAH. I JUST KNOW THERE'S SOMETHING HERE I'M SUPPOSED TO BE A PART OF.

YOU *WERE* A PART OF SOMETHING.

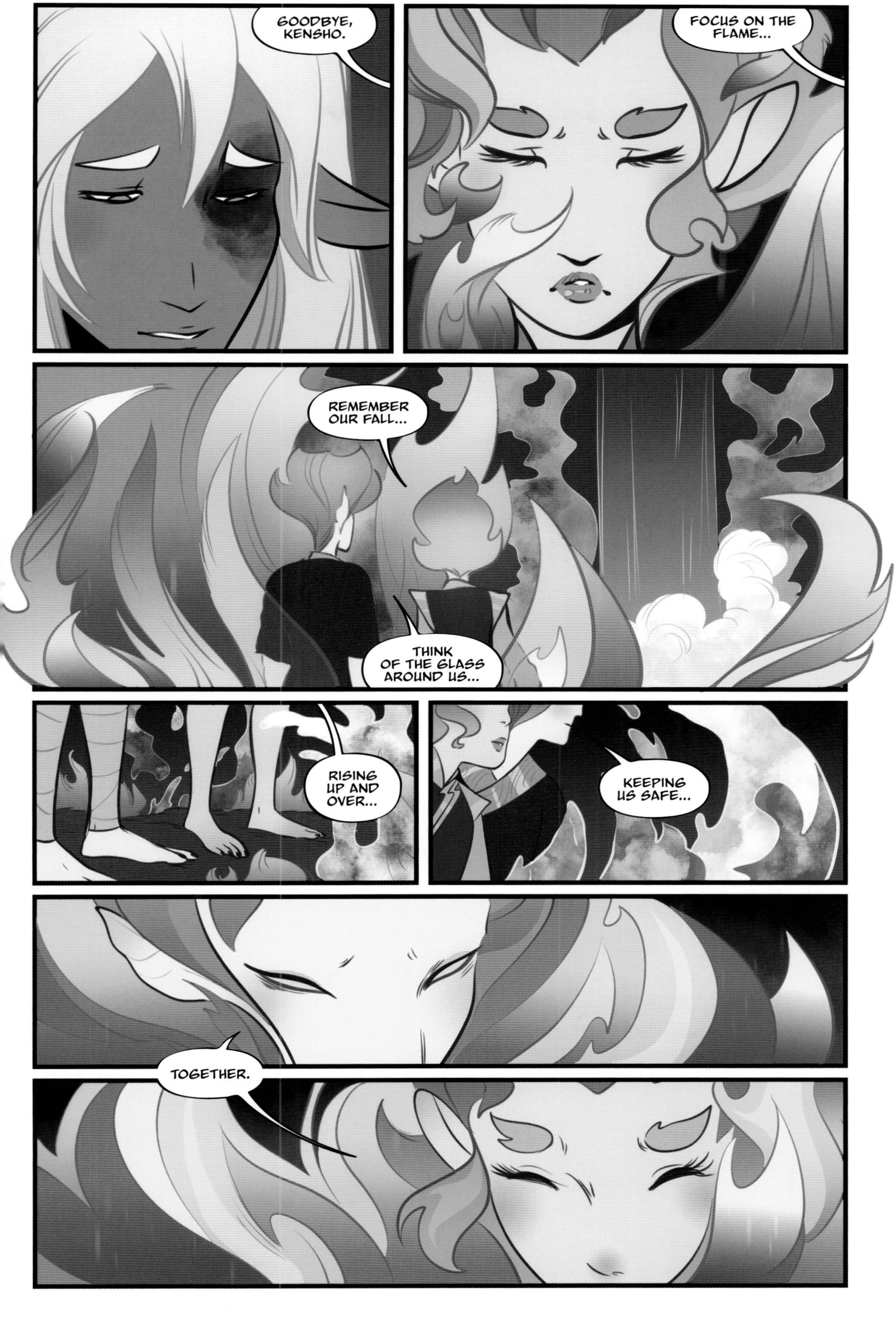
GOODBYE, KENSHO.
FOCUS ON THE FLAME...
REMEMBER OUR FALL...
THINK OF THE GLASS AROUND US...
RISING UP AND OVER...
KEEPING US SAFE...
TOGETHER.

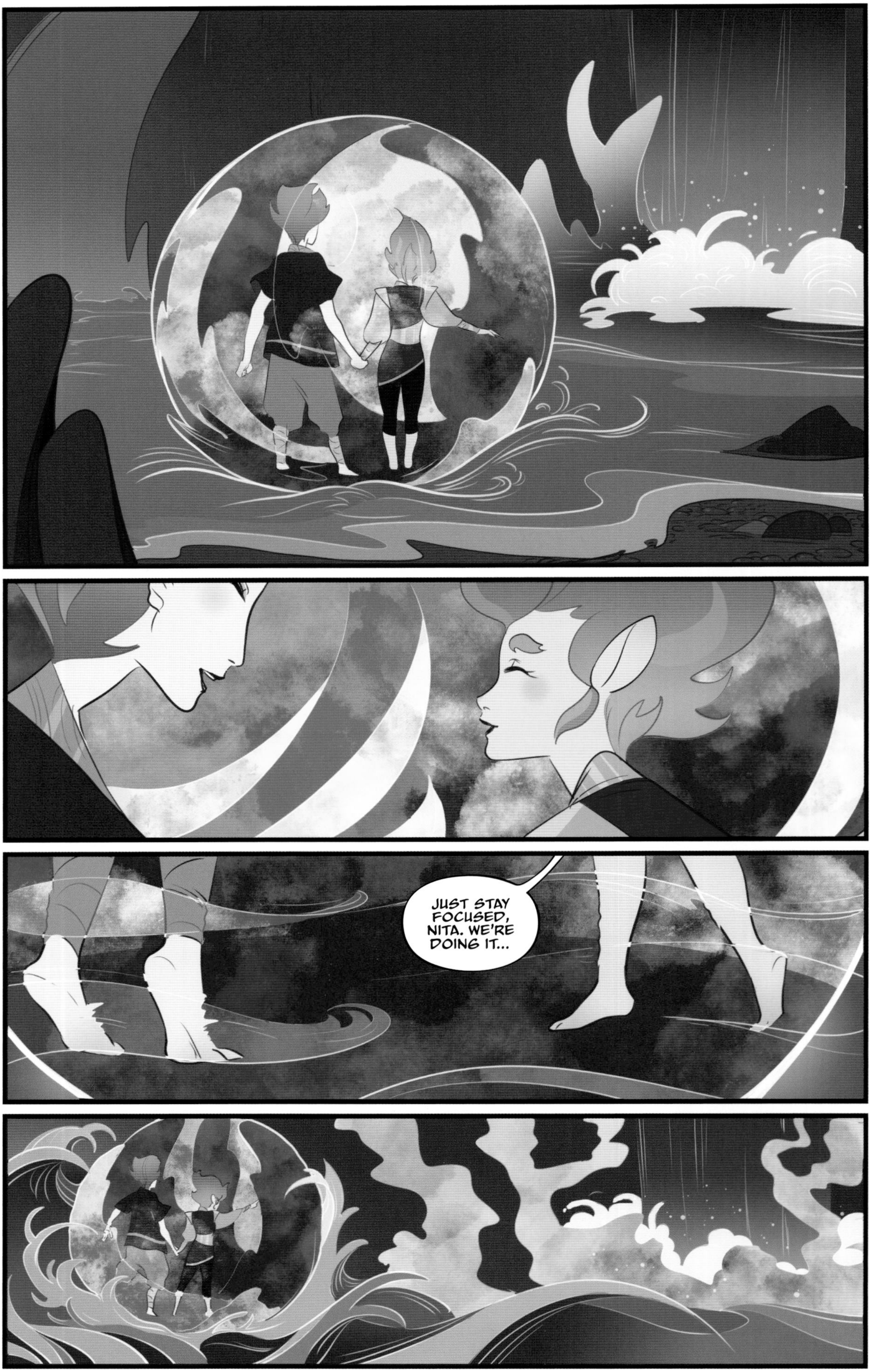
JUST STAY FOCUSED, NITA. WE'RE DOING IT...

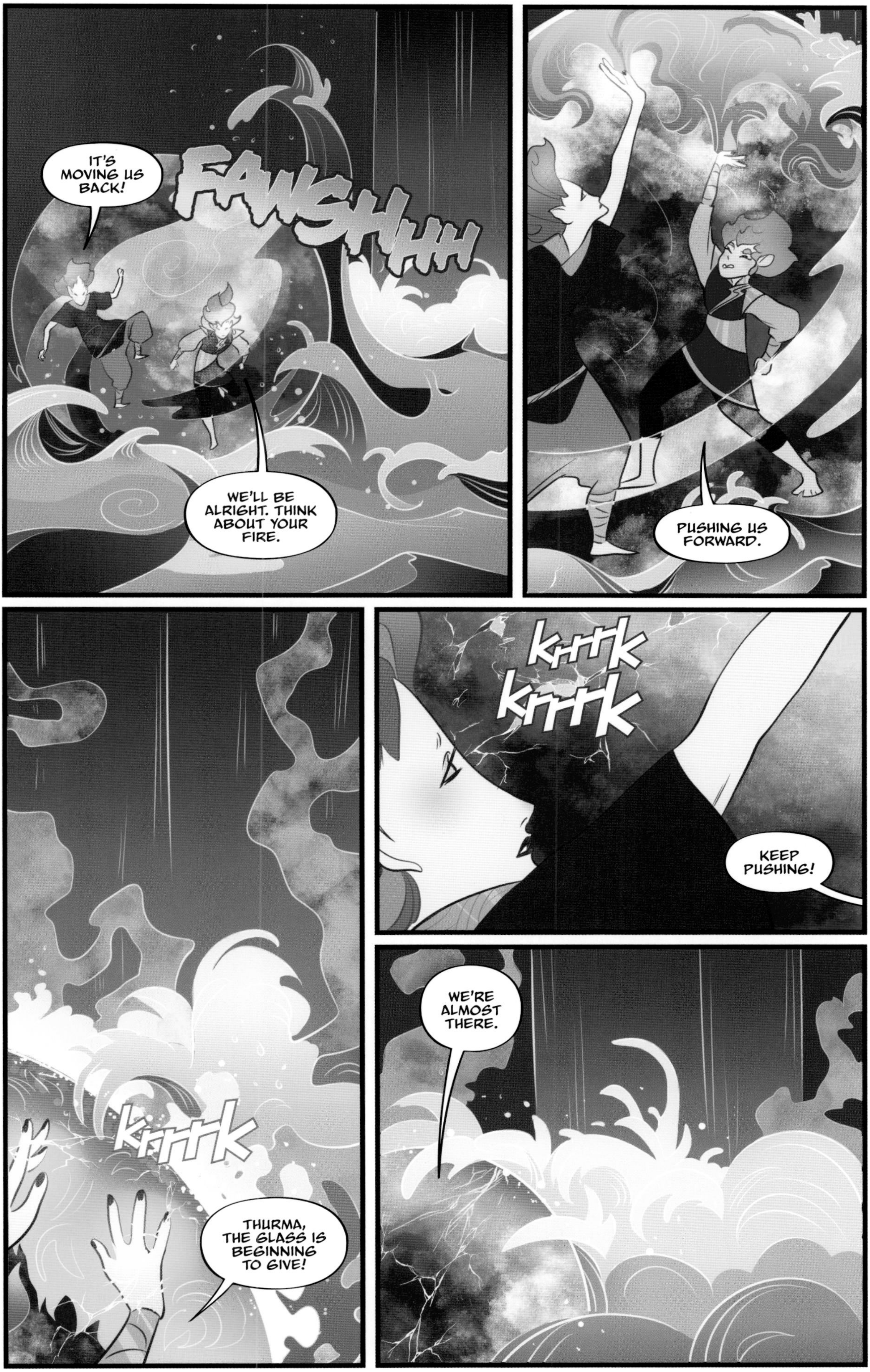
IT'S MOVING US BACK!
FAWSHHH
WE'LL BE ALRIGHT. THINK ABOUT YOUR FIRE.
PUSHING US FORWARD.
Krrrk
THURMA, THE GLASS IS BEGINNING TO GIVE!
Krrrk
Krrrk
KEEP PUSHING!
WE'RE ALMOST THERE.

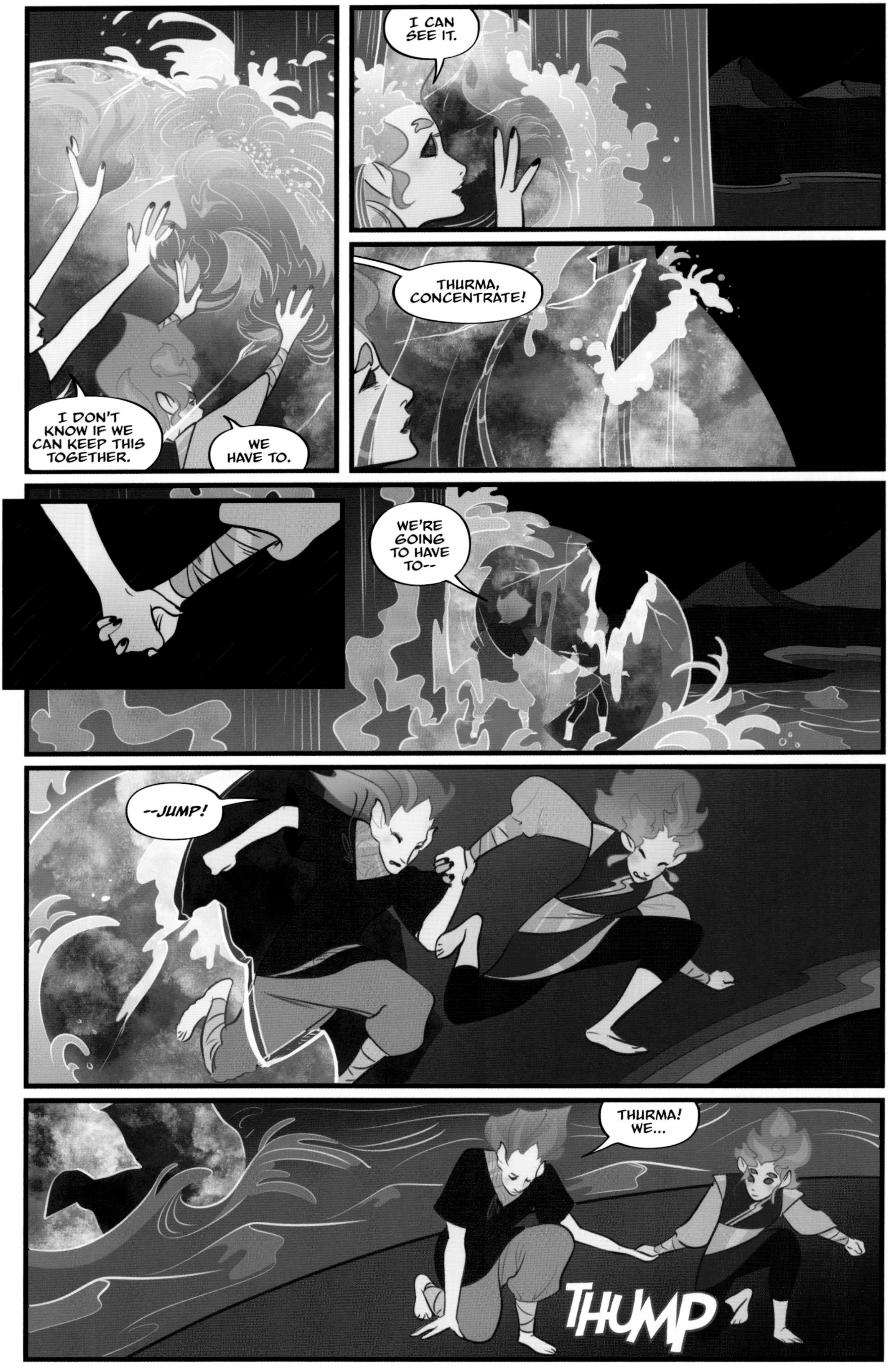
I CAN SEE IT.
I DON'T KNOW IF WE CAN KEEP THIS TOGETHER.
WE HAVE TO.
THURMA, CONCENTRATE!
WE'RE GOING TO HAVE TO--
--JUMP!
THURMA! WE...
THUMP

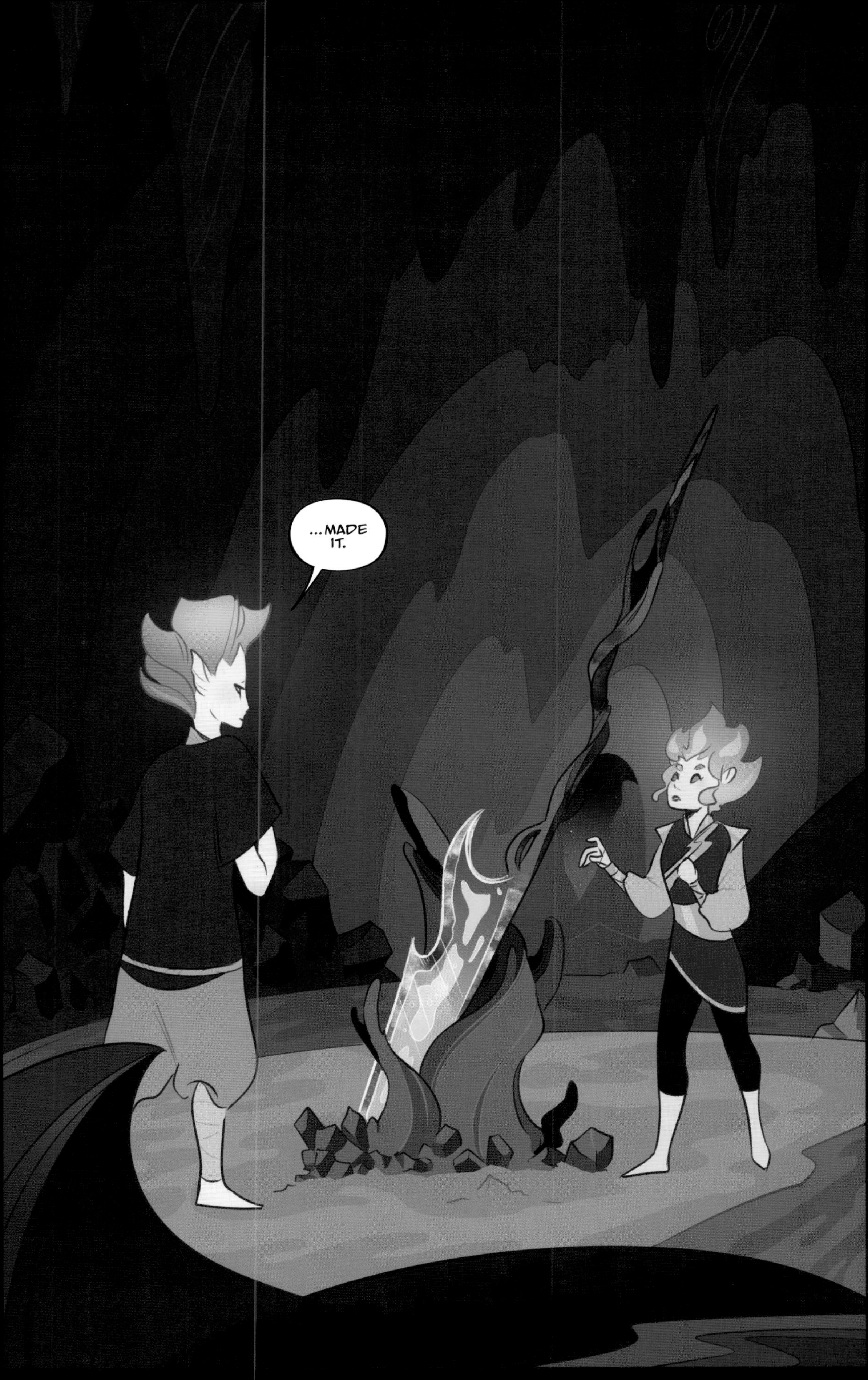
...MADE IT.

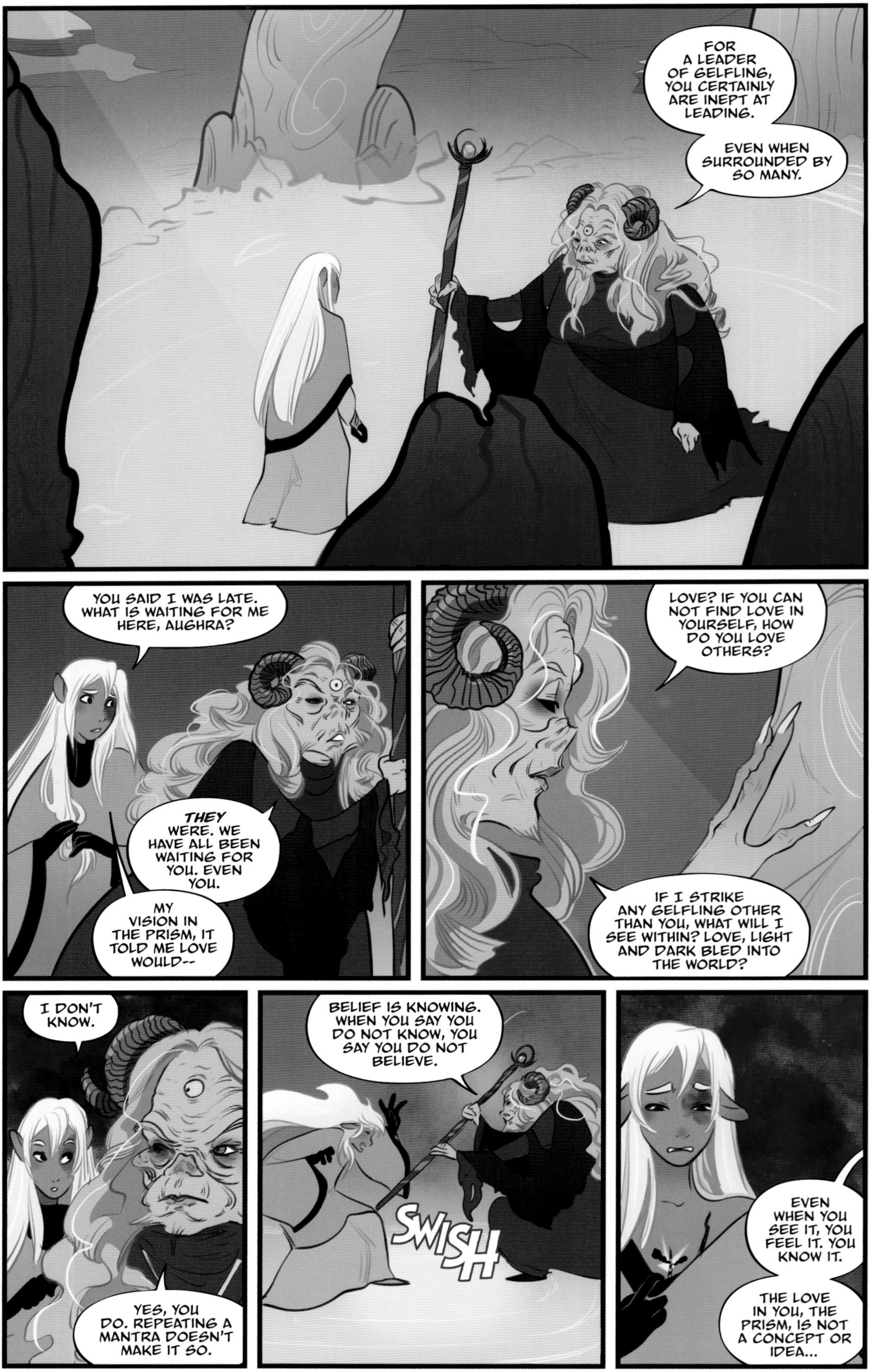

FOR A LEADER OF GELFLING, YOU CERTAINLY ARE INEPT AT LEADING.
EVEN WHEN SURROUNDED BY SO MANY.
YOU SAID I WAS LATE. WHAT IS WAITING FOR ME HERE, AUGHRA?
THEY WERE. WE HAVE ALL BEEN WAITING FOR YOU. EVEN YOU.
MY VISION IN THE PRISM, IT TOLD ME LOVE WOULD--
LOVE? IF YOU CAN NOT FIND LOVE IN YOURSELF, HOW DO YOU LOVE OTHERS?
IF I STRIKE ANY GELFLING OTHER THAN YOU, WHAT WILL I SEE WITHIN? LOVE, LIGHT AND DARK BLED INTO THE WORLD?
I DON'T KNOW.
YES, YOU DO. REPEATING A MANTRA DOESN'T MAKE IT SO.
BELIEF IS KNOWING. WHEN YOU SAY YOU DO NOT KNOW, YOU SAY YOU DO NOT BELIEVE.
SWISH
EVEN WHEN YOU SEE IT, YOU FEEL IT. YOU KNOW IT.
THE LOVE IN YOU, THE PRISM, IS NOT A CONCEPT OR IDEA...

...IT IS THE TRUTH.

BUT YOU HAVE RUN FROM IT AND EVERYONE FOR SO LONG. PUSHED BACK SO HARD AGAINST THOSE WHO NEED YOU, YOU'VE PUSHED AGAINST YOURSELF.

YOU HIDE A LIGHT FROM THE WORLD. YOU LET A SHADOW STRETCH AND BEND OVER MOUNTAINS AND RIVERS.

BUT HOW DOES THAT LIGHT HELP THRA?

IT HELPED DAGGER ROOT, DIDN'T IT? TALES OF YOUR LITTLE COUP HAVE INSPIRED ALREADY.

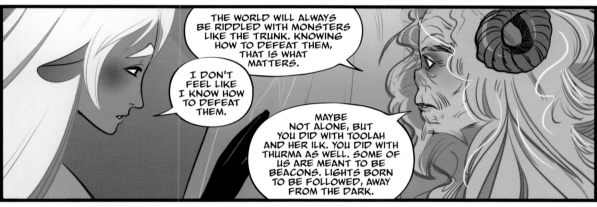

THE WORLD WILL ALWAYS BE RIDDLED WITH MONSTERS LIKE THE TRUNK. KNOWING HOW TO DEFEAT THEM, THAT IS WHAT MATTERS.

I DON'T FEEL LIKE I KNOW HOW TO DEFEAT THEM.

MAYBE NOT ALONE, BUT YOU DID WITH TOOLAH AND HER ILK. YOU DID WITH THURMA AS WELL. SOME OF US ARE MEANT TO BE BEACONS. LIGHTS BORN TO BE FOLLOWED, AWAY FROM THE DARK.

JUST AS THIS VALLEY WAS BUILT AS A SYMBOL OF THRA ITSELF.

WHEN YOU LET YOUR LIGHT INTO THE WORLD, YOU ARE A SYMBOL OF THE GELFLING...

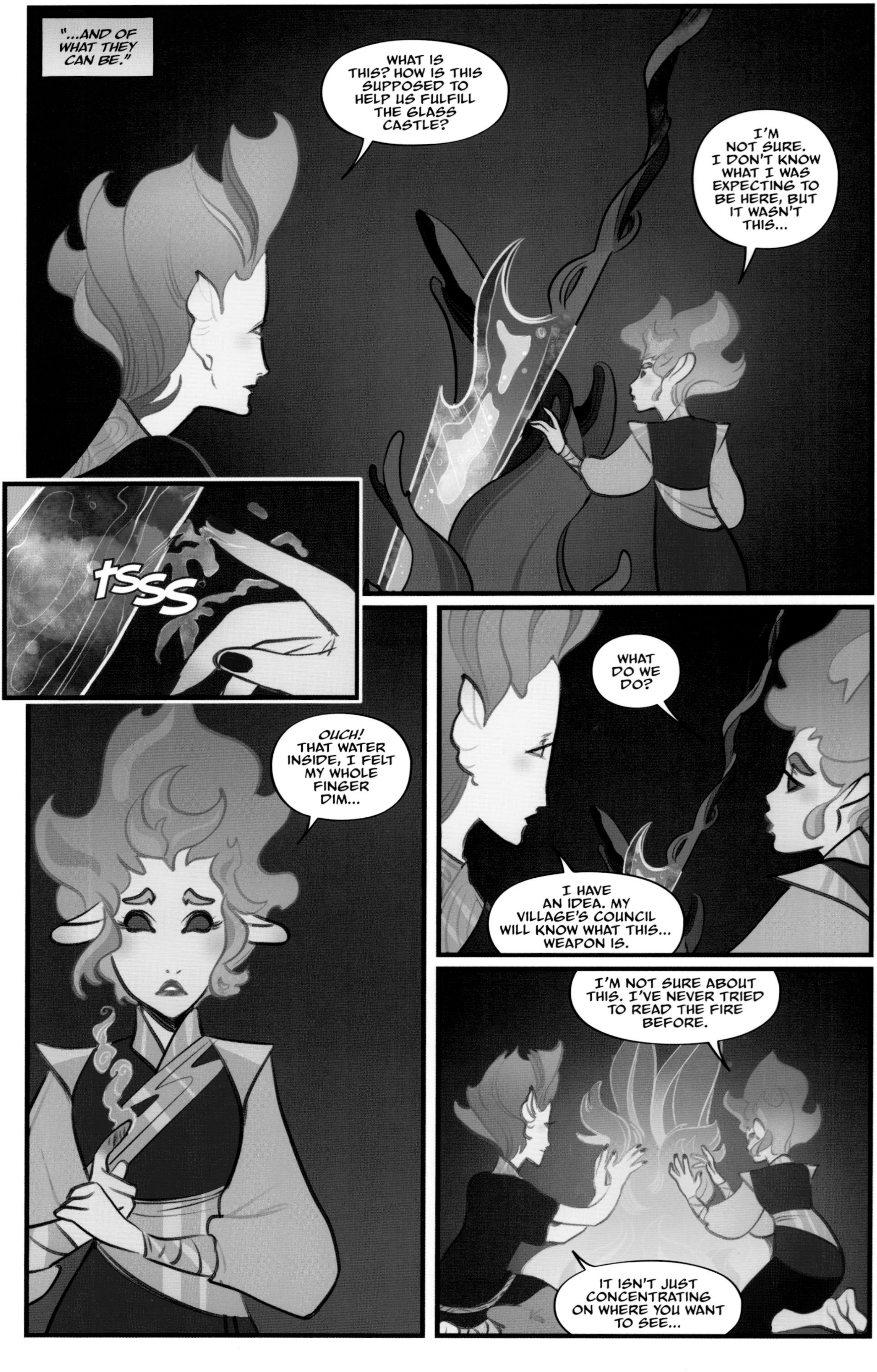
"...AND OF WHAT THEY CAN BE."
WHAT IS THIS? HOW IS THIS SUPPOSED TO HELP US FULFILL THE GLASS CASTLE?
I'M NOT SURE. I DON'T KNOW WHAT I WAS EXPECTING TO BE HERE, BUT IT WASN'T THIS...
tsss
OUCH! THAT WATER INSIDE, I FELT MY WHOLE FINGER DIM...
WHAT DO WE DO?
I HAVE AN IDEA. MY VILLAGE'S COUNCIL WILL KNOW WHAT THIS... WEAPON IS.
I'M NOT SURE ABOUT THIS. I'VE NEVER TRIED TO READ THE FIRE BEFORE.
IT ISN'T JUST CONCENTRATING ON WHERE YOU WANT TO SEE...

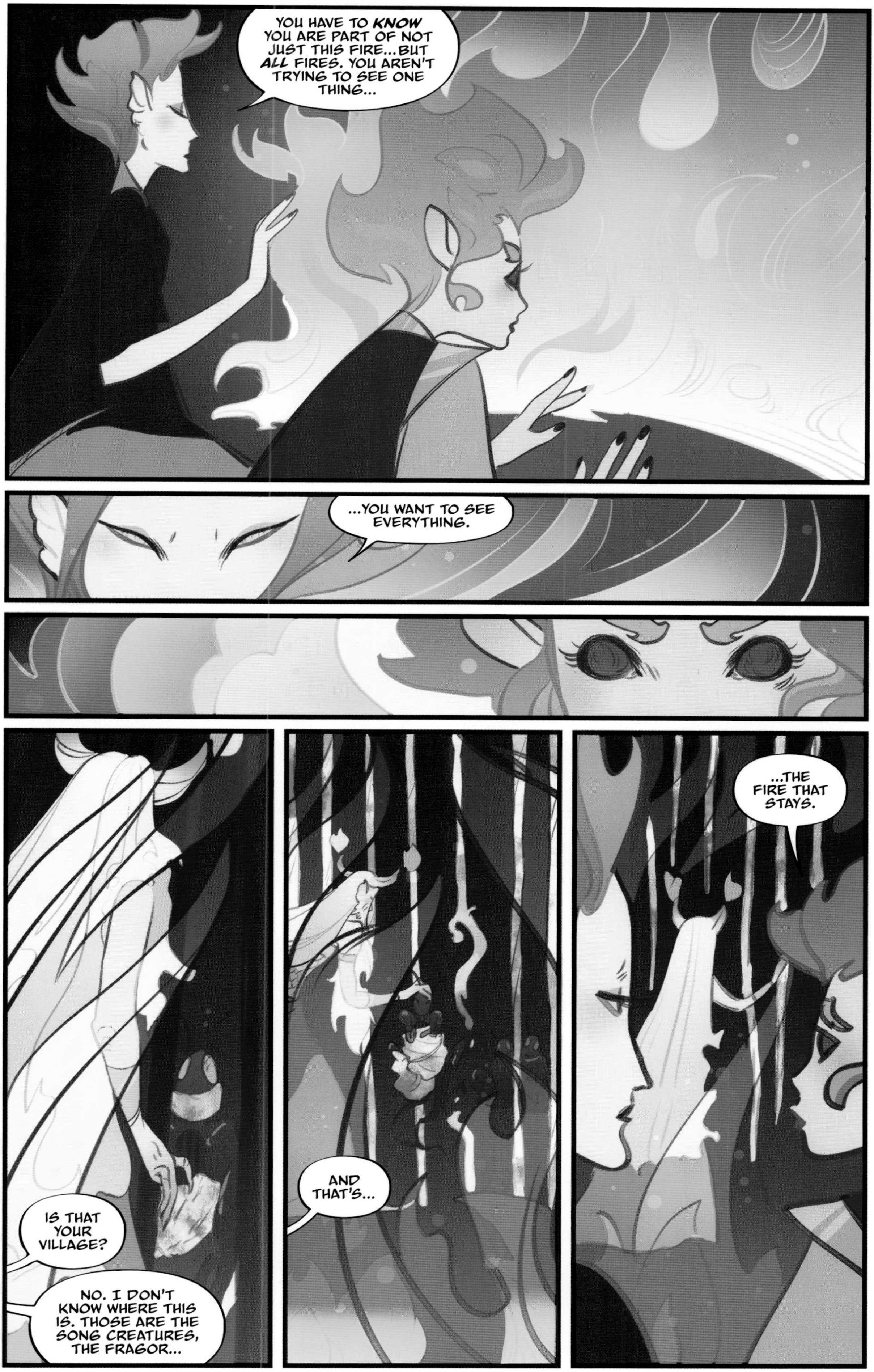
YOU HAVE TO KNOW YOU ARE PART OF NOT JUST THIS FIRE...BUT ALL FIRES. YOU AREN'T TRYING TO SEE ONE THING...
...YOU WANT TO SEE EVERYTHING.
IS THAT YOUR VILLAGE?
NO. I DON'T KNOW WHERE THIS IS. THOSE ARE THE SONG CREATURES, THE FRAGOR...
AND THAT'S...
...THE FIRE THAT STAYS.

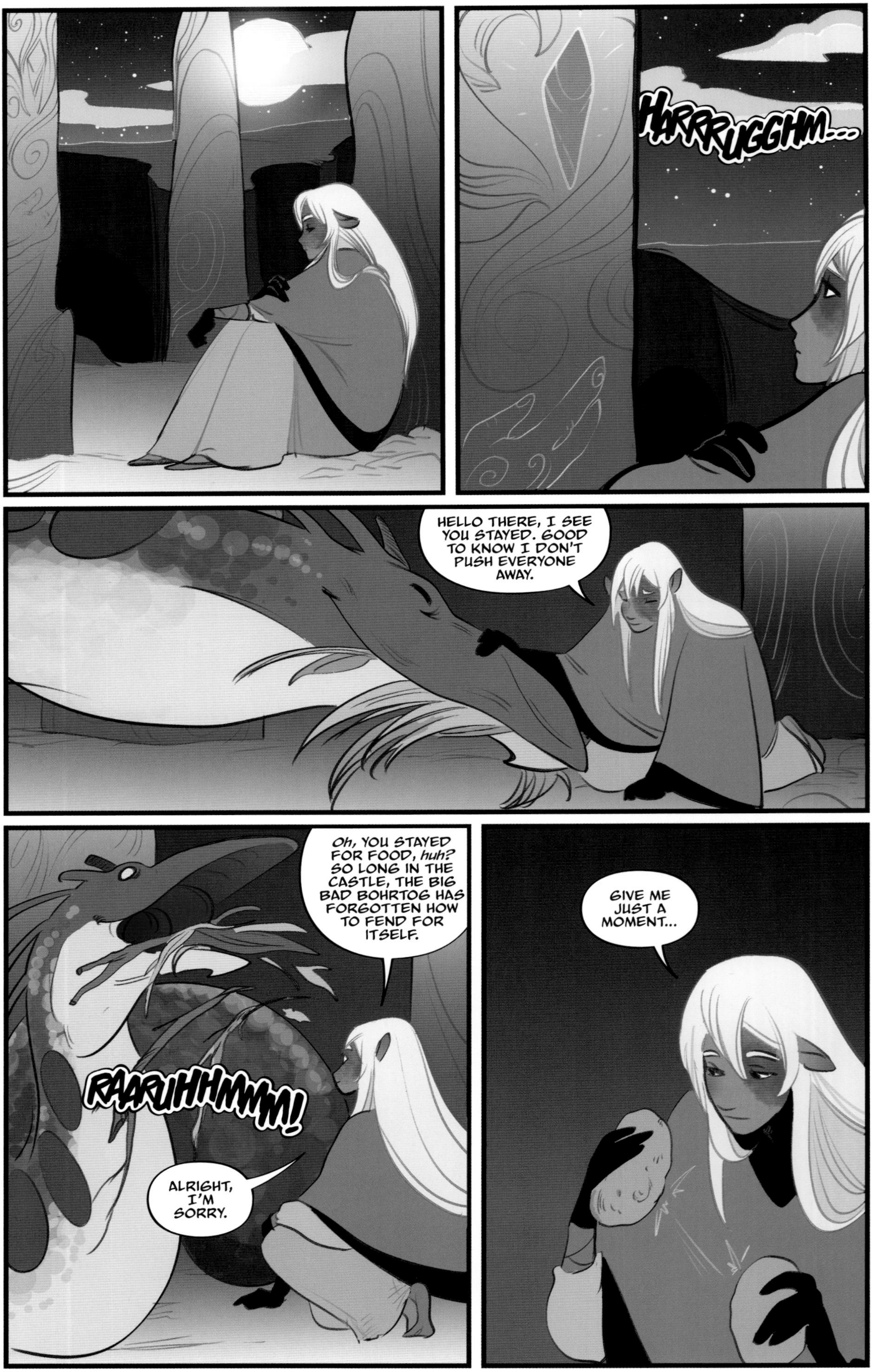
HARRRUGGHM...
HELLO THERE, I SEE YOU STAYED. GOOD TO KNOW I DON'T PUSH EVERYONE AWAY.
Oh, YOU STAYED FOR FOOD, *huh*? SO LONG IN THE CASTLE, THE BIG BAD BOHRTOG HAS FORGOTTEN HOW TO FEND FOR ITSELF.
RAARUHHMMM!
ALRIGHT, I'M SORRY.
GIVE ME JUST A MOMENT...

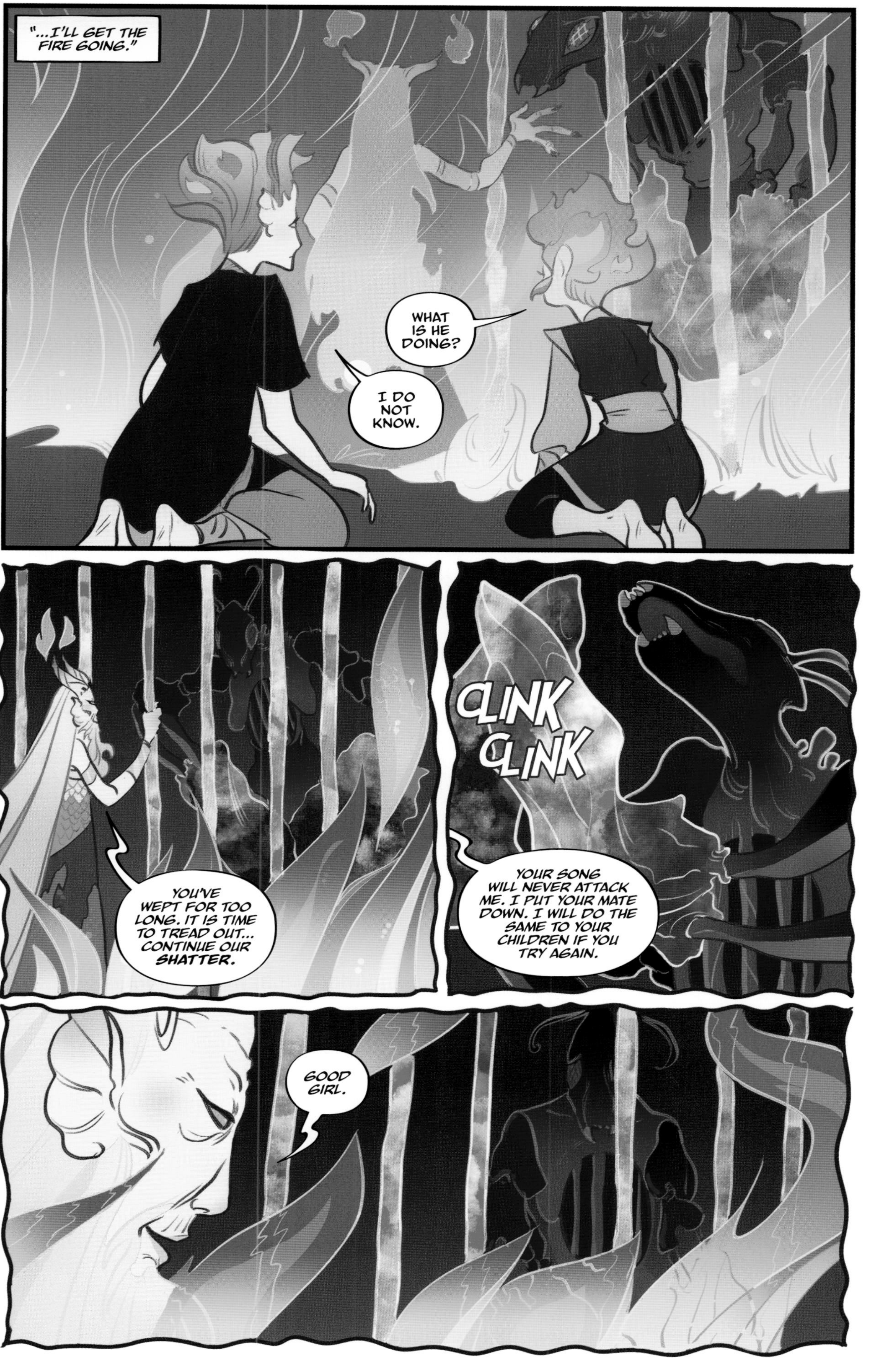
"...I'LL GET THE FIRE GOING."
WHAT IS HE DOING?
I DO NOT KNOW.
YOU'VE WEPT FOR TOO LONG. IT IS TIME TO TREAD OUT... CONTINUE OUR SHATTER.
CLINK CLINK
YOUR SONG WILL NEVER ATTACK ME. I PUT YOUR MATE DOWN. I WILL DO THE SAME TO YOUR CHILDREN IF YOU TRY AGAIN.
GOOD GIRL.

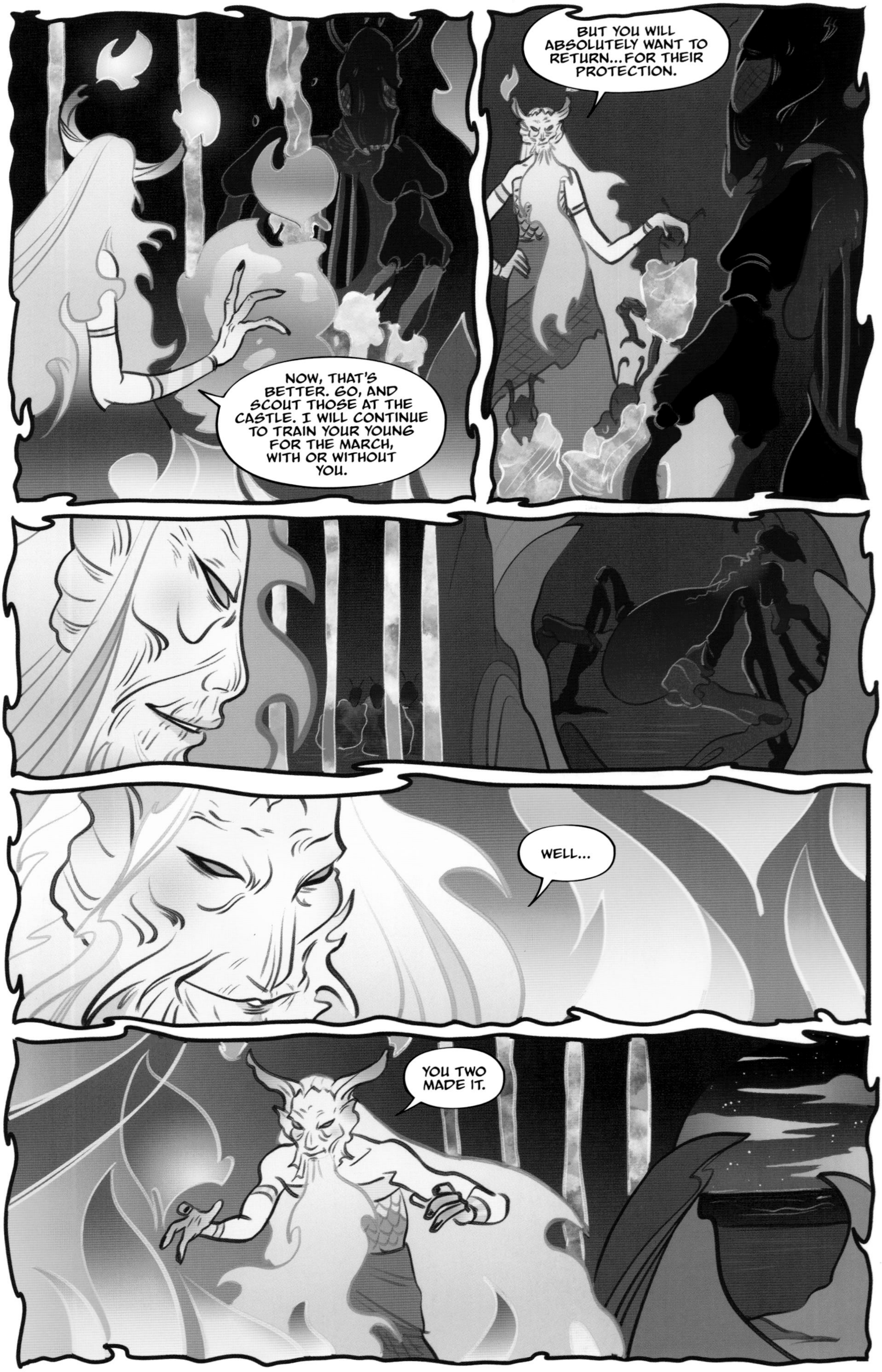
NOW, THAT'S BETTER. GO, AND SCOUT THOSE AT THE CASTLE. I WILL CONTINUE TO TRAIN YOUR YOUNG FOR THE MARCH, WITH OR WITHOUT YOU.
BUT YOU WILL ABSOLUTELY WANT TO RETURN...FOR THEIR PROTECTION.
WELL...
YOU TWO MADE IT.

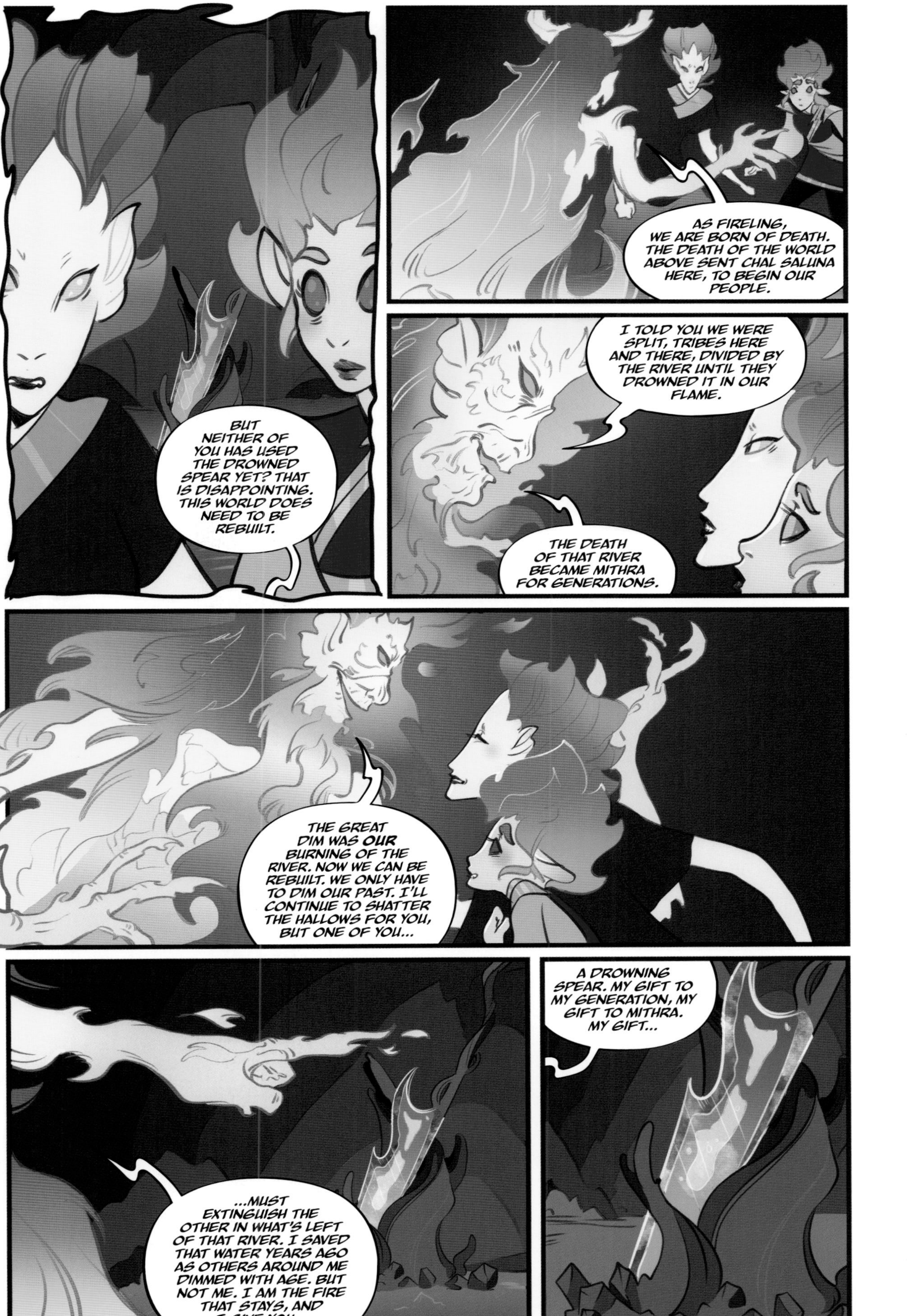
BUT NEITHER OF YOU HAS USED THE DROWNED SPEAR YET? THAT IS DISAPPOINTING. THIS WORLD DOES NEED TO BE REBUILT.
AS FIRELING, WE ARE BORN OF DEATH. THE DEATH OF THE WORLD ABOVE SENT CHAL SALUNA HERE, TO BEGIN OUR PEOPLE.
I TOLD YOU WE WERE SPLIT, TRIBES HERE AND THERE, DIVIDED BY THE RIVER UNTIL THEY DROWNED IT IN OUR FLAME.
THE DEATH OF THAT RIVER BECAME MITHRA FOR GENERATIONS.
THE GREAT DIM WAS **OUR** BURNING OF THE RIVER. NOW WE CAN BE REBUILT. WE ONLY HAVE TO DIM OUR PAST. I'LL CONTINUE TO SHATTER THE HALLOWS FOR YOU, BUT ONE OF YOU...
...MUST EXTINGUISH THE OTHER IN WHAT'S LEFT OF THAT RIVER. I SAVED THAT WATER YEARS AGO AS OTHERS AROUND ME DIMMED WITH AGE. BUT NOT ME. I AM THE FIRE THAT STAYS, AND I GIVE YOU...
A DROWNING SPEAR. MY GIFT TO MY GENERATION, MY GIFT TO MITHRA. MY GIFT...

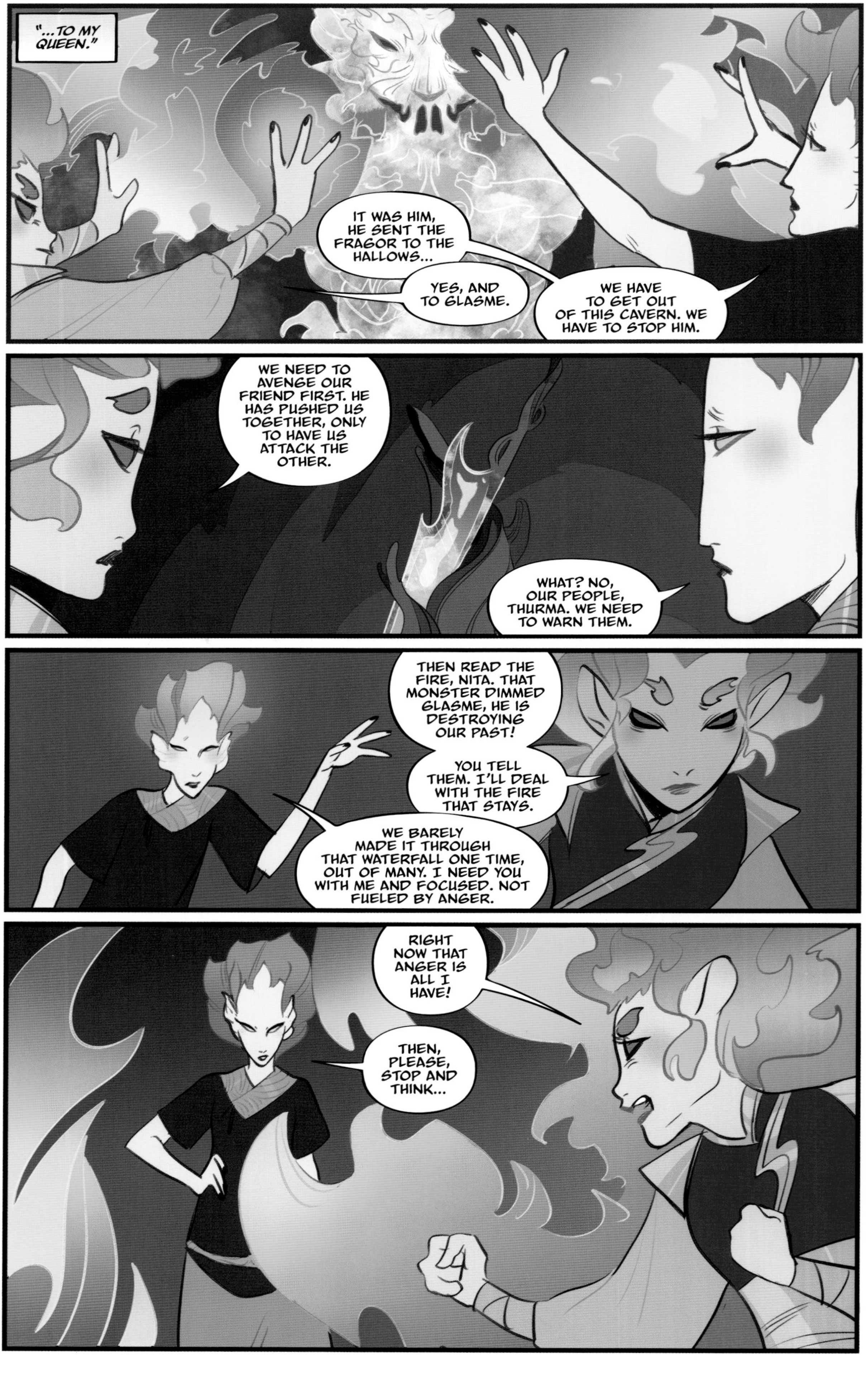
"...TO MY QUEEN."
IT WAS HIM, HE SENT THE FRAGOR TO THE HALLOWS...
YES, AND TO GLASME.
WE HAVE TO GET OUT OF THIS CAVERN. WE HAVE TO STOP HIM.
WE NEED TO AVENGE OUR FRIEND FIRST. HE HAS PUSHED US TOGETHER, ONLY TO HAVE US ATTACK THE OTHER.
WHAT? NO, OUR PEOPLE, THURMA. WE NEED TO WARN THEM.
THEN READ THE FIRE, NITA. THAT MONSTER DIMMED GLASME, HE IS DESTROYING OUR PAST!
YOU TELL THEM. I'LL DEAL WITH THE FIRE THAT STAYS.
WE BARELY MADE IT THROUGH THAT WATERFALL ONE TIME, OUT OF MANY. I NEED YOU WITH ME AND FOCUSED. NOT FUELED BY ANGER.
RIGHT NOW THAT ANGER IS ALL I HAVE!
THEN, PLEASE, STOP AND THINK...

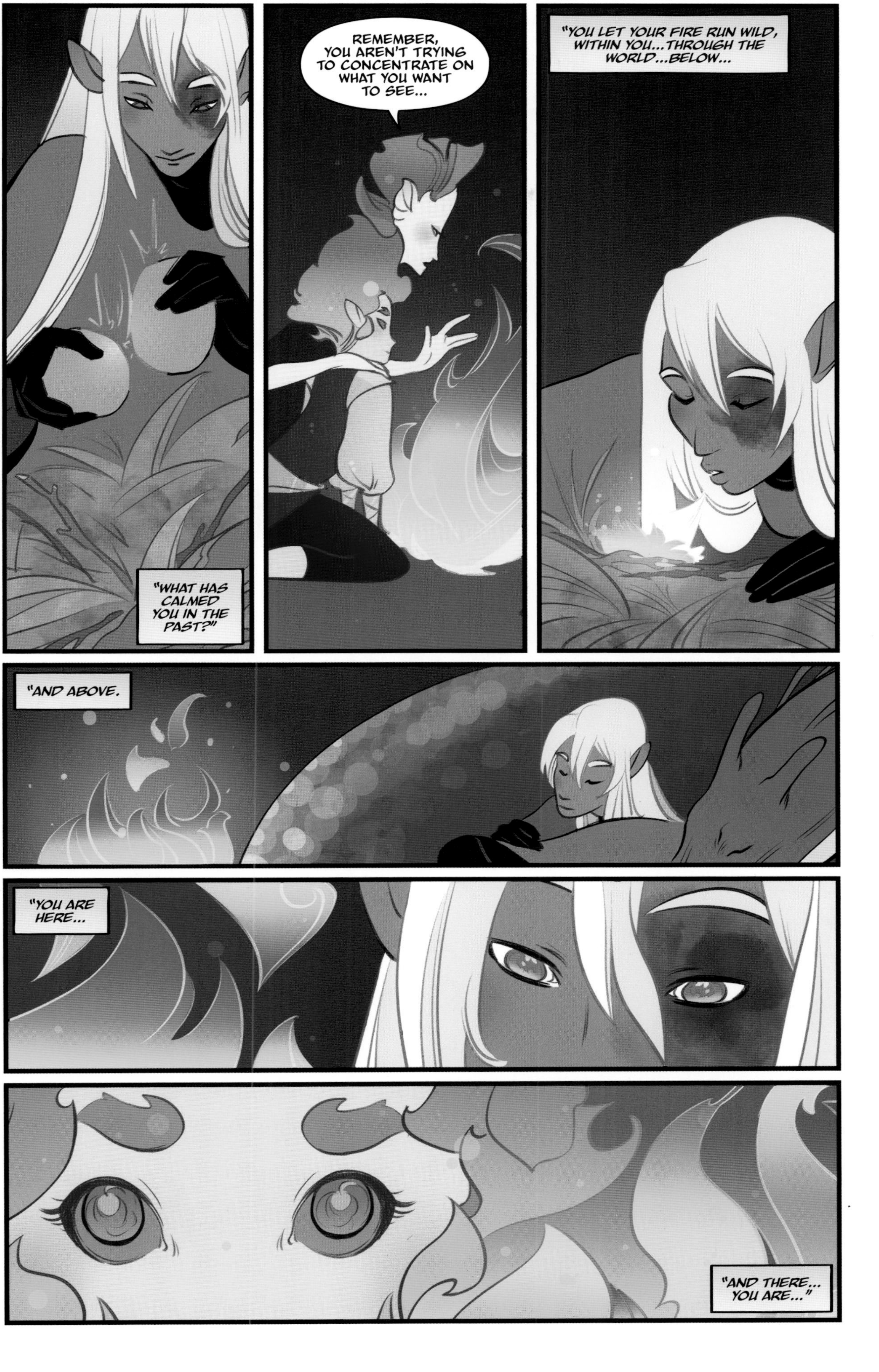
"WHAT HAS CALMED YOU IN THE PAST?"
REMEMBER, YOU AREN'T TRYING TO CONCENTRATE ON WHAT YOU WANT TO SEE...
"YOU LET YOUR FIRE RUN WILD, WITHIN YOU...THROUGH THE WORLD...BELOW...
"AND ABOVE.
"YOU ARE HERE...
"AND THERE... YOU ARE..."

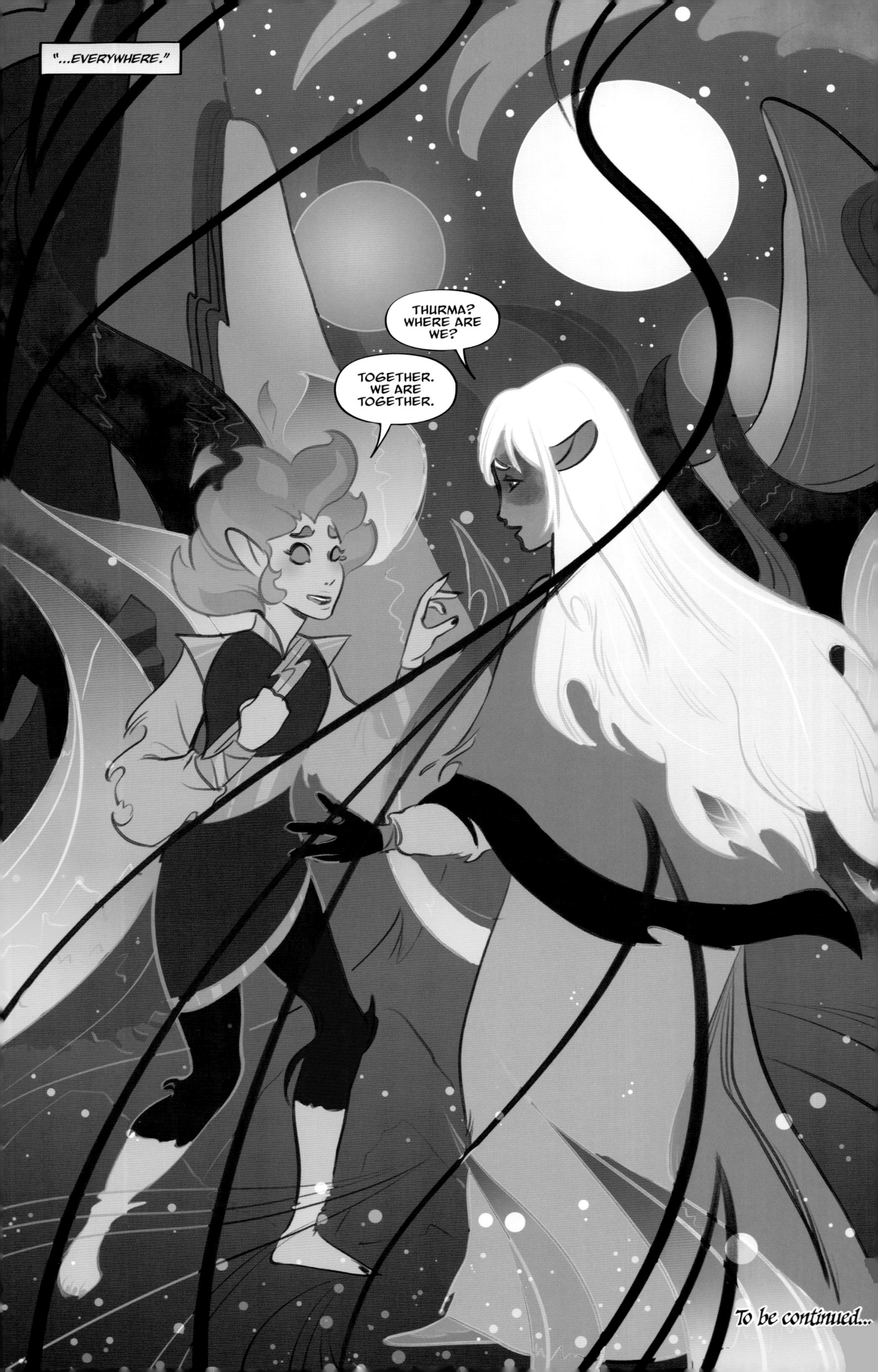
"...EVERYWHERE."
THURMA? WHERE ARE WE?
TOGETHER. WE ARE TOGETHER.
To be continued...

COVER GALLERY

Facing Page: Issue #5 Subscription Cover by David Petersen.
Following Pages: Issue #6-8 Subscription Covers by David Petersen.
Page 107: Issue #2 Variant Cover by Lee Garbett.
Page 108: Issue #3 Variant Cover by Lee Garbett.

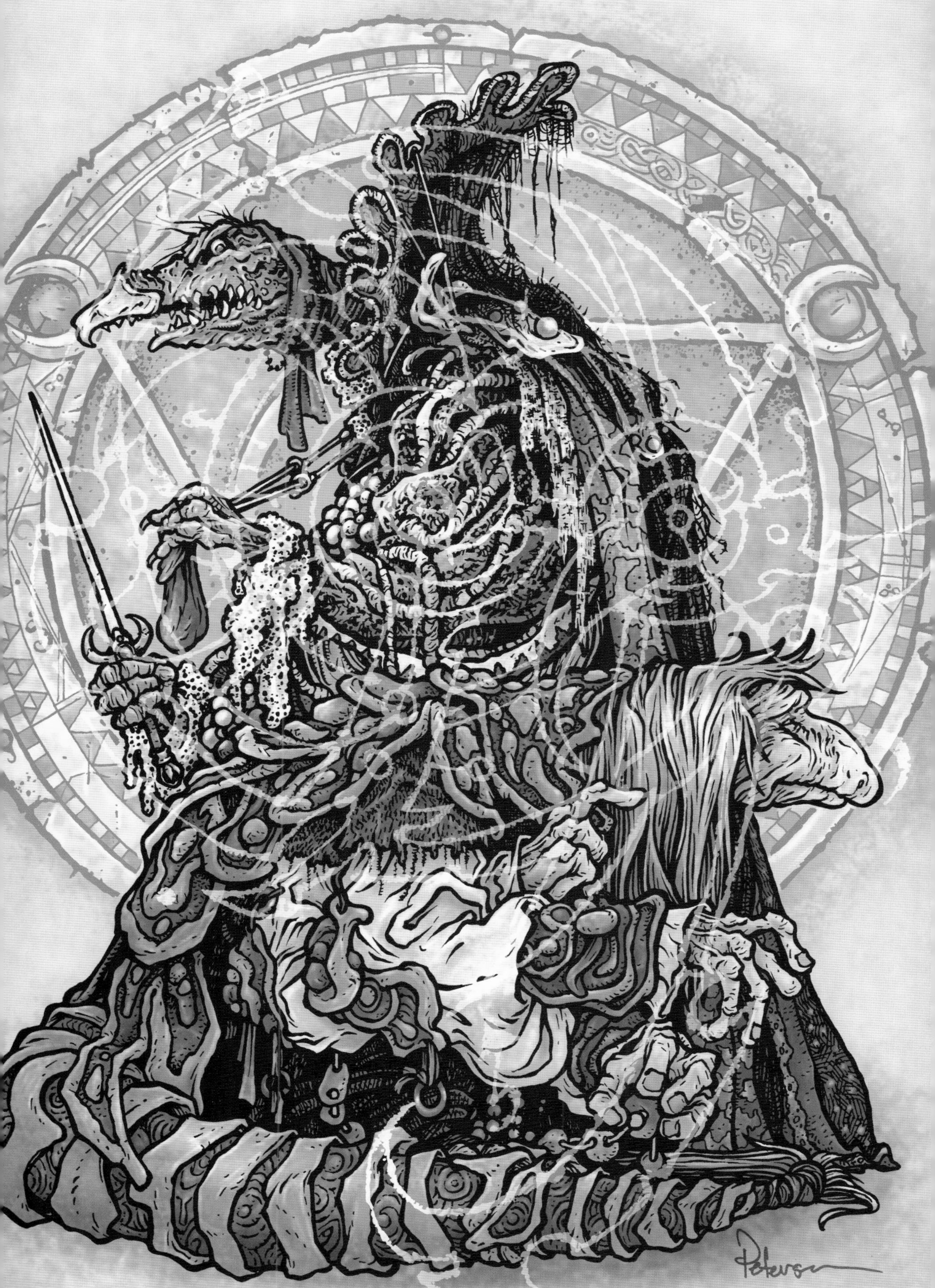

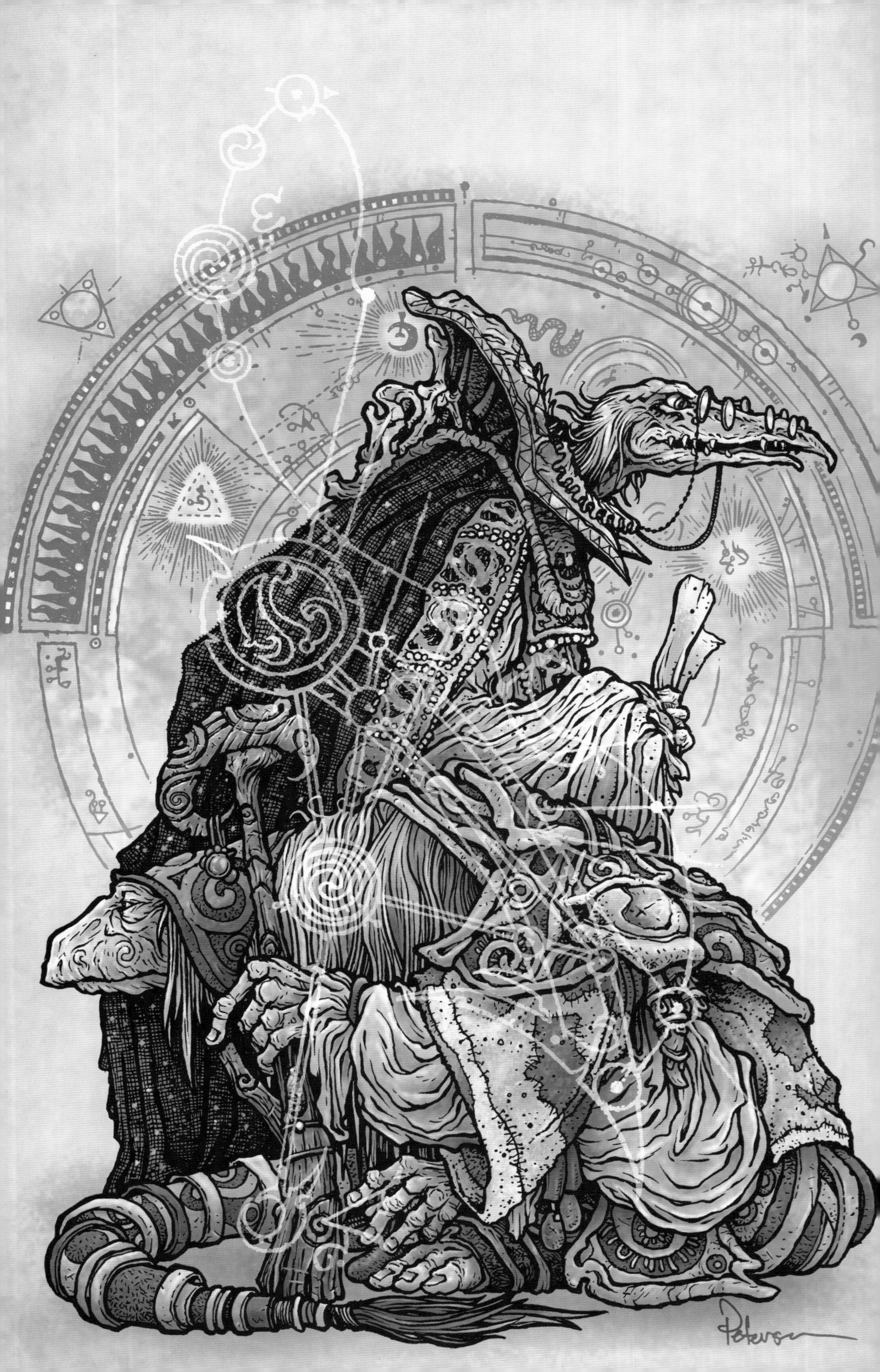

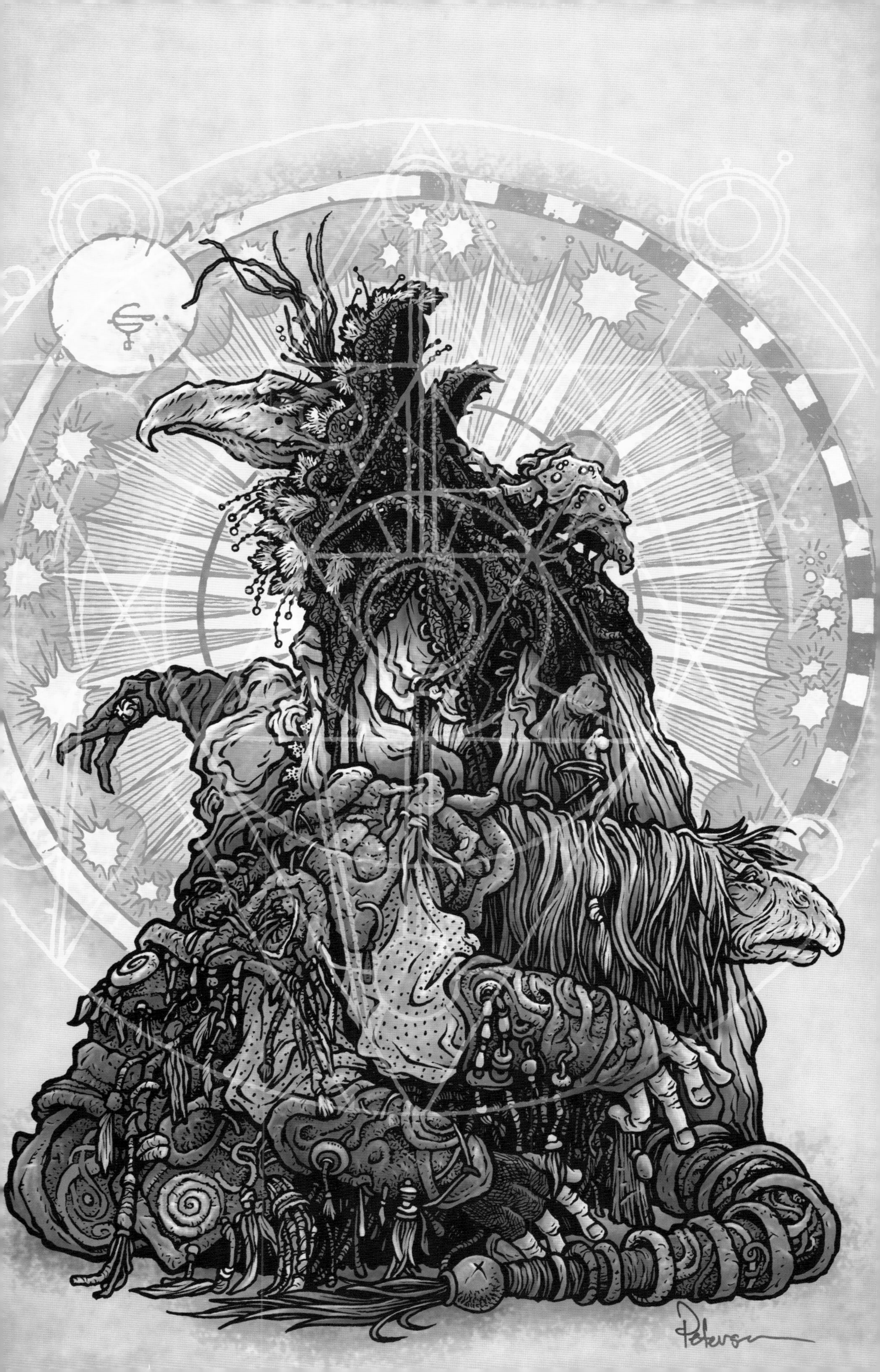

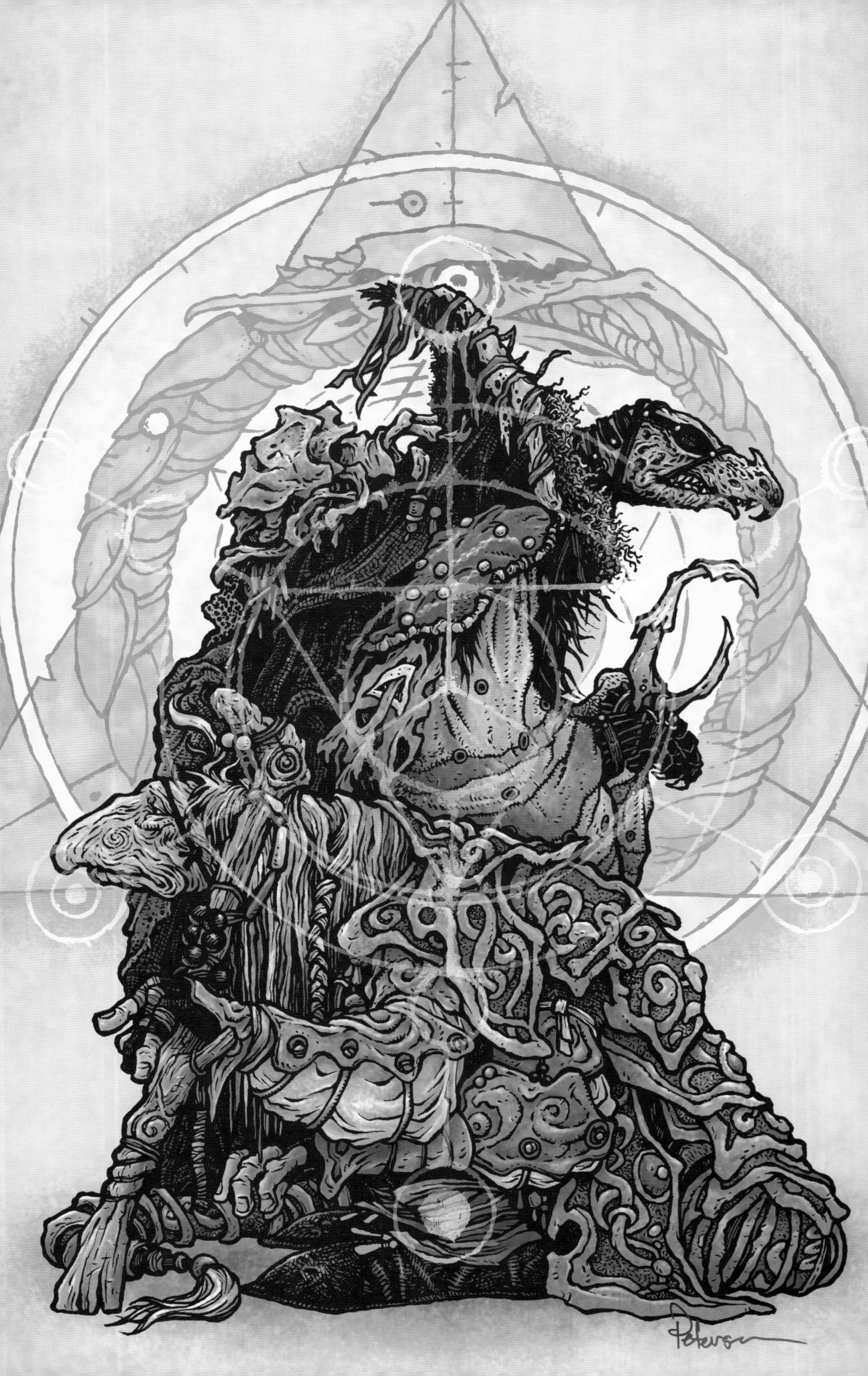

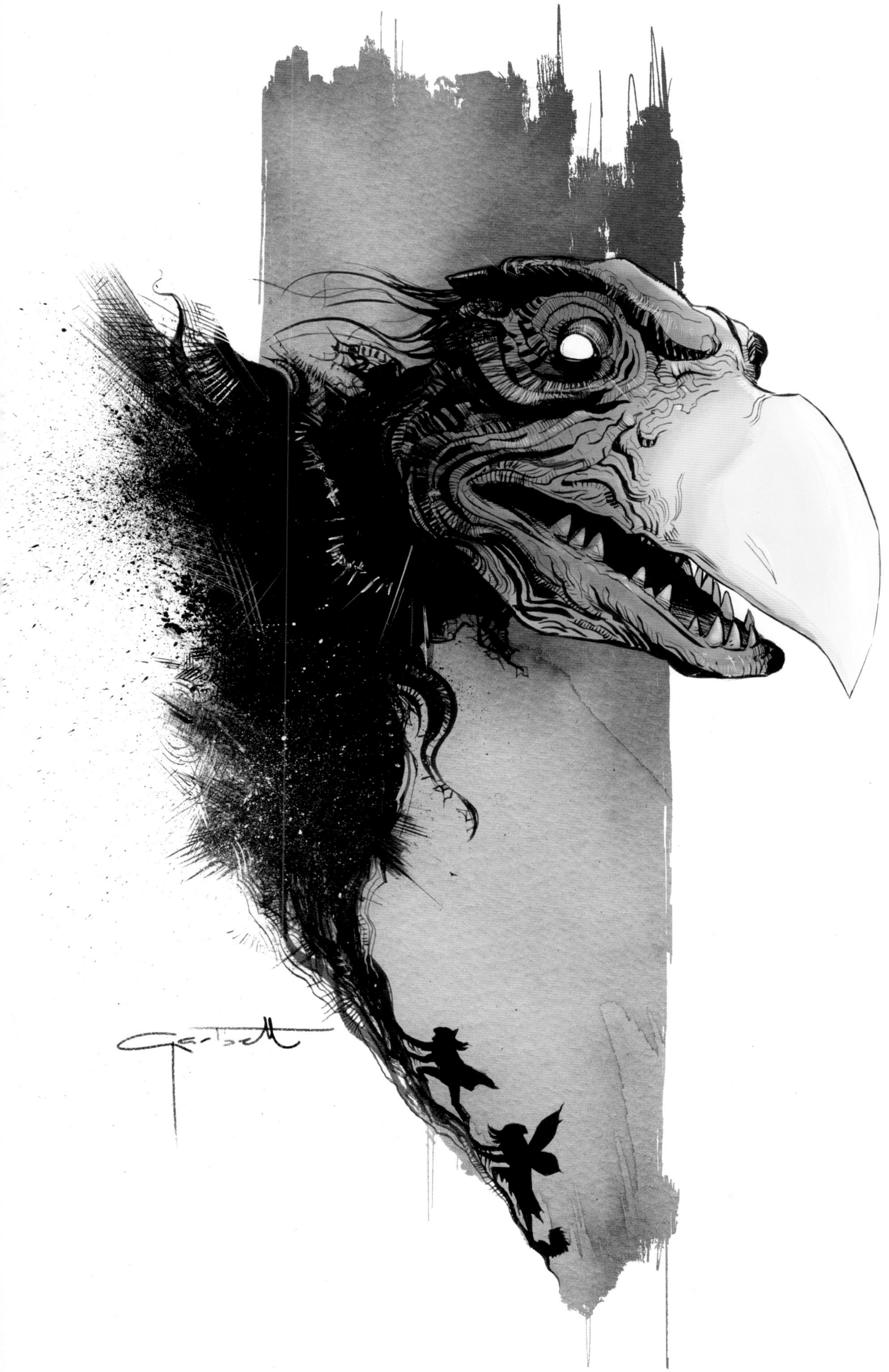

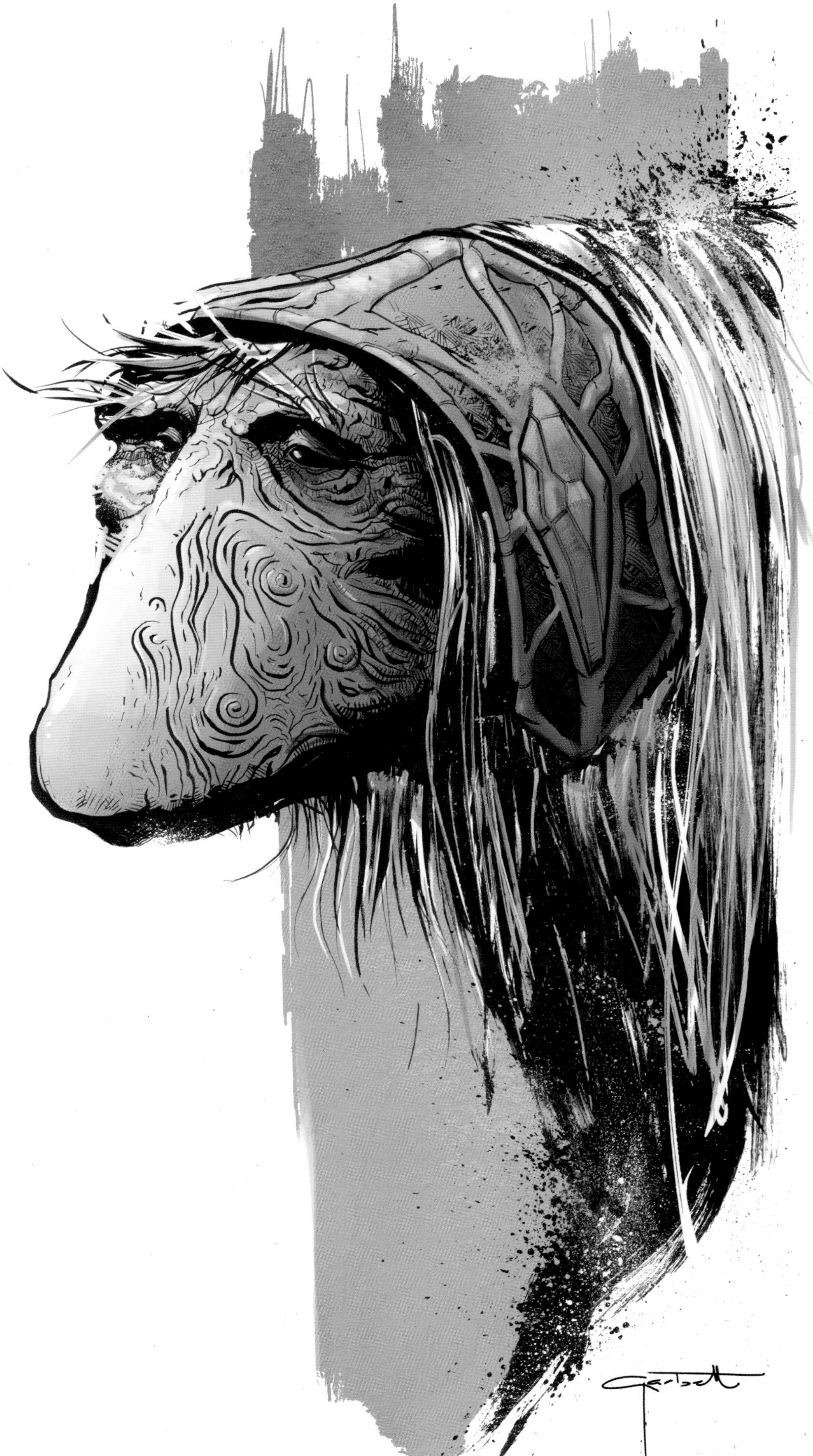

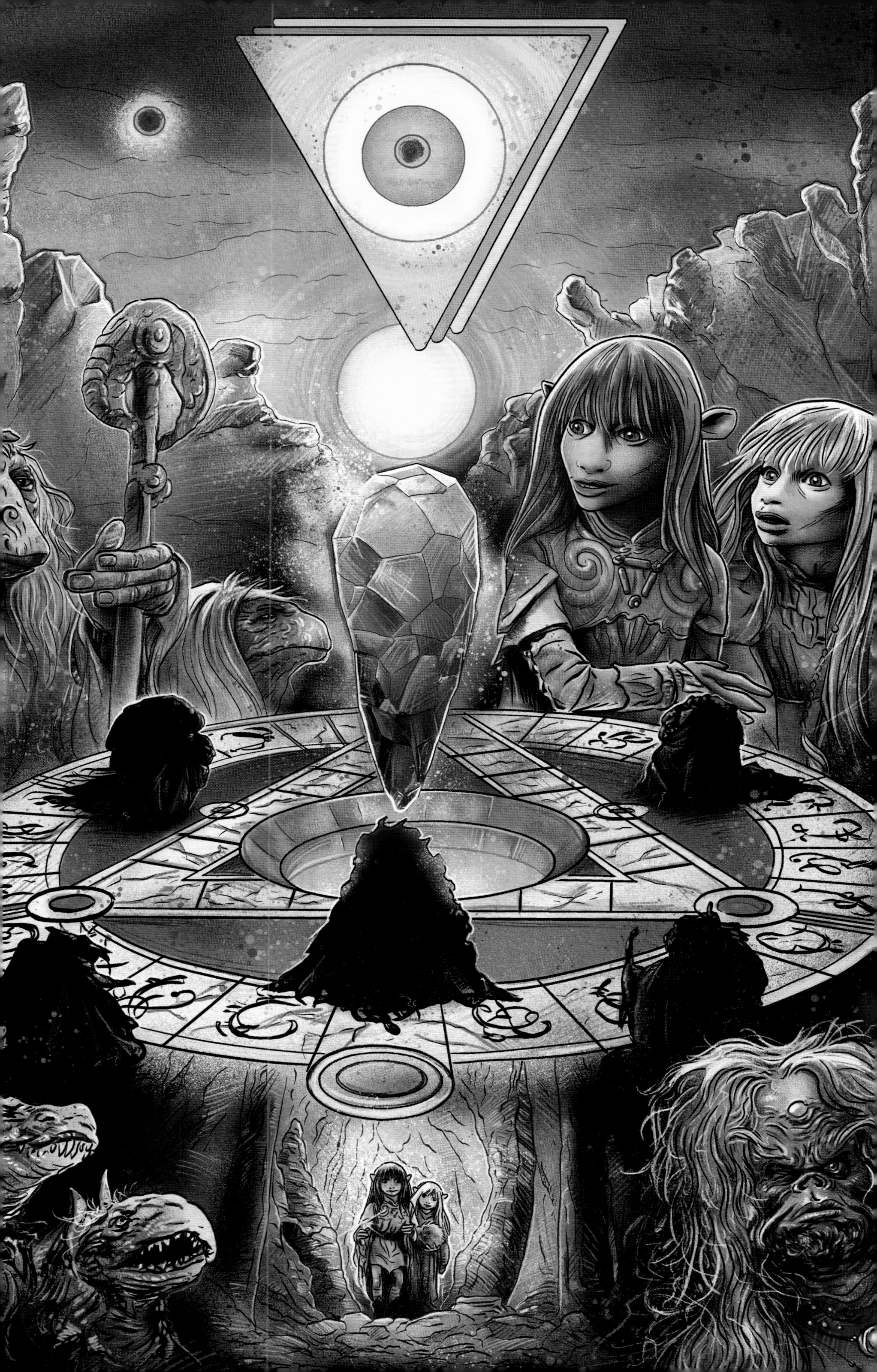

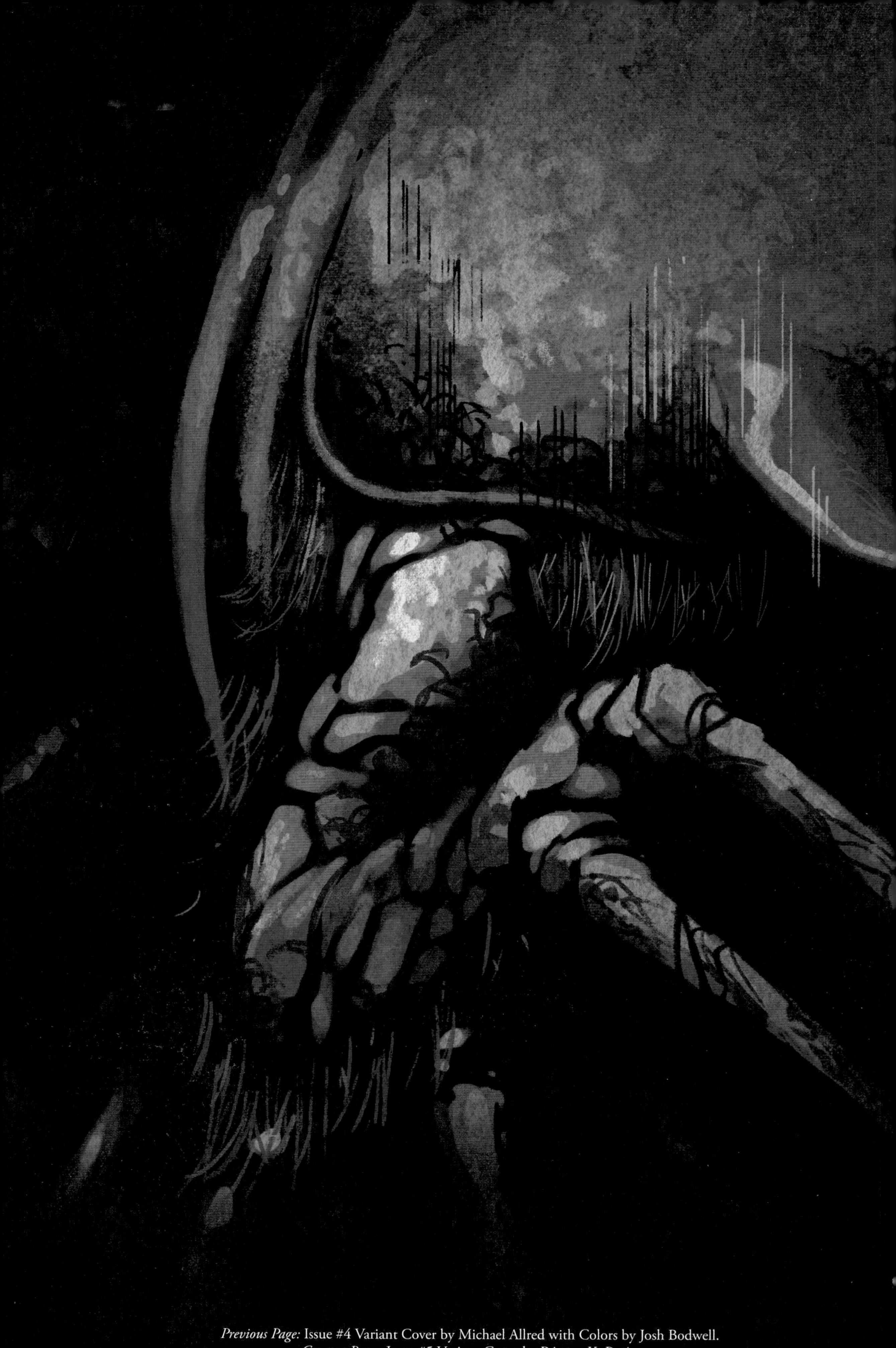

Previous Page: Issue #4 Variant Cover by Michael Allred with Colors by Josh Bodwell.
Current Pages: Issue #5 Variant Cover by Rámon K. Peréz.

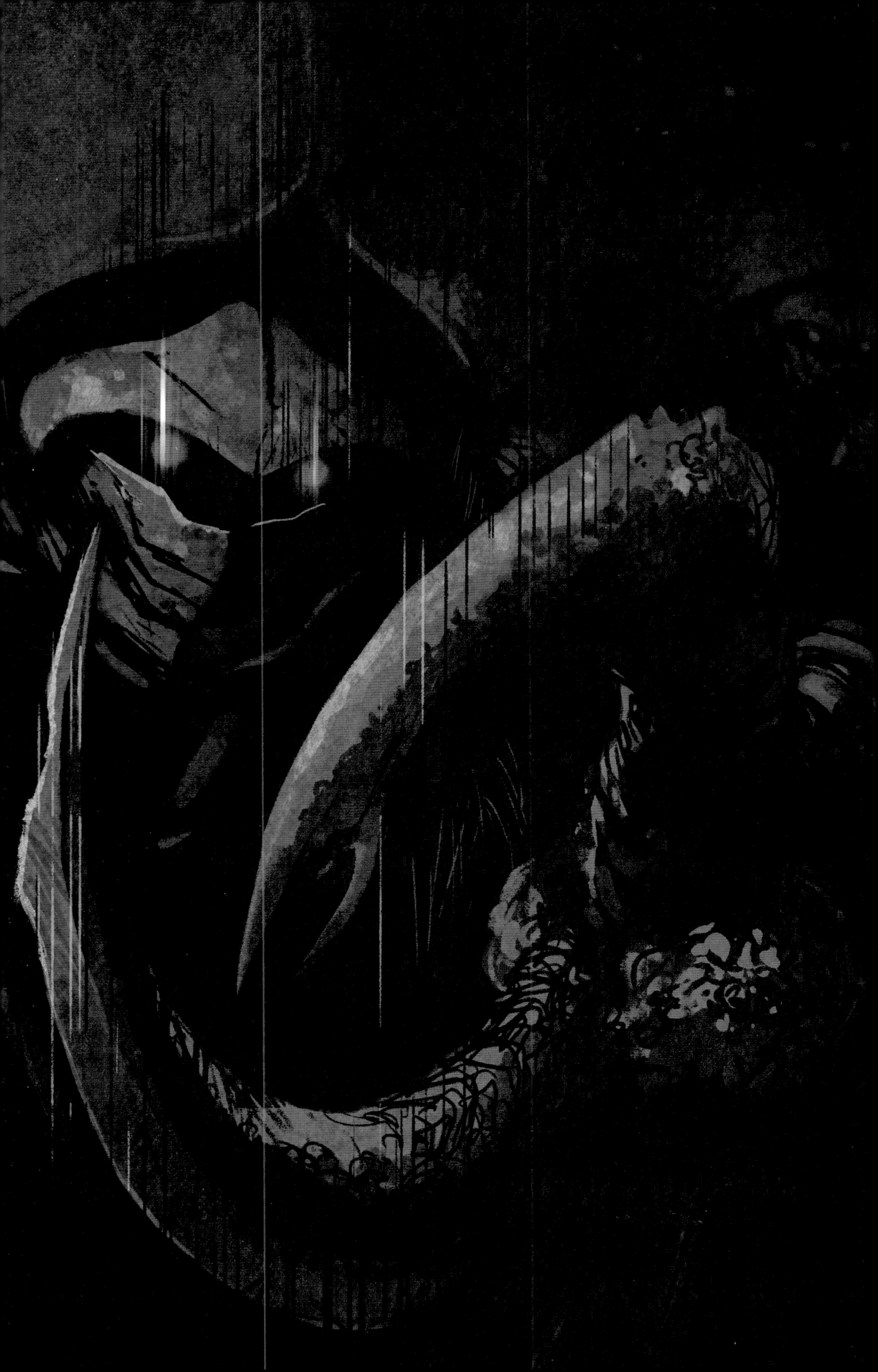

DISCOVER
GROUNDBREAKING TITLES

ASAF HANUKA
THE REALIST

LONG WALK TO VALHALLA
ADAM SMITH MATTHEW FOX

THE MARCH OF THE CRABS
THE CRABBY CONDITION
ARTHUR DE PINS

Jane
ALINE BROSH McKENNA
RAMÓN K. PÉREZ

ROYDEN LEPP
RUST
VOLUME ONE
VISITOR IN THE FIELD

MOUSE GUARD
THE BLACK AXE
DAVID PETERSEN

The Realist
Asaf Hanuka
ISBN: 978-1-60886-688-5 | $24.99 US

The Realist: Plug and Play
Asaf Hanuka
ISBN: 978-1-60886-953-4 | $24.99 US

Long Walk to Valhalla
Adam Smith, Matt Fox
ISBN: 978-1-60886-692-2 | $24.99 US

The March of The Crabs
Arthur De Pins
Volume 1: The Crabby Condition
ISBN: 978-1-60886-689-2 | $19.99 US
Volume 2: The Empire of the Crabs
ISBN: 978-1-68415-014-4 | $19.99 US

Jane
Aline Brosh McKenna, Ramón K. Pérez
ISBN: 978-1-60886-981-7 | $24.99 US

Rust
Royden Lepp
Volume 0: The Boy Soldier
ISBN: 978-1-60886-806-3 | $10.99 US
Volume 1: Visitor in the Field
ISBN: 978-1-60886-894-0 | $14.99 US
Volume 2: Secrets of the Cell
ISBN: 978-1-60886-895-7 | $14.99 US

Mouse Guard
David Petersen
Mouse Guard: Fall 1152
ISBN: 978-1-93238-657-8 | $24.95 US
Mouse Guard: Winter 1152
ISBN: 978-1-93238-674-5 | $24.95 US
Mouse Guard: The Black Axe
ISBN: 978-1-93639-306-0 | $24.95 US

The Cloud
K.I. Zachopoulos, Vincenzo Balzano
ISBN: 978-1-60886-725-7 | $24.99 US

Cursed Pirate Girl Coloring Book
Jeremy A. Bastian
ISBN: 978-1-60886-947-3 | $16.99 US

ARCHAIA™

AVAILABLE AT YOUR LOCAL COMICS SHOP AND BOOKSTORE
To find a comics shop in your area, visit www.comicshoplocator.com
WWW.**BOOM-STUDIOS**.COM

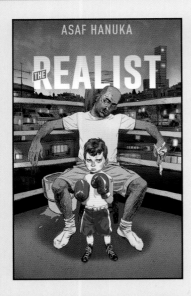

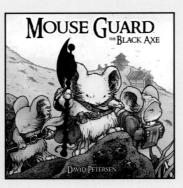